New Age Study of Humanity's Purpose, Inc.
P.O. Box 41883
Tucson, Arizona 85717

Cover and Illustrations by artist Sharon Nichols

Affirmations and Invocations reprinted here with permission of
Group Avatar

Manufactured in the United States of America

Library of Congress Cataloging in Publication Data
TXU 381 610
ISBN 0961528710
First Edition May 1, 1989
Second Printing January 11, 1990

THE
NEXT
STEP...

The New Age Study of Humanity's Purpose, Inc.
P.O. Box 41883
Tucson, Arizona 85717

DEDICATION 4/92

This book is Lovingly dedicated to those who have come to Love this Blessed Planet FREE; the men, women and children from every walk of Life.

The time has arrived for you to fulfill your mission, the most sacred mission ever embodied in human form. You are Messengers of Peace, exponents of God's Divine Love. You are "THE OPEN DOOR THAT NO ONE CAN SHUT." You are "the Light of the world" *and your time is at hand!*

ACKNOWLEDGMENTS

First and foremost I want to express my deepest Love and Gratitude to the entire Company of Heaven, Who ceaselessly blaze Their radiant Light through the dense veil of chaos and confusion to Illuminate our pathway Home.

I send my Heartfelt Love and Gratitude also to:

My dear friend and co-worker Kay Meyer who, in the face of seemingly overwhelming challenges, consistently chooses the Path of Light.

My Loving Husband whose support and encouragement perpetually sustain me.

My son Joao for his sense of Humor and his Strength.

My daughter Victoria for her Joy and her Inner Light.

The rest of my family for the Happiness I have experienced with them and the opportunities they have provided for my growth.

And last, but certainly not least, I want to thank all of my co-workers who devote hours of their precious time to self-lessly serve Humanity.

INTRODUCTION

We have moved VICTORIOUSLY through the threshhold into the Permanent Golden Age. Now, we are being called to take THE NEXT STEP which will assure our individual and planetary Victory, Freedom and Eternal Peace.

On August 17, 1987, a cosmic moment in the Earth's evolution, referred to as Harmonic Convergence, the Planet Earth and all Her Life moved forward into a new frequency of vibration. At that precise moment, the Masculine Polarity of God–Divine Will–and the Feminine Polarity of God–Divine Love–were brought into perfect balance resulting in the "birth" of the son/daughter principle which is Divine Illumination, Wisdom and Understanding. On August 17, 1987, an unparalleled frequency of God Illumination poured forth from the very Heart of God into the atmosphere of Earth. The Light was absorbed into the Heart Centers of aware Lightworkers on the Planet who had gathered at electro-magnetic power points throughout the globe. The Light was then projected on the Holy Breath into the Crystal Grid System of the Earth and anchored into the atomic substance of all Life on the Planet. The increased frequency of Illumination raised the vibration of every particle of Life evolving on this Sweet Earth, thus moving the Planet forward in the Light closer to Her rightful place in the Fourth Dimensional Realms of Perfection.

The veil has now been lifted on the Fourth Dimensional Plane, and Humanity has ascended into a new level of consciousness. From this new octave of awareness we have the opportunity to understand more clearly just how to implement the new qualities of Perfection pouring into the Planet and how to use them effectively in our everyday Lives.

It is obvious from outer appearances that there are extreme imbalances taking place on the Earth at this critical time. As the Light enters the atomic substance of physical matter, all discordant frequencies are being pushed to the surface to be Transmuted back into Light. It has the same effect as putting a pot on the stove to boil and all of the scum rising to the surface. This process is causing great challenges in our Lives, both individually and globally. Any situation we have been avoiding, or any block that is preventing us from moving forward, is being pushed to the surface in such a glaring way that we have no choice but to face it and deal with it.

The wonderful news is that darkness, which reflects agony, lack, limitation and all manner of suffering, cannot be sustained or exist in the presence of LIGHT. To do so would be in total conflict with both Physical and Spiritual Laws. If one walks into a dark room and turns on the Light, the darkness is dissipated. Consequently, we know clearly now that we do not have to do "battle" with the negativity surfacing in our Lives. We need merely to INVOKE THE LIGHT EFFECTIVELY AND LIFT OURSELVES UP OUT OF THE CHAOS INTO THE OCTAVES OF JOY!

In all former advancements of civilization and Golden Ages, the Spiritual Hierarchy was the sustaining force of the people. This time, it's going to be different. This Golden Age is being called *Permanent*, and the reason is clear. Now in the dawning Golden Age, Humanity is tapping the Wisdom WITHIN and reaching up in consciousness into the Realms of Illumined Truth. We are receiving every conceivable assistance from the Heavenly Realms, and each soul is being given the opportunity to embrace the Truth and Perfection of that dimension. Through this process, Humanity's consciousness will be lifted and *self*-sustained. As we begin to perpetually focus on the Light, our environment, through the Law of Attraction, will begin to reflect the beauty and Perfection of the Higher Realms. The actual Transformation of physical substance will occur, and the Earth will be projected forth into Her Divine birthright–HEAVEN ON EARTH.

Once the individual consciousness has awakened to the Power of God within and the patterns of beauty and Perfection from the Celestial Realms are blended in each person, there will be no retrogression or surcease from the expansion of Perfection, and the PERMANENT GOLDEN AGE will be manifest.

The Divine Plan for the Permanent Golden Age is so manifold in Its Glorious expression that, even if every second we received the Divine ideas that would take a whole Lifetime for us to accomplish, we would scarcely tap the unseen potent design which is awaiting fulfillment through the open door of Humanity's consciousness.

Our God Presence pulsating in our Hearts stands waiting to externalize through our physical and inner bodies. Each of us holds a thread of the Tapestry of Life which must be woven into the Divine design for Earth.

We can make a difference. By utilizing the new frequencies of Light now available to us, we can become the masters of our Lives and trigger a global shift in consciousness. We now have the ability to Transform our World.

Listen to your Inner Voice. You are now being called to assist this Blessed Planet. You are a Messenger of Peace, a bearer of the most sacred mission ever embodied in human form. You are one who can assist in changing the face of the World.

It is now time for your Supreme Initiation. This is the initiation into the Truth and Reality of your own Being. This cannot be accomplished through intellect. It will be attained ONLY through the perpetual practice of the Presence of God. It is now time for us to respond to the Inner call and time to take THE NEXT STEP.

This is the Cosmic Moment when Humanity will once again Unite in consciousness with the Universal flow of God's Will, God's Divine Love and God's Wisdom. This Unification will result in Humanity becoming One with our God Presence. It is now the time when the electronic nature of the God Presence (Fourth Dimension) must function through the atomic nature of the physical form (third dimension), and it is the melding of these two that is THE NEXT STEP.

In the third dimension, Humanity has been functioning as a Seven-fold Planetary Being with seven major physical chakras or energy centers active along the spinal column. With the Planetary shift in vibration that took place during Harmonic Convergence, Humanity was raised closer to the frequency of vibration that pulsates along the spine of the God Presence. This is a great shaft of Light that reverberates with the Twelve-fold Aspect of Deity. In order for this Earth to Ascend into the Realms of Light, the Twelve-fold Aspect of God's Perfection must be anchored into the physical plane. It is now necessary for Humanity to reflect the Twelve-fold Aspect of God by Living in at-one-ment with our God Presence, merging with the Twelve-fold Solar Spine. It is important for each of us to feel an entirely new identity as a Light Being as we are lifted into the Octaves of the Fourth Dimension.

Throughout this book, I will be sharing practical information on each of the Twelve Rays of God that comprise the Twelve-fold Aspect of Deity, and together we will learn tangible tools that will assist each of us as we reach our full potential, utilize the Twelve Rays effectively, and become the masters of our Lives. Our opportunity is unprecedented, and with perseverance, our VICTORY is assured!

SUGGESTIONS FOR GETTING THE MOST BENEFIT FROM THIS BOOK

THE NEXT STEP is a very important book filled with practical tools and exercises to help you reunite with the part of your Being that always aspires to the highest level of excellence.

To gain the most benefit from this book, first read it from cover to cover. Then, quiet yourself and ask the Presence of God, pulsating in your Heart, to reveal which chapter you should concentrate on first. Each chapter is filled with information, exercises and techniques to help you effectively utilize the particular Aspect of God being presented. Your God Presence always knows exactly what THE NEXT STEP is for your own individual path and will guide you, unerringly, to the correct chapter.

If you feel uncertain about being able to communicate with your God Presence just yet, listen to your inner feelings and choose the chapter that feels right to you.

Once a chapter has been selected, read it again carefully. Focus on the information presented. Apply the tools to your Life and practice them daily, until you feel a sense of completion. After you feel a sense of completion, ask your God Presence to reveal the next chapter you should concentrate on. Continue this process, until you have truly applied and experienced all Twelve Aspects of Deity.

As you proceed through the steps of the Twelve-fold Aspect of Deity, you will find yourself becoming more and more Illumined and Free. Your Life will change, and it will begin to reflect the Harmony and Success you have been striving to achieve for as long as you can remember. You will experience more Loving Relationships, Vibrant Health, Prosperity, Happiness, a Fulfilling Career, Spiritual Growth, Joyous Selfless Service and a sense of Inner Peace and Optimism.

The Purpose of this book is to provide you with the insight and techniques that will enable you to TAP THE POWER WITHIN YOUR OWN BEING. Then, once you have reconnected with your God Presence, you will be guided perpetually in the creation of a Life filled with *Joy, Fulfillment, Purpose and Excellence.*

I have produced a series of tapes to go along with the book. The tapes contain the information presented in each chapter, as well as all of the visualizations, exercises, affirmations and invocations for that particular Aspect of God. The tapes are an excellent way to reinforce and enhance your study of each chapter. We learn much faster when we include as many of our various senses as possible. The tapes are listed at the end of the chapter for your convenience, so you can order them, if you like. You may purchase the tapes separately or as a set. The order blank is in the back of the book.

I wish you Victory in all your endeavors.

NOTE

The use of capitalization in this book signifies the difference between the lower frequencies of the third dimensional plane and human consciousness, and the higher Divine frequencies of the Fourth Dimensional plane and God Consciousness.

All references to the aspects, qualities and frequencies of Divinity are capitalized.

TABLE OF CONTENTS

CHAPTER 1

THE FIRST ASPECT OF DEITY IS GOD'S WILL

COLOR – SAPPHIRE BLUE
FIRST RAY

THE FIRST UNIVERSAL LAW
OF ENERGY – LIGHT
THE FIRST CAUSE OF GOD
IS PERFECTION
"LET THERE BE LIGHT"

THE ATTRIBUTES OF GOD'S WILL ARE:

ILLUMINED FAITH
POWER
PROTECTION
DECISION
THE WILL TO DO
DIVINE ORDER
OBEDIENCE
INTUITION
UNITY
DISCRIMINATION
DISCRETION
PERCEPTION
VICTORY

THE WILL OF GOD
IS PERFECTION

Throughout the history of time, there has been much written about the Will of God. We often use this term to explain the painful things occurring in our Lives that we don't understand, and we use it to justify the atrocities taking place in the world. In the teachings available on Earth, the Will of God is so immersed in religious rhetoric and human conjecture that it is probably the most misunderstood of all the Aspects of Deity. As we proceed into the dawning age of Wisdom and Enlightenment, greater understanding is filtering into our consciousness, and the true meaning of God's Will is beginning to reveal Itself.

In order for us to grasp the real meaning of God's Will, we must first understand with greater clarity the meaning of FREE WILL. Free Will is a gift that is given to each Lifestream who comes forth from the Heart of God at the moment of creation. This gift is given to enable each of us, through conscious choice, to expand the borders of our Father's Kingdom by becoming Masters of our Lives, creating perfection in every dimension of our existence. It was never part of the Divine Plan for us to use this gift of Free Will to create anything other than good. Never was it intended that Humanity would choose to use our gift of Life to create chaos, confusion, disease, poverty, war, lack, limitation, fear, hatred and all other forms of grossly misqualified energy that are now manifesting in the world. This discord has become so prevalent on Earth that we have actually deceived ourselves into accepting that it is a natural part of Life, and even worse, we attribute it to, of all things, God's Will.

This duality of good and evil has become such an obvious part of our Earthly existence that we have even gone to the extreme of believing that without evil we cannot experience good. *This is, by far, the most destructive belief system we could have.* Our thoughts are creative, and as long as we believe good cannot exist without evil, we will continually create and perpetuate the negativity now existing on Earth. The Reality is the moment has arrived when the Lord's Prayer will be brought to fruition: THY KINGDOM COME, THY

WILL BE DONE ON EARTH AS IT IS IN HEAVEN. The frequencies of discord and disintegration now existing on Earth do not exist in the Octaves of Light. Nothing less than Perfection–God's Will–manifests in the Heavenly Realms, and that is the Divine Heritage of Earth.

The biblical allegory of Adam and Eve symbolically reflects this Truth. The Garden of Eden (Earth) was created to sustain human Life in the most Glorious way possible. Everything that Humanity (Adam and Eve) needed to survive in total Harmony was provided by God and the Kingdom of Nature. The gift of Free Will was given so that Humanity could choose each day how we would use our precious gift of Life . . . How today shall I expand the borders of my Father's Kingdom? How today shall I express God's Love, God's Truth, God's Wisdom, God's Power? How today shall I use my thoughts, words, actions and feelings to add to the Light of the World?

In all that perfection, there was only one admonition given to us by our God Parents, and that was *WE MUST NOT EAT OF THE TREE OF KNOWLEDGE OF GOOD AND EVIL.* But Humanity (Eve) did "eat the apple" and began experimenting with our Gift of Life in destructive ways, creating negative thoughtforms that reflected on the environment. This resulted in the eventual "Fall of Man". Humanity became so immersed in our self-created chaos and pain that we could no longer perceive our Divine Purpose. We continued creating denser and denser vibrations of negativity until we manifested such a chasm between ourselves and our knowledge of God that we felt isolated to struggle in our misery alone.

For aeons of time Illumined Souls have volunteered to come to Earth, penetrating into the dense, humanly created veil of maya and illusion to bring to the mankind of Earth the knowledge of God, and the realization of our own Divinity. Throughout history, the prophecy was made that there would come a time when Humanity would awaken to the Power WITHIN and develop our latent abilities, thus becoming the Masters of our Lives. This awakening would call to remembrance the vows we took in the Heart of God before even this world was. We would remember our Divine Purpose and reason for Being, and Paradise on Earth–the Garden of Eden–would be reclaimed.

THE COSMIC MOMENT HAS ARRIVED, THE TONE HAS SOUNDED, AND THE AWAKENING HAS BEGUN

As we awaken to the Power of God within, we will reach up into the Octaves of Illumined Truth and tap the Wisdom of the Ages. Then we will be able to clearly perceive the Reality of our True Beings. The humanly created world of illusion and limitation that we now live in will be exposed in the blazing Light of Truth. The Light of God will suddenly melt the distorted belief in separation that binds us to negativity. When this occurs, the Truth of God's Will, which is Perfection for all things, will reflect in every aspect of our Lives. The illusion of lack, limitation, poverty, disease, decay, war, pestilence and all manner of chaos will be Transmuted by the radiance of God's Light. Each of us will then realize and recognize as never before *"The Father and I are ONE!"* The Divinity within each of us is our REAL SELF and our point of Eternal contact with God.

As we Ascend into the vibration of God's Will, our bodies, our spheres of influence, and the Planet Earth with all Her Life will reflect God's Perfection and the PERMANENT GOLDEN AGE–Heaven on Earth will be manifest!

THE WILL OF GOD IS LIGHT.
THE WILL OF GOD IS GOOD.
THE WILL OF GOD IS HAPPINESS.
THE WILL OF GOD IS GRACE.
THE WILL OF GOD IS PEACE.
THE WILL OF GOD IS PURITY.
THE WILL OF GOD IS BALANCE.
THE WILL OF GOD IS HEALTH.
THE WILL OF GOD IS ABUNDANCE.
THE WILL OF GOD IS KINDNESS.
THE WILL OF GOD IS UNITY.
THE WILL OF GOD IS LOVE.
THE WILL OF GOD IS PERFECTION.

HUMANITY'S FALL FROM THE WILL OF GOD

Because of the negativity existing in our daily Lives, we sometimes feel hopeless and abandoned. Often God is the furthest thing from our minds, and it is impossible for us to believe that we could, in any way, be part of that Radiant Being of Light. We begin to look at outer world appearances and come to the conclusion that God either doesn't care about us at all or else He doesn't exist. We hear the words Mercy, Compassion and Forgiveness and wonder how a Loving God could possibly allow such pain and suffering. Our observation makes us cynical and callous; then these emotions begin to reflect in our behavior patterns as anger and resentment. The more disillusioned and frustrated we become, the more hopeless things seem and the more difficult our challenges are, intensifying the vicious circle of agony and fear. Our minds become confused, and we sink deeper into the darkness until our faculties of judgment and reason are muddled and distorted. This has been a constant pattern throughout time for the majority of Humanity, a pattern that must *now* come to an end.

With increased frequencies of Intuition, Discrimination, Discretion and Perception now pouring into the Planet, we are realizing greater Truths. We are understanding more clearly how the Earth got into Her present state of disarray and how Humanity, through the misqualification of our Gift of Life, became separated from God. It all began aeons ago prior to the "Fall of Man".

As we came forth from the Heart of God individualized as "I Am", we descended into denser and denser octaves of matter until we embodied on the physical plane of Earth. This is the process of INVOLUTION. As we proceed through our Earthly sojourn, we develop and become masters of the material plane on our return journey back to the Heart of God. This is the process of EVOLUTION. Every particle of Life, every electron of energy, is subject to this involutionary and evolutionary process.

Prior to the "Fall of Man", the Earth was a veritable

Paradise. Everything that Humanity needed to exist in Comfort and Harmony had been provided by the Elemental Kingdom in co-operation with our God Parents. The Human Beings in embodiment at that time would draw forth their Gift of Life, the electronic Light substance we use continually with our every breath, and they would use it for the expansion of God's Will on Earth. This Gift of Life went forth from each person on an electro-magnetic current of energy similar to a radio wave. As each person sent forth their thoughts, words, feelings and actions, the current of energy would proceed into the physical plane and go directly to the person, place, condition or thing the sender was thinking of at the time. After reaching its point of destination, determined by the thought of the sender, the current of energy (our Gift of Life) would begin the return journey back to its Source, returning first to the person who sent it forth and then, back to the Heart of God. In the beginning, this Gift of Life was used only for good, and it was a continual blessing to all it touched.

The experiences reflecting in each person's Life, as a result of the returning energy, qualified ONLY with the Will of God, were always joyous and mirrored the Perfection of God. This was the natural evolutionary process void of any trace of discord or negativity. This was the original Divine Plan for Earth and God's Will for all Life. In order to insure this Divine process and to insure that our gift of Free Will would never be misused, God gave ONE commandment: "DO NOT EAT OF THE TREE OF KNOWLEDGE OF GOOD AND EVIL."

As time passed, Humanity became curious about this commandment and eventually, through Free Will, chose to partake of the tree and "ate the apple". Upon doing so, for the very first time since we came forth from the Heart of God, we began to experiment with our Gift of Life in ways that were contrary to the Will of God. The currents of energy passing into the physical plane on our thoughts, words, feelings and actions no longer reflected just the Perfection of God. They were now tainted with the knowledge of evil. For the first time Humanity began to experience vibrations that were discordant and contaminated with negativity.

As these discordant thoughts were projected into the atmosphere of Earth, they began to reflect on the environment. Gradually, the beauty of the Elemental Kingdom began to reflect decay and disease. Our physical bodies, comprised of the same elements, also began to show signs of aging and degeneration. Humanity, inexperienced and unfamiliar with the vibrations of discord, became perplexed and fearful. The Glorious Gift of Life that used to flow so easily into the physical plane, qualified with God's Will, was now being misqualified by Humanity, and instead of pouring forth to bless all Life, it went forth from each person as a heavy inharmonious current. It then proceeded to the person, place, condition or thing held in the sender's thoughts, causing pain and friction along the way. After reaching its point of destination, it returned to the sender on its journey home to the Source.

But now there was a flaw. The energy could not pass through the sender's Heart on its return to God because it was contaminated and no longer vibrated with God's Will. The Law is, that in order for our Gift of Life to return to the Source, it must be vibrating with the same or a higher frequency than when it is first received. Now a greater problem ensued. Since the returning negative energy could not return to the Source until it had been Transmuted back into Light, and since Humanity didn't have the understanding or knowledge of how to accomplish that Purification, the destructive energy had no where to go and had to remain in the atmosphere of Earth. Gradually, as time passed, a cloud of negativity began to form around the Planet. It became denser and denser, creating a veil of maya, blinding Humanity from the Truth of our Reality and our Purpose for Being. This greatly added to the complexity of the problem.

Once Humanity lost the awareness of our God Reality and our Purpose for Being, we became more confused and frightened, consequently creating more negativity until the end result, known as "the Fall of Man", manifested on Earth. During this dark period of time, we separated ourselves from God so severely that today —millions of years later—we are still struggling to reconnect with our God Presence, and we are striving to Transmute the sea of negativity surrounding the Planet known as the humanly created psychic-astral realm.

In retrospect, it is clear why God gave a commandment "not to eat of the tree of knowledge of good and evil". Our Gift of Free Will is a Sacred Trust given to us by God and interpenetrates all realms of knowledge. God will *not* interfere with our Free Will REGARDLESS of how we choose to use it. Without the knowledge of evil we would not have been tempted to misqualify our Gift of Life, but once we partook of the fruit of that tree, we were subject to all the ramifications of that knowledge.

God does not release one electron of energy that is less than Perfection. Therefore, *anything* taking place on Earth that is less than God's Perfection is our own human creation, and it is in conflict with God's Will. It is a result of misqualifying our Gift of Life. With the realization and acceptance of this Truth, we can now proceed to Transmute this destructive energy and Transform our Lives into experiences of Joy and Harmony. Through concentrated effort, we will Transform this Planet into FREEDOM'S HOLY STAR. Once this occurs, Perfection will again be manifest in all our experiences, and God's Will shall be reflected in every facet of our Lives.

EXPOSING THE WORLD OF ILLUSION IN THE LIGHT OF REALITY

The confusion in our Lives is prevalent because of our distorted perception. We look at our environment and our world, and we believe the things we see are real. We believe the situations and relationships occurring in our Lives are just happenstance or coincidence. From outer appearances it looks as though we don't have any control over what's going on, and we often feel like victims. The Reality is that at any given moment we are a sum total of all our Earthly experiences. What is taking place in our Lives and our physical environment is a reflection of our consciousness. I know this is difficult to comprehend, but it is only because we have separated ourselves from our true God Self that this seems so complicated. Just for a moment try to disconnect from your attachment to physical matter and read these words with an open mind.

Much of the chaos Humanity experiences is because we perceive ourselves to be an intelligence *apart* from God. Some of us have even gone so far as to believe that we *are* our physical bodies. We have come to this conclusion because we look at the outer world and judge what we see to be real. We are truly multi-dimensional Beings and the physical plane, that which we interpret through our five physical senses, is just one of those dimensions. Our material senses; sight, touch, sound, smell and taste are limited and view only the physical plane. Consequently, they can't give us an accurate report of Reality.

Possibly you've heard the story of the three blind men who observed an elephant. One man held the tail in his hands and said, "An elephant is long and thin like a rope." The second man felt the elephant's leg and said, "No, an elephant is round and strong like a pillar." The third man touched the elephant's side and said, "You are both wrong. The elephant is huge and wide like a mountain."

This story symbolizes what it is like for us to try to accurately evaluate the Reality of the World by using only our limited material senses.

Actually the physical plane that we think is so real, is the *least* real of all. The physical plane is even called the "world of illusion" because it is so distorted. Our distorted perception of Reality is a direct result of our "fall" and separation from God. The denser the veil of maya became, the more distorted our perception was and the more we clung to the material plane to give us a sense of security.

Prior to our separation from God, we were very aware of the Law of Attraction, and we knew that we were the creators of the physical dimension. We knew that our thoughts, words, actions and feelings were continually being projected onto physical matter, thus manifesting in physical form. We realized that the Law of Attraction is a Creative Force, a Light from the Universal Source of All Life that flows through us constantly.

Even though we lost the awareness of this Law, it in no

way changed the Reality of Its existence. The Law of Attraction functions as follows: As Light (our Gift of Life) flows through us, it picks up the particular vibrations of our consciousness and expresses those vibrations in visible form, experiences, and circumstances. Our consciousness is always an accumulation of all our beliefs, thoughts, words, actions and feelings. As the Creative Force of the Law of Attraction passes through us and picks up the vibrations of our consciousness, the synthesis of all energy vibrating there is projected onto physical matter. Thus, everything manifesting in our Lives now, whether we are referring to our financial situation, health, relationships, careers, happiness, success or peace of mind, is a result of our beliefs, thoughts, words, actions and feelings.

As long as Humanity conceives that we are separate from God, we will experience distorted conditions of matter. Only when we realize our true God Reality, our Oneness with God, will we Ascend out of the world of illusion and reflect the Reality of the Heavenly Realms on Earth.

Humanity has given power to physical matter. We have given our physical bodies power to elevate us or bring us down. We have given the body power to incapacitate us through sickness, poverty, unhappiness, aging and on ad infinitum. We have allowed the distorted manifestation of physical matter to become our Reality when, in Truth, it is an illusion, created by our beliefs, thoughts, words, actions and feelings.

It is time for us to realize that our bodies and physical matter are not intelligent Life forms separate from God, but rather they are a mass of atomic energy controlled by our consciousness. NEVER does matter control consciousness. Our bodies and our physical environments are merely reflections of our consciousness. That is why matter cannot be changed by sheer human will power any more than a reflection in a mirror can be changed if we don't change the object causing the reflection.

Presently our worlds reflect our consciousness, and we have set about trying to change the reflection or picture instead of changing our consciousness. This concept again comes from a belief in separation.

When we actually accept our God Presence AS ourselves and not some separate "self", our environment and our world will reflect an entirely new picture. Instead of disease we will manifest Health. In place of poverty we will reflect Abundance. Instead of pain we will outpicture Joy. The recognition of our own Divinity will begin to instantly reflect on the physical matter around us.

This process is beyond the reasoning of our outer minds, but it will be revealed as an Inner Knowing. As we Heal our separation from God, again become One with our God Presence, our power is withdrawn from matter. Matter is then seen as a mass of atoms waiting to take on our consciousness and reflect the Perfection of God. It is only when we recognize the God within as the master of our bodies and environments that we experience true Freedom from limitation. The Light of God suddenly melts all distorted beliefs and the separation that binds us to negativity.

It is time for us to begin developing our consciousness by recognizing and ACCEPTING our true Reality. We must now go within and re-establish a Loving relationship with our God Presence, the part of ourselves that is One with God. When we begin to recognize our God Reality, we glimpse our true potential. Then we realize that the Power of God is within each of us *NOW*. It is all Knowing, all Caring, all Loving, and all Powerful.

"I AM" THE DIVINE IMAGE OF GOD

"I AM" the Divine Image of God manifesting Perfection in my Being and world, and for the Children of God, everyone, everywhere in God's Supreme Name FOREVER.

Wherever "I AM", my very Presence in the Universe is a constant outpouring and release of God Life and Light, God Truth and God Freedom to all I contact, every day, in every way.

HUMANITY'S RETURN JOURNEY BACK TO THE WILL OF GOD

The long awaited moment has arrived. The Age has dawned long foretold by the ancient prophets, when Humanity will attain our Victory in the Light. We need only to lift up our consciousness and step through the open door into our Eternal Freedom.

This is the Age of Enlightenment and Wisdom, the Age when our humanly created, self-inflicted separation from God will be Healed, and the Truth of our own Divinity will be revealed. The awakening is now taking place within each one of us and change is being experienced by every Lifestream. Transformation is occurring subtly and deeply at an atomic, cellular level. The Power of God is penetrating into every electron of precious Life energy evolving on the Earth. This process of Transformation has been a dormant seed in our consciousness that is being activated now by a tremendous influx of God's Light. The seed of Transformation is growing and expanding, filling our entire Beings with Light, lifting us up to touch the Realms of Illumined Truth, enabling us to manifest the Reality of our true God Self now in the world of form.

As the seed of awareness grows in our consciousness, it begins to blaze like the Sun radiating forth Rays of Light that connect with every other Lightbearer on the Planet. This activity of Light is creating a Powerful Forcefield around the Earth, an actual network of Light. The collective radiance of this network of Light is the most Powerful force on the Planet. It has created a Bridge of Light that spans the abyss from the lowest vibrations on Earth to the Highest Realms of Light, a Bridge over which this Earth and all Her Life will Ascend into the Octaves of Perfection. The Victorious Light of God has returned, and the Permanent Golden Age has begun.

The Power of God pulsating through all Life is the Power of Unity, the Power of Reverence for all Life, the Power of Inner Peace, the Power of Divine Order, the Power of Faith, and the Power of Victory. This Power is working through each of us ceaselessly to activate within us the Inner knowing and remembrance of the Oneness of All Life. Our strength lies in this greater knowing and in the unification of our Hearts and Minds with the billions of Lifestreams joining us on the return journey back to the Heart of God.

As we attune to the Power of God, we become portals

through which the totality of God's Perfection will flow to Bless all Life. As the Light of "I Am" floods the physical plane of Earth, the humanly created shadows of discord will be Transmuted in the purifying Radiance. Daily and hourly, more and more of Humanity are awakening to realize their Divine Purpose. As this occurs, the effect becomes exponential, and the collective Light Force attains a critical mass causing change to manifest suddenly everywhere.

There are critical points in time when the incoming Power of God's Transforming Light builds to great intensity. These points signal the Higher Realms to begin projecting forth the energy to stimulate the Spiritual growth of Humanity. As Humanity awakens, more and more Lifestreams are becoming aware of these peak transmission periods. Thus, people begin to co-operate with the Divine Plan by anchoring the incoming Light into the consciousness and physical substance of Earth. This is happening more frequently through synchronized global activities.

1986 was the year signaling the initial impulse of the return of God's Will to Earth. As this knowledge was absorbed into the consciousness of Humanity, many wonderful activities were reflected in the outer world. 1986 was heralded as a year of Transformation and declared the INTERNATIONAL YEAR OF PEACE by the United Nations for the first time in history.

We have often heard the expression "Where your attention is, there you are". That is a very profound statement from the Realm of Truth. In 1986 the full magnitude of Truth within that statement began to well up in the Hearts of all Humanity, and throughout the world people turned their attention toward Hope, Peace, Love, Prosperity, Health, Happiness, Joy and Harmony. People began to gradually learn that, by focusing on the negativity and chaos of the world, we are actually intensifying it. Several activities transpired that assisted Humanity in drawing our attention away from despair and separation toward Hope and Unity.

The first major activity was called "The Great Peace March: A Step Forward". On March 1, 1986, several thousand people began a march that took them from Los Angeles, California, to Washington, D.C. In an attitude of World

Peace and Reverence for all Life, they began a journey to end the threat of nuclear war and to sustain Eternal Peace. Along the path, they were met by thousands of fellow citizens who joined the march into Washington, D.C. Through the media, this Peace March was brought to the attention of millions and millions of people throughout the World. Every nation and world leader was given the message: The People of the World long for and demand that Peace be a priority in ALL governmental affairs. The People of the World will lead their leaders.

A second major activity that was building in momentum in 1986 is called "Peace the 21st". "Peace the 21st" is a simple, but tremendously effective concept. We know now that there is Power in thought, and we know the collective thought of Humanity is the most Powerful force on Earth. The objective of this activity is to harness this force in the interest of World Peace. "Peace the 21st" is designed to gather together those who desire to participate in forming a massive and United "Thought Image of Peace".

This global effort for World Peace involves an ever-expanding number of participants. It is a concept based on Universal Love and Co-operation. The activity is planned to take maximum advantage of the increased flow of Light on the Equinoxes and the Solstices. On the 21st day of the months of March, June, September and December of EACH YEAR from 7:00 to 7:30 P.M. local time, Lifestreams throughout the world join together in consciousness to energize a Thought-Image of Peace. We can participate in any way that is comfortable for us; prayer, meditation, affirmations, music etc. Whatever we decide to do should be positive and constructive, emphasizing the theme of Peace and Love. It is the focused effort of a multitude joining their thought images together at the same time for the same purpose that is important.

The third major activity to invoke worldwide attention in 1986 was "HANDS ACROSS AMERICA". The goal of this project was to raise funds to combat hunger and homelessness in America. But, by far, the greatest benefit was the joining together of literally millions of people around the world in a consciousness of Humanity reaching out to help each other. Through this activity, millions of people joined hands forming a human chain which created a Unified Forcefield that extended from the Statue of Liberty across America to the Pacific Ocean in Los Angeles, California. Imagine the Power of millions of people joining hands across this sacred nation singing "America the Beautiful" and "We Are The World".

The fourth very special activity was called "The First Earth Run". The Vision of this activity was to create an event of such magnitude that all Humanity would be compelled to action by the image it generated . . . a great thread of Light passed around the World by tens of thousands of people, linking us and showing us that we are together, igniting a global sense of Hope for the future.

The First Earth Run began at the United Nations in September, 1986, and culminated back at the United Nations in December, 1986, after having carried a torch of Light around the World.

The goals of The First Earth Run were accomplished in a five phase program:

1. The torch relay itself, in which a flame serving as a visual symbol of co-operation connected nation to nation as runners from every country were invited to relay the fire around the Earth. Through the everchanging and endless landscapes of our Earth—the torch was held aloft, passed from Russian runner to American runner to Chinese runner to Jamaican runner to Kenyan runner . . . a co-operative effort against time, distance and physical limitations.

2. At local ceremonies along the route, people received the flame from torch bearing runners onto candles,

torches and miner's lamps, then spread it from individual to individual, community to community. By the end of the Earth Run, a substantial portion of the people of the World had received the flame onto their own personal candles. To culminate the event, the torch was brought into the United Nations at which point people world-wide relit their candles.

3. Concert celebrations took place in major cities along the route to coincide with the arrival of the flame.

4. The "Olympics of Co-operation" encouraged communities along the route to acknowledge projects which demonstrated the spirit of co-operation. Those projects were publicly recognized, and medals and financial grants were awarded to those which most effectively met local challenges.

5. There was endorsement of, and participation in, the Earth Run by the world leaders along the route and also in the opening and closing ceremonies at the United Nations. Their support was an example to people everywhere that global co-operation and cross-cultural understanding is achievable.

Hundreds of thousands of people lined the streets of New York City as the torch wound its way to the United Nations to complete its epic around-the-world journey. The Secretary General of the United Nations and the world leaders gathered to receive the energy from millions now embodied in the torch and passed it from one to another.

The final major activity scheduled for 1986 was the most enthusiastic undertaking of all. This project was called The Planetary Commission. The Planetary Commission called for 500 million people around the world to consent to the Healing and Harmonizing of this Planet and all forms of Life hereon. The activity is described in detail in a book titled THE PLANETARY COMMISSION by John Randolph Price. The book states:

"Our objective is obvious. Why not reverse the polarity of the Forcefield and achieve a critical mass of positive energy? Why not insure a chain reaction of self-sustaining good in and around and through this Planet? It can be done, and it will be! We will achieve a critical mass of Spiritual Consciousness to heal the sense of separation and restore mankind to Godkind. The fact that we can do it has already been demonstrated in the laboratory. One of the major universities on the west coast took the figure of 50 million people with a spiritual consciousness and through the use of computers and measurements of spiritual energy radiation, made this observation: if these men and women would meditate simultaneously and release their energy into the Earth's magnetic field, the entire vibration of the Planet would begin to change, and if there were no massive and dedicated counter forces to offset the benefits, war, poverty, crime, hunger and disease and other problems of mankind would be eliminated.

In order to reach the critical mass of Spiritual Consciousness our objective by December, 1986, is to have 500 million people on Earth simply consenting to a Healing of this Planet with no less than 50 million meditating at the same time on December 31, 1986, 12:00 Noon Greenwich Time."

People added to this Light in any way that was comfortable for them with Love, Music, Prayer, Guided Visualization, Meditation, Positive Thought or any other constructive release of positive energy.

Approximately 400 million people participated in this God Victorious activity, and organizations throughout the world are continuing to energize this Glorious thoughtform on the last day of each month. Then, on December 31st of each year, at 12:00 Noon Greenwich Mean Time, the Lightworkers of the World join together to amplify this Powerful "World Healing Meditation" and project it onto the physical plane of Earth.

WORLD HEALING MEDITATION

In the beginning—In the beginning God. In the beginning God created Heaven and Earth. And God said Let there be Light, and there was Light.

Now is the time of the new beginning. I Am a co-creator with God, and it is a new Heaven that comes as the Good Will of God is expressed on Earth through me. It is the Kingdom of Light, Love, Peace and Understanding, and I Am doing my part to reveal Its Reality.

I begin with me. I Am a Living Soul, and the Spirit of God dwells in me, as me. I and the Father are one, and all that the Father has is mine. In Truth, I Am the Christ of God.

What is true of me is true of everyone, for God is all and all is God. I see only the Spirit of God in every Soul, and to every man, woman and child on Earth, I say: I Love you, for you are me. You are my Holy Self.

I now open my Heart, and let the pure essence of Unconditional Love pour out. I see it as a Golden Light radiating from the center of my being, and I feel its Divine Vibration in and through me, above and below me.

I Am one with the Light. I Am filled with the Light. I Am Illumined by the Light. I Am the Light of the World.

With purpose of mind, I send forth the Light. I let the radiance go before me to join the other Lights. I know this is happening all over the World at this very moment. I see the merging Lights. There is now one Light. We are the Light of the World.

The one Light of Love, Peace and Understanding is moving and expanding as it flows across the face of the Earth, touching and Illuminating every soul trapped in the shadow of the illusion, and where there was darkness, there is now the Light of Reality.

And the Radiance grows, permeating, saturating every form of Life. There is only the vibration of one Perfect Life now. All the kingdoms of the Earth respond, and the Planet is alive with Light and Love.

There is total Oneness, and in this Oneness we speak the Word. Let the sense of separation be dissolved. Let mankind now be returned to Godkind.

Let Peace come forth in every mind. Let Love flow forth from every Heart. Let Forgiveness reign in every soul. Let Understanding be the common bond.

And now from the Light of the World, the One Presence and Power of the Universe responds. The Activity of God is Healing and Harmonizing Planet Earth. Omnipotence is made manifest.

I Am seeing the salvation of the Planet before my very eyes as all false beliefs and error patterns are dissolved. The sense of separation is no more; the Healing has taken place, and the World is restored to sanity.

This is the beginning of Peace on Earth and Good Will toward all, as Love flows forth from every Heart, Forgiveness reigns in every soul, and all Hearts and minds are one in perfect Understanding.

It is done. And it is so. I Am.

for further information contact:
Quartus Report
PO Box 1768
Boerne, Texas 78006-6768

The Power of Light magnetized into the consciousness of Humanity in 1986, increased in Radiance and momentum throughout 1987, building to a crescendo that culminated on August 15th, 16th and 17th, 1987. This time was a Cosmic Moment in the evolution of this Planet that had been prophesied for hundreds of years.

Much information poured forth into the consciousness of Humanity to help us prepare for this Sacred event. I would like to share with you now some of the clearest articles.

HARMONIC CONVERGENCE
AUGUST 16 & 17, 1987

The following is an article that was printed in EROSPIRIT in 1987)

The Cosmic Moment is NOW!!!

According to Julian Spalding, publisher and editor of Ero-Spirit, "Harmonic Convergence is an impending planetary event which is being heralded as a quantum leap for the entire collective consciousness of humankind.

"The Earth is approaching its spiritual initiation of Illumination and each human being, in order to survive the resulting increase of Light on the Planet, is going through a time of preparation. We have all been in preparation on unconscious (and conscious) levels for a time. The process, of which we are all an integral part, is now becoming conscious to a greater number of people than ever before as the energy builds toward a critical mass.

"Critical mass is the term used by scientists to denote the point at which one predominant state gives way to another. It is the point at which a shift is made away from one paradigm, or cultural belief system, into a new one. It is the point at which the scales tip toward a new consensus. We are fast approaching that point as a species and as a planetary organism.

"The dates, August 16-17, 1987, have been long prophesied as a critical turning point for the Planet. The Hopi and other Indians prophesied that on August 17, 1987, 144,000 Sun Dance Enlightened Teachers will totally awaken in their dream-mind bodies . . . and the Rainbow Lights will be seen all over the world, and these Rainbow Light Dreams will help awaken the rest of Humanity.' The Aztec Calendar ends on August 17, 1987, and according to the ancient Maya, the dates August 16-17, 1987 are 'precise calibration points in a harmonic scale that mark the moment when the process of global civilization climaxes,' says anthropologist and art historian Jose Arguelles. He has dubbed the event Harmonic Convergence.

"During the days of Harmonic Convergence, 144,000 + people are being called to sacred sites around the globe to channel the healing energies that will be directed to the Earth. Many people are planning to return to these natural shrines or timeless temples, while others are creating new sites, believing that, in truth, every site is sacred. The Sacred Sites Festival is designed to facilitate the process of reaching the Light Workers, the so-called 144,000, with the information regarding the Earth's powerspots.

"Jose Arguelles describes the kind of changes people can expect to experience as we go through this intensification of energy on the Earth. In an interview in 'Magical Blend' magazine, Arguelles says that 'those people who are attuned–not just the 144,000 who are called out to ritually interface with the geomantic hotspots of the Planet–but a half a billion to a billion others who are tuned into the possibility of something actually happening–(will experience) a kind of ripple that goes through the Planet, producing a period of time feeling like a highly extended deja vu. This is literally the dissipation of the old mental frame and imprinting of the new mental frame. There will be a release of archetypal memory that has been dormant a long time. A highly renewed inspiration will occur.'

"John Randolph Price, one of the instigators of World Healing/Meditation Day, December 31, 1986, talks of Harmonic Convergence in his June, 1987 'Quartus Report': 'In very pragmatic terms, August 16-17 seems to provide an 'escape hatch' from the race fears which will manifest'. He recalls a vivid dream he had on April 5, in which his 'Old Man' said: 'The time of August 16-17 is very important to your world. The analogous words are soft clay, as opposed to gaseous substance, the soft clay being the condition of the Mother Substance (on those days). That which shall be impressed at that time will be expressed most quickly, for never has the world's consciousness been so vulnerable to impression as it will be on those days. Those who do not impress their visions will reap what Humanity's consciousness will sow. Those in spiritual Light, imprinting a higher vision, will share in a new beginning. The vision to be impressed must come from the Highest Aspect within and not from the lower nature. Let the vision gather strength in mind and impress it upon the clay. Those who do so will remove themselves from the effects of men's race fears, which through ignorance, shall surely be manifest on Earth.'

"Price interprets the dream: 'The message clearly calls for the Vision, that which we can see from the Highest Aspect, to impress it upon the 'soft clay,' the Mothering Energy of

Creation, which will be most receptive on August 16-17. Through this purposeful imprinting, the individual will actually be shaping his/her personal future. Without the desire and will to do this, the individual is consenting to participate in the collective impression to be made by the race mind of Humanity, according to its vibrations on those particular days, and choosing to partake of the race mind expression to follow.'

"In the January-February issue 'Integrity International', the journal of Emissary Foundation, Lord Exeter says that 'there is this rising tide or movement of spirit which is bringing change. There are evidences of something being put together, something coming together. This is an entirely new state of affairs, inconceivable at present to the human capacity to comprehend. There are those who are sensing this, and this is a sign of the times.'

Great change has been portended by many. Two generations ago the late modern mystic, Joel Goldsmith, predicted that in three generations there would be no more war or disease on the Planet. Dr. Joseph Jockmans, who authored the book, 'Rolling Thunder, The Coming Earth Changes,' has devoted his life to 'teaching others how to return to humankind's forgotten role as both energizers and co-creators of the Planet,' which he says 'will also be our net global level of spiritual initiation.' He says that 'both the Earth and all of Humanity have now entered a wonderful time of transition as we move together into new vibration and new planetary awareness'."

For further information contact:
EroSpirit
P.O. Box 35188
Albuquerque, New Mexico 87176

SACRED SITES FESTIVAL
by Jim Berenholtz

"August 16-17, 1987, is Harmonic Convergence, the conclusion of one world and beginning of another, where we lift to a new level of awareness and activate our prayers for planetary peace. According to ancient prophecies, many enlightened beings and teachers are due to return around that time, among them the Lord of Unified Opposites, Quetzalcoatl. Alongside the ancient prophecies, the guidance of the moment indicates the manner in which the prophecies are to be fulfilled. And so it is being seen that the Sacred Sites of Planet Earth, be they natural shrines or timeless temples, are calling us back to reactivate their energies and link them in the ways that are appropriate to now. These sites are here to help us do what must be done. Like acupuncture points, they channel the healing energies. Our ancestors have left us a great gift, knowing the Time of Remembrance would come. NEVER BEFORE HAVE HUMAN BEINGS SIMULTANEOUSLY COORDINATED THEIR PRAYERS, MEDITATIONS AND CEREMONIES AT SACRED SITES THROUGHOUT THE WORLD. What a remarkable opportunity we have. If we can focus our energies as clearly as our ancestors have focused the creation of the sites we will be using, imagine the potential for healing and positive change.

" 'THE INTERNATIONAL SACRED SITES FESTIVAL,' as it is being termed, is one aspect of Harmonic Convergence. People can answer the calling for two days of prayer and ceremony from wherever they are, knowing that everywhere is also a sacred site, and at every moment we stand in the center of the Universe. But the organic unfolding of the prophecy will naturally lead many of us to 'recognized' sacred sites. It is to this end that the information that follows is being supplied.

A VISION FOR THE FESTIVAL

"The ancient prophecies of Mesoamerica pinpoint the return of Quetzalcoatl, Lord of the Dawn, to the time that correlates with August 16-17, 1987, on the Gregorian Calendar.

Quetzalcoatl represents the force of cosmic intelligence, the spiraling, serpentine pattern that governs that movement of all things in this Universe. Quetzalcoatl is the enlightened state, the kundalini energy soaring to the crown chakra. Quetzalcoatl lives as a potentiality, a seed on the day of Harmonic Convergence and will grow to flower and seed again towards the awakening of all Humanity in the years that follow.

"The number 9 (1 + 4 + 4) is the number of Quetzalcoatl, indicating both a deepening and a heightening of the seven chakras (energy centers of the body), a unifying of duality that brings the enlightened state. The guidance I have received is to use the number 9 as a building block for the re-webbing of sacred sites that will create the mandala of our planetary ceremonial. Sixteen is four times four, the Four Seasons of the Four Directions, the cross of time and space, spirit and matter, which is the cross of Quetzalcoatl. When embraced in a Circle of Peace, it is the symbol of our Planet, or as the Hopi says, 'Land and Life.' Nine times 16 is 144, the harmonic of light, correlating to the 144,000 that will facilitate the Great Awakening. According to the ancient Maya, God and Mathematics are One. Through activating the proper formulas, we are able to experience our Divinity.

"Sacred Sites include Mystery Schools (Center of Knowledge), World Centers (Axis of the Universe), Sacred Mountains (Abodes of the Gods), Holy Waters (Sources of Life), Emergence Places (Sipapus: Wombs of Origination), Places of Enlightenment, Temples of Healing, Halls of Records (presently hidden from the world, but soon to re-emerge (Atlantis, Shambala and Paititi)..

"In North America: Chaco Canyon, New Mexico; Serpentmound, Ohio; Sedona, Arizona; Harney Peak in the Black Hills, South Dakota; Mt. Shasta, California; Niagara Falls, USA/Canada; Grand Canyon, Arizona.

"In Middle America: Teotihuacan, Mexico; Palenque, Mexico; Tenochtitlan (Mexico City), Mexico; Popcatepetl Mtn., Mexico; Agua Azul, Chipas, Mexico; Lake Atitlan, Guatemala; Tule Tree, Oaxaca, Mexico (Quetzalcoatl); Tikal Temple, Guatemala.

"In South America: Machu Picchu, Peru; Tiahuanaco,

Bolivia; Cuzco, Peru; Chimborazo Mtn., Ecuador; Iguazzo Falls, Brazil/Argentina; Island of the Sun, Lake Titicaca, Bolivia.

"In Europe: Temples of Delphi and Mt. Olympus, Greece; Standing Stones of Calenish and Iona, Scotland; Hill of Tara, Ireland; Chartre Cathedral, France; Tor of Glastonbury, England; Prague, Czechoslavakia.

"In the Middle East: Sphinx and Great Pyramids, Egypt; Temples of Karnak and Luxor, Egypt; Jerusalem; Tree of Gethsemane, Jerusalem (Christ); Mt. Sinai; The Dead Sea, Israel/Jordan; Mt. Hermon, Lebanon/Israel/Syria; Babylonia Ziggurat at Ur, Iraq.

"In Africa: Dogon Cliff Dwellings, Bandiagara; Mali; Lalibela Bedrock Churches, Ethiopia; Ruwenzori Peak, Uganda; Mt. Kilamanjaro, Tanzania; Mosi-oa-Tunya (Victoria Falls), Zimbabwe; Ngorongoro Crater, Tanzania.

"In Asia: Abshar Monastery, Afghanistan; Borobudur, Java; Kailas Mtn., Tibet; Mt. Fuji, Japan; River Ganges at Sangam (near Alahabad), India; Bodhi Tree, Bophgaya, India (Buddha); Angor Wat, Cambodia; Lake Baifal, Russia.

"In the South Pacific: Ponape, Micronesia; Rapanui (Easter Island), Polynesia; Tetiaroa, Tahiti; Haleakala Mtn., Maui and Diamond Head, Oahu, Hawaii.

"In Oceania: Uluru (Ayer's Rock), Australia; Rotorua, Aotearoa (New Zealand); Katatjuta, Australia.

"The above list is by no means exclusive or comprehensive. There are numerous other sacred sites and categories to consider. The form is evolving.

"Specific sites share important correspondences, which are to be acknowledged and rebalanced through 'seed' plantings and ceremonials. Among these are: 1) Palenque, Mexico/Jerusalem (as the cultural and geographical centers of their respective hemispheres); 2) Easter Island/Giza (as key sites for the preservation of Lemurian and Atlantean knowledge); Haida, Queen Charlotte Islands/New Zealand (Maori: voyagers of the Pacific Rim); The Hopi Mesas/The Dogon Cliffs (keeper of the ceremonies and prophecies); San Francisco Bay/Rio de Janeiro Bay.

"An additional two sites, one in North America, one in South America, illustrate the principal of Union of Duality through their natural formations as well as in balance to each other. They are "The Mittens" at Monument Valley, Arizona, and the confluence of the Amazon River and Rio Negro, just east of Manaus, Brazil. These sacred sites are centered within "National Sacrifice Areas," targeted by the governments of their respective countries, and calling attention to them, as to many other ecologically threatened sacred sites (such as Iguazzu Falls, The Black Hills, etc.) will ceremonially facilitate a healing of the thoughtforms that allow such sites to be destroyed. In combination with the twenty sites in Mesoamerica, these two sites yield a total of twenty-two, being the number of 52 year cycles we are completing in the conclusion of our present fifth world.

"Another ancient prophecy, this from the Lakota Sioux Indians, moves towards fulfillment as the Sacred Pipe of Ta Tanka Wian Ska (White Buffalo Cow Woman) is brought out at Summer Solstice, 1987. "The Buffalo" are coming again, and the Ghost Dance prophecy of Native America at last comes into its time. A great pyramid of purification is to be activated between the Sacred Peaks of Mt. Shasta, the Grand Teton, and Taos Mountain, its center on the island of the buffalo in the Great Salt Lake. A ceremony at Pyramid Lake grounds the historical roots of the vision, and a linking from Mt. Tamalpais, San Francisco Bay to Harney Peak, the Black Hills, allows the new energy to stream in as the Buffalo come out of the West.

"Perhaps most crucial in this year is our ability to embrace the unknown. Political and natural upheavals may test our abilities to adapt and release. We may be guided to go to certain sites or do certain things without knowing precisely why. But revelations will come with each step along the way. An old order is dying, and our ceremonies at ancient sites are partly a cleansing to prepare the field for an entirely new cycle. New sacred sites shall emerge. We are learning to work in harmony with the Planetary Being to co-create our shared reality. Like our ancestors were, we are again Technicians of the Sacred."

For further information contact:
Jim Berenholtz
PO Box 902
Taos, New Mexico 87551

PROPHECIES OF
INTERTRIBAL MEDICINE SOCIETIES
OF THE NATIVE AMERICAN INDIANS
Transcribed from a tape of a lecture given
by Harley Swiftdeer   April, 1983

"Throughout the ages, Humanity has sought out the prophecies of the spiritually gifted to instill a clear hope and vision into Life. During this time, many prophecies come to us trying to lead us in many different directions. Some prophecies point to disaster, hopelessness, and the annihilation of mankind. But other prophecies create a vision of Joyful Transformation through quantum leaps into Love and Light.

"We are dreamers, and we create physical reality through the thoughtforms we hold. As things stand now, the human race is dreaming a hell. But as individuals and as a collective Humanity, it is our potential to dream of paradise and to create the Kingdom of Heaven on our Mother Earth.

"Could it be that the pain in our Hearts, caused by the hell we have created, will spur us on into visions and creations of a world formed in Love? It is my prayer and dream, along with a multitude of others who have taught me to dream the Rainbow Dream, that each and every one of you learn to dream, both while awake and sleeping, the dream of Unity and Love through Divine Transformation.

"The prophecy that follows is a dream and a vision that is a potential reality for mankind. It is not an ultimatum. But it is ours to behold and to create, if we only dare to dream it together.

THE PROPHECY

"1987–144,000 Sun Dance enlightened teachers will totally awaken in their dream-mind bodies. They will begin to meet in their own feathered serpent or winged serpent wheels and become a major force of the Light to help the rest of Humanity to dance their dream awake. A Sun Dance teacher is any human being who has awakened, who has balanced his shield, who has gained the dream-mind body and who honors all paths, all teachers, and all ways. I look for the day when I can sit down with my pipe and the Buddhists with theirs. You will see me sit down with my dagger and my Sufi drum, with my sword, my Shinto way, my pipe, my Indian way. We're going to put our Soul out on the table and say, 'I Love you all.' This is a sacred dance. That's what 1987 is all about. That's a Sun Dancer. You cannot say that you have the only true way, for all ways are true. In 1987, 144,000 enlightened souls will sit down in gathering together circles, saying, 'Here it is, Brothers and Sisters. Openly, totally– Come and receive it.' A lot of these are going to be common people and not the people you see up there now. On August 17, 1987, the various winged serpent wheels will begin to turn, to dance once again and when they do the Rainbow Lights will be seen in dreams all over the world, and those Rainbow Light dreams will help awaken the rest of Humanity."

BILLION WATTS OF NEW ENERGY BOMBARDING EARTH
Science Confirms What We Already Know
Quartus Report by John Randolph Price

"For years we have been talking about the new energy that is coming in from the Higher Planes–enabling Earth to rise into a higher electromagnetic field 'with a dramatic accelera-tion taking place in this century' . . . 'spiritual energy as cosmic rays has been focused on the field of Humanity's con-sciousness . . . in the form of a gentle radiation to soften hearts and open minds. As the radiation continues, a new

Love vibration will be the instrument to modify behavior, change attitudes, and dissolve the destructive patterns buried deeply in the collective consciousness.' (Quotes from *With Wings As Eagles*)

"We have also discussed how this new energy can cause great strain in the mental-emotion-physical system as it works to root out false beliefs and lift us into a higher consciousness.

"Now the Associated Press, in an article on the possible causes of the ozone depletion (May 22, 1987), reports that 'electron showers have been detected by an instrument aboard a satellite. Each of the showers dumps about a billion watts of energy a second into the atmosphere, according to the Los Alamos National Laboratory. The electrons tend to spiral down the Planet's magnetic field lines. The electron showers, which hit every 27 days and last 2½ days, appear to come from Jupiter, the sun, or both, the lab said.'

"Electrons are the electrical charges whirling around the nucleus of atoms, which cause atoms to cluster in an energy field. So an 'electron shower' would seem to indicate the appearance of new energy field being stepped down to the physical plane.

"Let's look again at the primary source as given in the report: Jupiter. And what is the significance of this Planet? In Rodney Collin's *Celestial Influence* he writes: 'The system of Jupiter seems to present an exact model of the Solar System. There are a number of implications of the highly developed state of Jupiter's system . . . in the first place, the influence or radiation produced by such a system must be an extremely subtle one (gentle radiation?) incorporating a large number of different frequencies in a harmonic relation. Moreover, the fact that Jupiter's system is a scale-model of the whole Solar System brings other implications. We supposed the structure of man to be an image of that of the Solar System, and the endocrine glands in him to correspond to the various planets . . . Jupiter by its place in the Solar System appears to emit a 'note' or frequency which activates the posterior pituitary gland and produces in it a corresponding rhythm . . . a feminine significance (energy) in the posterior lobe.'

"Recall Patti Cota-Robles' comment . . . 'For several years the Love nature of God, the Feminine Aspect of Deity, has been pouring into the Planet in ever-increasing frequencies.'

"Referring back now to Rodney Collin's book, we find that the energy radiation from Jupiter is a 'healing and harmonizing' energy (words used consistently throughout Chapter One of *The Planetary Commission* and the call for the global mind-link). Collin goes on to say that the energy of Jupiter 'should be reflected in a universal fluctuation of the gentler and more Humanitarian instincts of man . . . in general in the more humane aspects of human life.'

"The AP report mentioned that the energy hits Earth every 27 days. Is it just a coincidence that in numerology, 27 is nine–the ancient number symbolizing initiation? It was also called the number of man.

"And while it may be a totally unrelated phenomena, the New York Times Service reported on May 24th that 'The violent stellar explosion that flared into view over the Southern Hemisphere on February 23 has apparently spawned a mysterious twin, according to scientists at the Harvard-Smithsonian Center for Astrophysics. The observations show that the bright exploding star, or supernova, is two points of light, close together, one about 10 times brighter than its companion. Since neither was present before the explosion, astronomers assume that, mysteriously, both arose from the same blast.'

"What was released in that explosion? Yes, 'two points of light, one about 10 times brighter than its companion.' But what/who do the lights represent? Regardless of the light year-time factor, the effect in Humanity's consciousness is now.

"Perhaps the lights are the symbol of a revelation. In her book, *From Bethlehem to Calvary*, Alice Bailey writes: 'Christ Himself tells us that at the end of the age the sign of the Son of Many will be seen in the Heavens (Matt. 24:30). Just as the Birth at Bethlehem was ushered in by a Sign, that of the Star, so shall that birth toward which the race is hastening be likewise ushered in by a heavenly Sign. The appeal which goes up from the hearts of all true aspirants to initiation is beautifully embodied in the following prayer:

There is a Peace that passeth understanding; it abides in the Hearts of those who Live in the Eternal. There is a Power which maketh all things new. It Lives and moves in those who know the Self as One. May that Peace brood over us; that Power uplift us, till we stand where the One Initiator is invoked, till we see His star shine forth.

"When that Sign is seen and the Word is heard, the next step will be the recording of the Vision.'

"As I typed the above lines I began to feel a tingling sensation all over–and my mind instantly recalled the dream on April 5th: 'Those in spiritual light, imprinting a higher vision, will share in a new beginning.' Suddenly everything seems to come together . . . the Global Mind-Link on World Healing Day, December 31st . . . the stellar explosion on February 23rd . . . the discovery of the twin lights which was actually made on March 24 . . . the dream about the vision and the soft clay on April 5th . . . the showers of new energy bombarding the Earth reported on May 22nd . . . the opportunity to impress the new Vision on August 16th and 17th. Is 'something' shaping up? Is a pattern emerging? Is there any reality to all of this?

"We shall see."

RADIATION AND MESSAGE
OF LORD GAUTAMA
May 13, 1987, Wesak Festival–Full Moon
from Group Avatar

"Blessed Exponents of God's First Cause of Perfection, I bow to the Light of God blazing in your Heart Flames. This sacred day, I come to enfold you in the radiance of Gratitude from the Universal Source of all Life "I AM" for your service to Life.

"As you have been apprised, 1987 is a Cosmic Moment in the history of this Dear Planet, and I, who currently hold the office of Planetary Logos to Earth, now invoke your assistance. Because of the need of the hour, on Easter Morn the

Karmic Board was drawn into special session under the direction of Cosmic Law. This August Body of Beings has been drawing before It, in their finer bodies, every man, woman and child evolving on Earth. As each soul passes before the Karmic Board, a special request is made by these Beings of Limitless Mercy and Compassion. Each soul is being asked to now fulfill the vows it took in the Heart of God before this embodiment to assist in this urgent hour. Each soul is being asked to release the good stored in its Causal Body, to draw forth every gift, every talent, every skill or ability that has ever been developed in any existence, in any dimension, and release it now for the benefit of all Life on Earth. The Karmic Board is asking each soul to recommit and dedicate itself to increased service to the Light.

"The Light of God, expended by those of Us in the Heavenly Realms, is always used with great reverence and efficiency. Therefore, you must realize for this unique activity to be taking place, the need for Humanity's assistance is extremely critical. The Cosmic push to bring the Masculine and Feminine Polarity of Deity into perfect balance is being accelerated. When these dual aspects of God–Divine Will (Masculine) and Divine Love (Feminine)–are in perfect HARMONY (balance), the birth of Divine Illumination (the Son/Daughter or the Christ) will occur. The Christing of this Planet and all Her Life is the next step in moving Earth forward into the Fourth Dimensional Octaves of Perfection where She will manifest Her Divine Heritage–Heaven on Earth.

"This sacred night, during the full moon of the Wesak Festival, a Cosmic dispension has been granted by the Karmic Board. Due to the increased commitment of Humanity and the petitions and promises of greater service, Cosmic Law has allowed a Galactic Being from the Great Silence to enter the atmosphere of Earth. This majestic Being's name resonates with celestial tones; the closest sound of your third dimensional frequency is LuElla. She has come with Her Regal Court for an unprecedented service to Life. She has come to EMPOWER and ACTIVATE the Crystal System of Earth. The full gathered momentum of Her radiant Light, drawn from the very Heart of God, is the glittering essence of

Emerald Green and Sapphire Blue Crystal. The qualities and frequencies of this scintillating substance are beyond anything experienced in the physical plane of Earth.

"She has taken Her strategic position in the etheric realms above the sacred focus of Diamond Head in Hawaii within the Temples of Harmony and Eternal Peace that pulsate there.

"Diamond Head is a sacred mountain that resonates with Eternal Truth. At the inception of this Planet, prior to the fall of man, Diamond Head was a tremendous vortex of Power on the continent of Lemuria or Mu. Through this vortex, the Crystal Grid System of the Planet was empowered with perfect Harmony and the totality of God's Perfection. After the fall of man, when Humanity became so immersed in his own miscreation, the Crystal System, amplifying all in Its radiance including mankind's discord, became a source of pain and destruction for Humanity. As a merciful activity to Life, the power was withdrawn from the Crystals until there was a mere flicker of Its original glory. Now, through the invocations and assistance of the mankind of Earth and through your rededication to service, the Crystal System of Earth shall again, one day soon, express all Its potential and power.

"The name of this sacred mountain, Diamond Head, signifies the crystal Purity of the CROWN CHAKRA of GOD ILLUMINATION for the Planet Earth. On August 17, 1987, when the Masculine and Feminine Polarity of Deity are brought into Perfect Harmony, the Light of God Illumination will pour into this forcefield at Diamond Head and will be anchored into the Crown Chakra of the Planet through the Heart Flames of the Light Workers gathered there. This Light will then be transmitted through the Crystal Grid System of the Planet to every other Chakra Center and anchored into the Earth through the Light Workers gathered at sacred sites all over the world.

"Beloved LuElla has directed Her Court to traverse this Planet, and a member of Her Legions has descended into EVERY power point on the Planet. From this sacred night until the influx of God Illumination on August 17, 1987, these selfless servants of God will prepare each power point to receive the maximum frequency of Light. After the Light of Illumination has been transmitted throughout the Planet on August 17th, Beloved LuElla will begin magnetizing from the Heart of God the Electronic Light Substance that will empower the Crystal System and restore It to Its original glory and service. This Light will be transmitted into the crystals ever so gently, so this power will ONLY Bless Life as this Planet is raised into the Octaves of Perfection.

"We in Heaven's Realms ask you each one to be the PEACE COMMANDING PRESENCE you are capable of being. Invoke the Violet Transmuting Flame as never before into every electron of Humanity's misqualified energy, past or present, known or unknown. The more mankind's misqualified energy has been Transmuted into Light, the more power God can transmit into the Crystal System and the greater the forward movement of the Planet and all Life into Light.

"Dear Ones, go within, and ask your God Presence how you can be the most powerful force of God's Light at this Cosmic Moment. We in Heaven's Realms await your assistance. Remember always: You are the open door which no man can shut."

"I AM" "I AM" "I AM"

Group Avatar
PO Box 41505
Tucson, Arizona 85717

VINCENT SELLECK
SHEKINAH FOUNDATION
HARMONIC CONVERGENCE

"On the 16-17th of August, 1987, millions of Lightbearers worldwide celebrated an event known as Harmonic Convergence. For the first time in aeons people throughout the World celebrated a common Holy moment at sacred sites, creating a geosynchus network of Light spanning the globe.

Operating as one body of Love in attunement to the resonance of the Planet, these Servants of Light helped to re-
align the crystal network within the Earth, restoring balance
between the mind and body of our Living sphere. As a result, pure currents of Cosmic Intelligence are now afforded
access to the mind-field of our Planet. In the sacred places an
in-spiraling of celestial energy began, setting the wheels of
planetary activation turning.

"Like chakras awakening, the spinning centers of Earth
energy have increased the vibrational frequency of the
planetary mind. The Earth as a resonant body is being lifted
into the next orbital level of the Universal Mind. Pure Light
Images from the Pleiades, Sirius, Arcturus and Orion are
now informing the resonant core of our Planet, creating a
phase shift in the morphogenetic field which imprints Galactic information upon the D.N.A. spiral of the human species.
By way of planetary crystal radiogenesis our bodies are being
informed with the Light frequencies which bring the Light-
body, our electrobiomagnetic intelligence envelope, into active conscious articulation.

"We can no longer limit our mental association of self to
our physical, emotional and mental bodies. Like the quantum transformation of matter which occurred with the split-
ting of the atom, every cell within us is being transformed,
releasing Light into our world and our bodies. Once again
we are experiencing the Sacred Presence of the Holy Spirit
within the form. The Holy Spirit is being released from the
heart of every atom of created matter like waves of Light, returning the sand castles of war and industrial society into the
random scatter resonance of pulsations emanating from the
central informing Light of our universe.

"Harmonic Convergence began a five year resonant
awakening of our Planet which will culminate in a consciously articulated, unified, planetary Intelligence field
known as the Light body of the Earth. The Human Kingdom
is to form the exo-nervous system of the planetary body.
Every human cell in this larger system will experience the
inclusive unity of a larger body of Light or Christ consciousness. We will experience a total paradigm shift as the old
mental house of industrial society is replaced by the informa-

tion beam of the Galactic Hierarchy, which will reharmonize the human kingdom with the nature forces of the Planet. Even now, as you read, the changes are taking place within you.

"In one sacred act we have broken the seals of our age, transmuting the prophesies of armegeddon, global catastrophe and war. In one unprecedented act all of the negative entropy of our world has been overruled by a constructive unified consciousness aligned with causal levels of creation. The prophesies of St. John, Nostradamus and other prophets of the former age, need not apply because they could not foresee or take into account the instant of co-operation that occurred on August 17, 1987. We are now free to live in peace and bring Heaven to Earth."

For futher information contact:
SHEKINAH FOUNDATION
P.O. THORA
N.S.W. AUSTRALIA 2454

WORLD CONGRESS ON ILLUMINATION
DIAMOND HEAD, HONOLULU, HAWAII
AUGUST 16th through AUGUST 22nd, 1987
Patricia Diane Cota-Robles

The New Age Study of Humanity's Purpose organized a global activity in Hawaii at Diamond Head. Our inner direction indicated that it was necessary for Light Workers from all over the World to gather at that Sacred Site to create a Unified Cup through which the initial impulse of Illumination would flow into the Crown Chakra of Earth.

The World Congress On Illumination was a Joyous Celebration that fulfilled the following purpose:

1. A Celebration of the Awakening; the Dawning of the New Age of Wisdom and Understanding.
2. A Celebration of a new awareness and major shift in consciousness toward Peace, Love, Healing, Joy, Spirituality, Wholeness.

3. A bringing together of major enlightened and awakened teachers for the purpose of sharing their experiences and visions of the future.

4. Defining of the Vision of the New Genesis.

5. Sharing of visions, dreams, Illuminations and Enlightenment on the Pathway toward unfoldment.

6. To more clearly understand the nature of Humanity and the purpose of Life.

7. Increase our awareness of the vision of the New Age by bringing together Illumined energies and expanding the Light.

8. To serve as a Spiritual Body in support of the Unification of the Planet.

9. To fulfill the concept of a Planetary Network of Light.

10. To create a Unified "Cup" through which that Light of God will be anchored into the world of form.

THE FAMILY OF HUMANITY CREATING A UNIFIED CUP THROUGH WHICH THE LIGHT OF GOD WILL POUR INTO PLANET EARTH

"My experience in Hawaii confirmed for me what I have been receiving in meditation for quite some time, and that is, that the greatest honor and privilege for any Lifestream in any dimension, in any stage of evolvement, is physical embodiment on Planet Earth during this Cosmic Moment of Transformation.

"Since that Sacred event in August, I have been assimilating the magnitude of what actually transpired, and I have perceived clearly the rejoicing of all the Realms of Heaven as Archangel Gabriel sounds His trumpet heralding the Immaculate Concept of the new Cosmic Day–Heaven on Earth.

"The Victorious accomplishment of Harmonic Convergence and the World Congress On Illumination far surpassed even the greatest expectations of the entire Company of Heaven. On August 17, 1987, the Feminine Ray of Divine Love was anchored into the core of the Eternal Sun of Even Pressure in the center of the Earth. That radiance of Divine Love then began to pulsate in, through and around every electron of precious Life energy belonging to or serving the

Earth at this time. The Feminine Ray of Divine Love called forth the Cosmic Love Nature at the core of every electron which is the fundamental building block of all creation in the Universe. This activity of Light built in momentum and intensity until the Autumn Equinox on September 23, 1987. During the birth of the New Moon, there was an eclipse of the Sun. The Sun and Moon blended their Rays at the moment of balance when day and night were of equal duration. At that symbolic moment the Masculine Ray of Divine Will and the Feminine Ray of Divine Love were permanently sealed in perfect balance within every electron of energy in the physical plane of Earth. The Cosmic Forces are now in place in perfect balance, and an aura of indisputable, impersonal Divine Love penetrates all Life. Through this unparalleled event, an atmosphere of safety has been created to allow the HOLY CHRIST SELF WITHIN THE HEARTS OF *ALL* HUMANITY TO NOW BE CALLED FORTH. The Feminine Nature of God–Divine Love–represented by the Divine Mother Principle–is now holding a protecting, nurturing forcefield around each Lifestream enabling the unfolding Christ Nature of all Humanity to grow safely to full stature. What a Glorious, God Victorious moment on Earth!

"As the Christ within begins to take dominion, we will experience greater and greater levels of self-mastery. Soon our Lives will no longer reflect the world of Illusion but will reflect only the totality of God's Perfection.

"The World Congress On Illumination was a magnificent activity of Light, and we have been directed from within to hold it annually in various locations on the Planet to magnetize the Light of God into the physical plane of Earth."

If you would like information regarding this event, you may contact:

The New Age Study of Humanity's Purpose
P.O. Box 41883
Tucson, Arizona 85717

Interesting Observations: If we will be more conscious and observe the things occurring in the outer world, we will see tangible proof that this knowledge is piercing into the consciousness of Humanity in all phases of existence. For example:

1987 was the year of the return of the Feminine Aspect of Deity–the Divine Mother Principle. Throughout history, Mother Mary has SYMBOLICALLY represented this aspect of God. On January 1st, 1987, Pope John Paul dedicated the year to Mother Mary.

The Beings of Light have indicated to us that the Masculine Polarity of God enters the Earth as a tremendous shaft of Light in the Himalayan Mountains. That masculine power had been the predominent influence flowing into the Planet up until 1954 when the main thrust of Light was transferred to the Feminine Polarity of God which enters the Planet as a tremendous shaft of Light in Mt. Meru in the Andes Mountains of South America. The Feminine Ray built in momentum from 1954 until the Cosmic Moment of August 17, 1987, 33 years. Thirty-three is the mystical number that symbolizes the Christ Consciousness. Jesus fulfilled His Divine mission at the age of 33. Interestingly, the last time a Pope dedicated the year to Mother Mary was 1954, the year the power was transferred to the Feminine Aspect of God.

Mother Mary's Ascension Day is celebrated on the 15th of August each year. It is not a coincidence that the Feminine Ray was anchored into the Earth at that time. On August 15th, 1987, the Light began increasing and intensified for three days until It reached the point of perfect balance. Then the Cosmic Tone sounded, and the Feminine Ray of God was anchored into the Divine Forcefield of the Sun of Even Pressure that pulsates in the center of the Earth.

Many of the ancient prophecies seemed to reflect the "end" of the world. The Aztec Calendar ended on August 17, 1987. The reason is that the seers of ancient times could not "see" beyond the power of the Masculine Ray into the more refined vibrations of the Love Nature of the

Feminine Ray. Quite the contrary, instead of the "end", it was truly the "Birth" and a new beginning.

Another interesting occurrence in 1987 was the signing of the missile treaty by President Reagan and General Secretary Mikhail Gorbachev. In 1987, Mother Mary had been appearing to several children in Medjugorje, Yugoslavia for quite some time. Her message was clearly the need for World Peace and Harmony among countries, especially the United States of America and the Soviet Union. The missile treaty was signed on December 8, 1987, the date long celebrated as Mother Mary's Feast of the Immaculate Conception. The Immaculate Concept is the "Perfect Thoughtform" or "Divine Blueprint" of any physical manifestation. What a perfect day to be initiating the very first step *ever* for arms reduction.

In 1987 my son was traveling with the wonderful Peace Ambassadors "Up With People". That year, they were invited FOR THE FIRST TIME to tour the Soviet Union. The official invitation reached the "Up With People" headquarters the same day President Reagan and Mikhail Gorbachev signed the missile treaty, December 8, 1987, Mother Mary's Feast of the Immaculate Concept.

Everything is being greatly accelerated, and if we will be alert, we will experience continual confirmation of the "moment at hand."

The exceptional expansion of Light occurring in 1986 and 1987 continued to increase in 1988, *as it will each and every year from now on* until the Permanent Golden Age is manifest in every sacred detail.

In 1988 the Twelve-fold Aspect of Deity was activated within the axis of the Planet and within the Solar Spine of every Lifestream evolving on Earth. This activity signaled the return of the "I AM" Presence to Earth, the HEALING OF OUR SEPARATION FROM GOD.

Each month throughout the twelve month cycle, a Solar Chakra, radiating one of the Twelve-fold Aspects of God, was activated within the Solar Spine of Humanity. Month by month, an aspect of God's Perfection poured through the Humanity of Earth to Bless all Life.

A key event in 1988 took place on February 13th. This activity was referred to as EARTH LINK-88. The interim stage between Harmonic Convergence and Earth Link-88 represented a turning point in the direction of world endeavor. Vincent Selleck of the Shekinah Foundation described it as follows:

"The critical mass that occurred within causal levels of creation during Harmonic Convergence was externalized as an explosion of Light on February 13, 1988. People everywhere experienced a resonant shift in their level of conscious awareness. The collective ceiling of human thought opened to the Spiritual Realms allowing a stream of Light to enter each person's sphere of consciousness, Illuminating a vision of higher Truth. Light was released from the Heart of every created atom, from within every Living cell in the human body, restructuring the genetic blueprint with higher Life Codes. Humanity literally awakened as our "I AM" Consciousness was brought into alignment with the Universal 'I AM' That 'I AM'."

Vincent explained the time frame and the event thusly:

"You may ask, 'Why will this happen on the 13th of February? What is so significant about this date?'

"The answer to this question is etched in the sky by the Great Architect who designed the cycle of the planetary spheres. Saturn and Uranus will reach their exact conjunction point on that date. The metal Uranium, named after Uranus and Saturn, represents the principle of density of form. Together they combine to create the 'critical mass' explosion of Light demonstrated by nuclear physics. Unlike the situation that occurred in 1945 after the previous conjunction of these two planets in Taurus, sign of the release of secret power from the depths of the Earth, which resulted in the destruction of Nagasaki and Hiroshima, the 1988 conjunction occurs in the final degree of Sagittarius, sign of the spiritual goals and aspirations of Humanity. This potent release of Light will Illuminate a new direction and purpose for the spiritual development of Humanity. Suddenly, like the lightning flash of Uranian electricity, a powerful new mental structure will be revealed that will revolutionize our concept of ourselves and the universe. This revelation will change the foundations of science, religion and philosophy and bring forth a collective global vision that will suddenly transport our world into a new age of co-operation, unified purpose and spiritual vision."

Vincent continues:

STARS OF SYNCHRONIZATION

"There is a direct astrological link between Earth Link 88 and Harmonic Convergence. During Earth Link 88, the sun's relative position from the Earth will be directly opposite (180° from) the position that it was in at the time of the Harmonic Convergence. Because the Sun was 144° from the Vernal Equinox point at 1° Aries during the Harmonic Convergence this means that the Sun will be 144° from the point of the Autumnal Equinox (Northern Hemisphere) on February 13th. Diagramatically, this can be expressed by two five pointed stars, 144° being the angle between interconnected points.

Position of the Sun during
Harmonic Convergence
at 25° Leo

Position of the Sun during
Earth Link '88 at
25° Aquarius

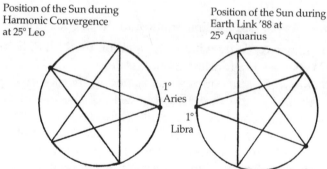

1°
Aries

1°
Libra

"These stars trace parallel lines across the circle of the zodiac indicating the parallel relationship between Earth Link 88 and Harmonic Convergence.

"The opposing stars that they form demonstrate the reconciling of the opposing forces of spirit and matter. When both of these stars are united in our consciousness as part of one experience, the forces they represent are harmonized within us. The separation of the five heavenly elements and their reflected five earthly elements disappears.

$$5 + 5 = 10(1 + 0) = 1 \text{ THE RETURN TO UNITY}$$

"While the Harmonic Convergence represented the rising Sun and the inflow of cosmic information that began a new cycle, Earth Link 88 represents the setting Sun and the death of the old age and its disharmonic structures.

SEQUENCE OF PLANETARY ACTIVATION

"It is difficult to draw one moment out of the constantly changing sea of time and separate it from the moment immediately before and immediately after. The height of one wave crest is only of significance when measured from the trough. The lightning bolt activation of Earth Link 88 cannot be seen separately from the steady build of electrical potential before or the peace and stillness after. One moment unfolds into the next. Change is constantly everywhere.

"The energy of Earth Link 88 is a cyclic transformation in three stages or movements of change which reach their optimum potential during these moments:

1. 12:30 a.m. G.M.T. 13th February 1988. Festival of Human Commission. World wide synchronized meditation peaks at the exact time of the conjunction between Uranus and Saturn in the 30th degree of Sagittarius.

2. 10:33 p.m. 13th February 1988 G.M.T. crystallization of Radiant pathways in the Earth matrix. Saturn transits from Sagittarius (Fire) to Capricorn (Earth).

3. 10:00 p.m. 14th February 1988 G.M.T. Ignition of crystal fire–Image within Earth Matrix. Uranus transits from Sagittarius (Fire) to Capricorn (Earth).

FESTIVAL OF HUMAN COMMISSION

"The exact conjunction point of Saturn and Uranus in February presents us with a unique opportunity for cosmic attunement. Unutilized, this moment may pass by as any other. However, if a sufficient number of incarnated souls can resonate their Hearts and minds together and fill the sky with the song of their burning desire for paradise and perfection in the Kingdom, then a mighty force from Heaven will come and shake the foundations of the World, bringing the return of Intelligent order to the scheme of our Lives. This intervention into the World by Higher Intelligence can only occur if permission is granted by the vibrational majority of human thought-impulse upon the Earth. The synchronized global meditation scheduled for midnight to 1:00 A.M. G.M.T. on the 13th of February 1988 is the vehicle through which permission will be granted. The wave of the global invocation of the redemptive Christ Light will overrule the limited mental paradigm of the fallen consciousness, and our Earth will become Holy again. The vibrations of Glory will return to the heart of every atom as the forms of our World once again radiate with the Light of the Holy Spirit.

"The conjunction of Uranus and Saturn acts as a cosmic gateway allowing a stream of Manasic force to enter the Earth's bio-magnetic fields. Manas is the Intelligent Will of the higher Evolution, the active purpose or fixed idea which brings about existence, utilizes form and processes effects and causes through discrimination. Earth Link 88 is such a time, and provided that critical mass of human thought is united in appealing to the Karmic Board for redemption, the influence of the Masters of Light will return 'and the functions of the faculties reserved for the Ascended Masters are passed on to the Saints of Light who have overcome darkness with the power of God's Word . . . ' (Key 206:63k "The Keys of Enoch").

"Our solar system is a complete body of Intelligence, the planets of which operate in much the same way as Chakra centers in that larger body. This inter-connectedness of the planets is expressed mathematically in astronomy through the harmonic relationship of one planet's orbit to another. This relationship, brought to Light by Kepler, allowed astronomers to discover Uranus, Neptune and Pluto through the detection of slight aberrations in the orbits of other planets. Central to the whole scheme is the Sun, whose electro-magnetic intelligence field or Heliocosm envelops all of the planetary spheres. The central Intelligence of the Sun, the 'Solar Logos', intermediates between the planets and incoming radiations from the Stellar Logi. Jose Arguelles in 'The Mayan Factor' enlarges on this process.

'The information flow between a planet body like Earth and the galactic core is maintained and mediated by the Solar activity known as the binary sunspots. Both Sun and planet operate with the same galactic information bank. Whenever a stellar body, such as our Sun, begins its evolutionary course, it is imprinted with the 260-unit galactic code. Once a planet such as ours attains a point of resonant activation, the galactic information flow mediated through the sunspots imprints the outer electromagnetic sheath with the basics of the planetary memory programme'. (Page 109 'The Mayan Factor')

"In 'A treatise on Cosmic Fire' by A. Bailey we are told:

'For some time the (Solar) Logos has turned His Attention to the *Earth Scheme* and to *Saturn*, whilst *Uranus* is receiving stimulation. Much is therefore accentuated and increased evolutionary development is the consequence of this divine attention'. (Page 357-8 'A Treatise on Cosmic Fire')

"Hence a conjunction of Uranus and Saturn has great consequences for the evolving Intelligence on the Earth.

CRYSTALLIZATION OF RADIANT PATHWAYS

"Once the appeal has been sent forth, the chalice must be prepared for the wine. The 'chalice' in this case is the Light Network that we have helped to weave between the sacred sites of our Earth. One can equate this preparation process to the wiring of the electrical circuits in our electrobiomagnetic Planetary temple. On the 13th of February at 10:33 p.m. G.M.T., when Saturn transits into Capricorn, the Galactic electricity commission will inspect our wiring and advise us of any final work that is necessary before the power is connected.

"Our consciousness has acted as a bridge for the reharmonizing of the planetary crystalline grid, receiving and implementing instructions from divine source which led to the resonant activation called 'Harmonic Convergence'. As Saturn changes signs, we are asked to complete the resonant structure by attuning to inner advice at sacred sites throughout the globe. The final imprint of our collective aspiration will then occur, and the resultant neurological pathways of the rebalanced and enlarged global mind will be locked into crystal form as the reservoir of Life-patterning information for the next Aeon. It is extremely important that only the highest and best vision for the future Earth be imprinted at this time.

"Fortunately, the Earth is endowed with a protective mechanism to ensure that only pure spiritual patterns can enter the data base for future program. Information can only be entered into the program from the vortex areas of the 1745 sacred sites by programmers possessing the resonant vibrations of the Holy Names and a capacity for maintaining Love Vibration. The threshold level of the minimum vibrational requirement has been set, though the success of the final program is governed by how high a vision can be sustained above that threshold level.

"As Saturn moves from Sagittarius to Capricorn, the fire of matter, the Kundalini force of Sagittarius is brought into the crystalline Earth of Capricorn. The spiralling energy of the sacred fire is the force that animates material form and causes it to become biological Life. The spiral sacred fire force also imprints the basic building block of Life, the D.N.A., with its pattern.

"When the Earth-fire re-crystallizes into a new structural form, the entire biological program of Life is affected. As the Human Kingdom evolves further into its role as co-creators of Life, we are offered an opportunity to imprint the best qualities of our consciousness into the new biological model of the next race. The new age will be built on the foundations of our achievements now.

IGNITION OF THE CRYSTAL FIRE-IMAGE

"At 10 p.m. G.M.T. on the 14th of February 1988, a bolt of lightning will unite the two poles of creation. Uranus, the electrical fire of the spirit, will enter into the density of Earth in Capricorn sending an electrical charge from the crown of planetary Humanity to the root of creation. Spirit will enter matter revealing the radiance of the inner worlds that lie beneath the structure of form.

"The resonant pathways that were crystallized into the energy matrix of the Planetary mind through the service of the faithful will become charged pathways of electrical Light intensity. Throughout the world, the lid of material reality will be lifted revealing the webs of Light that constitute the causal levels of matter. Light will emmanate from all created substance. Thus will the Holy Spirit be revealed!

"The Regenesis of Humanity will begin as the Life model controlling the D.N.A. pattern is brought onto a new level of evolution. The Image of Perfection, empowered by the crystal reservoir within the now electrically brilliant Earth, will be applied upon our physical garments causing deep transformation to occur within every created cell of our Beings. The spark will begin at Uluru in Central Australia and travel throughout the world network like lightning. Radiance will be everywhere. Matter will be transformed into Light.

"We cannot, in our limited consciouisness, even begin to imagine what this will be like,'...*as Hosannah* is united with the unspeakable splendor of God as He really is–utterly beyond comprehension'. (Key 206:63, 'The Keys of Enoch')

"Everyone, in every country, in every religion, in every place everywhere will see the Light, because the Light will be within them. The spark will ignite the soul into wakefulness, and a vision of purpose and higher attainment will become clear to the whole Being. Then, as quickly as the Light came, it will disappear. Those who can retain the perspective of their soul will be empowered to bring their vision into attainment. Others will simply go back to their old ways and try to forget that it ever happened, denying everything.

"One week later, Mars will transit the conjunction point bringing the thrust of this inner-light awakening into physical expression in the material world."

This information was taken from an excellent book titled *Earth Link 88–A Guide to the Planetary Awakening* by Vincent Selleck. It can be ordered through

The Shekinah Foundation
P.O. Thora
N.S.W., Australia 2454

The following article appeared in *The Arizona Daily Star* on October 11, 1988. This enhances the information reflecting the shift in vibration occurring on the Planet and our increased awareness.

PHYSICISTS THEORIZE BEAM
IN SPACE HAS NEW PARTICLES

ALBUQUERQUE (AP)–A powerful beam striking the Earth from a twin star system 14,000 light years away could herald a new type of particle that physicists said confounds the standard theories of physics.

The beam, carrying a million billion electron volts of energy, comes from a neutron star, half of a binary star system named Hercules X-1 in the constellation Hercules, said Dr. Guarang Yodh, a physicist at the University of California at Irvine.

The neutron star is nearly the size of Earth's moon, but is extremely dense with a mass nearly double the sun's.

The other half of the star system, about 4 million miles from the neutron star, is a star similar to the Sun.

The neutron star is a large, spinning magnet, generating massive electromagnetic fields and giving off powerful radiation.

The beam, first detected at Los Alamos National Laboratory in July 1986, initially was believed to be electrically neutral gamma rays, which are high-energy light waves or photons.

The problem with that interpretation was that the beam "hits way up in the atmosphere and produces a shower of particles," Yodh said Friday in a telephone interview.

Gamma rays are not supposed to do that, said Dr. Darragh Nagle, a physicist at the Los Alamos lab.

"That's the thing that's interesting and puzzling about the finding," he said. "There is the possible presence of a new particle that is coming out of the study of a powerful neutral beam.

"It isn't the power of the neutral beam; it's this peculiar interaction in the Earth's atmosphere," Nagle said, in a telephone interview.

Yodh said the discovery should lead to new insights about sources of energy in the universe and about the elementary structure of matter.

"Both of them are extremely relevant to our understanding of our universe. I think that is the main impact it will make on society," Yodh said.

Yodh said scientists have come up with several explanations for the strange beam, which also has been detected by observatories in Arizona and Hawaii. One explanation is that it is made of a previously unknown particle.

*   *   *

The information regarding these synchronized global activities is presented as tangible proof that Humanity is truly awakening to the need of the hour. There is definitely a shift taking place in the awareness of people as we realize the Oneness of all Life.

The most critical time of any age is at its inception, and the Lifestreams in embodiment at this time are responsible for magnetizing the flow of Light from the Godhead into the physical world of form.

At this Cosmic Moment, THE INCEPTION OF THE PERMANENT GOLDEN AGE, our responsibility is unparalleled in the history of time. It is critical that each and every one of us goes within to the Perfection of God blazing in our Hearts. We must draw forth guidance and assistance to fulfill our Purpose and Reason for Being NOW!!!

EFFECTIVELY UTILIZING GOD'S WILL IN OUR DAILY LIVES

The Law of Attraction magnetizes into our Lives whatever we focus our attention on. Therefore, if we want to experience God's Will in our daily activities we need merely hold our attention on that Divine Quality.

The First Ray of God's Will reverberates through the atmosphere of Earth on a frequency of Sapphire Blue Light. It resonates through our Solar Spine in the vicinity of our Throat Chakra.

The Sapphire Blue Ray of God's Will contains within It the resonance of Decision and the Will to Do. Everything that has ever been accomplished on the physical plane of Earth or in the Heavenly Realms has been accomplished by men and women of Decision. Without Decision and the Will to Do, there is no permanence of accomplishment.

Preceeding all action and all manifestation, there must be the WILL TO DO within the consciousness. We can easily see how important it is for each of us to become adept at utilizing this sacred Gift from God. What we WILL manifests. What we WILL to be, we WILL be. What we WILL to CREATE must come, for it is Law. Knowing this Divine Law, each of us should continually affirm: "I WILL to be God FREE!"

We are the open doors through which the Divine Design of the Permanent Golden Age is being passed into the world of form. As the Divine Ideas are lowered into our consciousness, we must vitalize them with our heartfelt desire and feelings. Then we must, through Decision and the Will to do, precipitate them into manifest expression for the blessing of all Life.

God's Will for Humanity is the fullness of all good; all opulence, all beauty, all FREEDOM. The Will of God must now be impressed with such Strength and Power into the consciousness of Humanity that there will no longer be any delay in all Lifestreams lifting up out of the shadows of limitation and suffering. We must now be willing to accept ONLY God's Will in our Lives, which is Perfection for all things.

Within the Power of God's Will is Mastery, and within the full gathered momentum of God pulsating in our Hearts is the Faith to attain that Mastery, a Faith that stands in the face of seemingly insurmountable odds, a Faith that stands in the face of "reason", a Faith that stands in the face of human appearances.

Faith is a constant state of our Being every second of Eternity. It is not a quality we have to acquire. It is already present within us. What we *do* need to realize is that we have the ability to train ourselves to allow the quality of Faith to sustain only those manifestations which we desire to sustain.

How many of us, through the Power of our attention, have placed our Faith in poverty, disease, loneliness, pain, suffering and despair? Faith is self-perpetuating. The more we focus our attention on the negativity of the world, the more Faith we have that it will continue. Conversely, the more we focus our attention on the Will of God, the more

Faith we have that It will manifest.

We have the Power to let go of the situations in our Lives that are creating obstacles. We need simply to adjust our consciousness and focus on God's Will, and invoke the highest good for all concerned. Through the Law of Attraction, God's Will will be projected through our consciousness into the atomic substance of the material plane. Then, our environment and Life situations will be Transformed. This may seem too simple and too good to be true, but it is the accurate application of the Natural Law of the Universe, and works consistently and scientifically to the letter.

The wonderful thing about Natural Law is that we are all subject to it regardless of whether we believe in it or not. Consequently, we don't have to accept this Truth. We don't have to believe it. We don't even need to understand it. All we have to do is APPLY it.

Our consciousness has become embedded and engrained with much imperfection through our Life experience, but now as we focus our attention on Truth and God's Will, our ability to interpret Life and our Perception of Life will become more accurate. Then, we will be much more receptive to Divine Will. The Light of God shall NEVER again recede, and the fullest manifestation for the Divine potential of Earth and all Humanity is now abundantly evident.

The Will of God is that we must now EXTERNALIZE the perfection already existing at Inner Levels. We must draw the visions, ideas, patterns, and plans that have already manifested in the Octaves of Perfection into the physical plane. This can be accomplished by all sincere, practical, willing students on the path of Light.

In the flow of Divine Will even our human ego with all its treachery cannot block God's First Cause of Perfection. We each have great momentums that we have built through time. We each have a different heritage that we are bringing to Earth to offer as our service to Life. Within our Causal Bodies, our storehouse of good, we have tremendous momentums of Perfection upon which we can draw to assist in the Transformation of our own Lives as well as the salvation of the Planet.

Each diverse human being is bringing their unique thread

of the tapestry of Life to weave into the Unified purpose of the Planet. In Perfect Harmony Humanity will begin to expand the borders of the Kingdom of our Father-Mother God. This Unified effort is beginning to reveal itself now. There must be Unity of Purpose in the Hearts of all on the Planet for the Earth to outpicture the Plan of Perfection ordained for Her.

Unity of Purpose, in God's Name, means to individually be obedient to the Will of God and function at all times from the Heart of our God Presence. If we will do this, we will have such a Glorious experience that words cannot describe it. Unity and Oneness with God and all Life is a goal we shall one day soon attain.

In order to fulfill our Unified Purpose we must become the fullness of our God Nature. Through that endeavor, we will bless all Life, not by pressing the strength of our personal opinions and human will on other Lifestreams, but by being a clear crystal through which the Light of God will flow unobstructed to nourish Humanity and every particle of Life.

We must go within to the well-spring of our Hearts and listen in the Great Silence for the guidance of our true God Self. To receive directions from our God Presence accurately is an accomplishment in itself, but to then draw the energies and substance together to OBEY those directives involves the full Power of the First Ray of God's Will, Decision and the WILL TO DO. This is the first step of our self-mastery. The First Ray is in a unique position in the Great evolutionary plan of Creation because it is the initial impulse by which the ideas born out of the Mind and Heart of God are given Life. As we reach deep within ourselves, we will realize our God Presence is anxiously awaiting the opportunity to express Itself. It is time to liberate our God Presence from the confines of our lower human consciousness. Only then will we be able to reach our full potential and effectively participate in the Divine Plan unfolding.

Change of any kind, even for the better, seems to stir our individual energies causing our outer human consciousness to resist. But, if we will rhythmically and consistently do the exercise of "Getting in Touch with our Higher Self," we will experience miraculous changes in our Lives as we begin to tap the Power of God within and respond to the infallible guidance of our true God Self.

This exercise is a very simple, yet incredibly Powerful way to reach our God Self. Practice it daily and BE Transformed.

GETTING IN TOUCH WITH YOUR HIGHER SELF–YOUR GOD PRESENCE "I AM"

Communing with the God Presence within is the key to our Spiritual Freedom and ultimately our Ascension in the Light. There are myriad ways of accomplishing this communion, and each person will have their own individual, unique variations. Here, in five basic steps, are some simple guidelines that are amazingly effective:

1. Become quiet and relax. "BE STILL AND KNOW."
2. Call forth a Forcefield of Protection.
3. Reach up into the Octaves of Light.
4. Invoke Your God Presence.
5. Listen. "BE STILL AND KNOW THAT 'I AM' GOD."

BECOME QUIET AND RELAX

Begin by commanding every cell and organ of your body to relax.

"BE STILL AND KNOW"

Being still is known in many ways: "entering the Silence," "being in tune with the Infinite," "going within." This is a Stillness that permeates every level of your Being. It begins with your physical body. Speak to each portion of your body and tell it to relax. Start with your feet and move all the way up to your scalp. Gradually, you will become more and more proficient, and one day you will only have to command the body to relax, and instantaneously, it will respond.

The etheric body (memories of the past), the mental body (thoughts), and the emotional body (feelings) must also be silenced. Cleanse your Heart and Mind of everything less than Harmony and cover everything else that may distract you in a blanket of pink Love.

When your relaxation is complete affirm deep in your Heart Flame:

"I AM" that "I AM". (Repeat 9 Times)

Now gently move to the next step.

CALL FORTH A FORCEFIELD OF PROTECTION

Light is the most Powerful emanation of all Creation. In this step you Invoke the full Power of God's First Ray of Protection and Divine Will.

In the Name of the Almighty Presence of God "I AM", I invoke from the very Heart of God an invincible shaft of God's First Cause of Protection. This shaft of Sapphire Blue Light extends from the Heavenly Realms into the Earth below me. It surrounds every electron of my Being encapsulating me in an invincible forcefield of God's Holy Will and Protection. This forcefield cuts Free anything that is not of the Light from within me and prevents anything that is not of the Light from penetrating into my forcefield of Protection. I feel and know that "I Am" absolutely Protected.

Only when you feel perfectly protected do you proceed to the next step.

REACH UP INTO THE OCTAVES OF LIGHT

This step is used to raise the vibratory level of your four lower bodies (physical, etheric, mental and emotional), enabling you to reach up past the chaos of the psychic-astral plane into the Octaves of Illumined Truth.

I invoke the Golden-White Christ Light from the Heart of God to flood my Being. I now consciously direct this Light into every electron of my four lower bodies. I visualize the Sacred Light expanding through my brain structure and my seven major chakra centers. The scintillating Light calms my

*thoughts and activates the dormant centers of my brain enabl-
ing me to clearly perceive the voice of my God Presence. Every
fiber of my Being is now pulsating with Christ Light.*

*"I AM" now ready to Ascend into the Octaves of Light. I
start with my feet and see the Golden-White Christ Light spinning around my feet and ankles. The swirling vortex of energy
begins to build, rising up my legs into my torso. It rises higher
and higher until my entire body is surrounded in a whirling
forcefield of electronic Light.*

*I now feel myself Ascending up the Sapphire Blue shaft of
God's Holy Will into the Realm of Eternal Light.*

*Very slowly I let the Light unwind back down to my feet,
and I remain in the Realm of Eternal Light.*

*"I AM" able to see myself now AS my God Presence. I feel
the Oneness—the separation is no more.*

Gently move to the next step.

INVOKING MY GOD PRESENCE

Now ask for guidance and direction to assist you in fulfilling your Divine Plan.

*Through the Power of God pulsating in my Heart, I invoke my
Mighty "I AM" Presence, My True God Reality, to take command of my four lower bodies and walk through me. Blessed
One, raise me back up to my Source and reunite me with the
One Presence of all Life. Bring forth the God energies necessary for me to know only the Perfection of God in all Life, and
let me experience only God's Love, Life and Light in all I see,
feel, speak and do this day!*

So Be It!   *"I AM"*

Now ask your God Presence whatever question you may
have. Ask for clarity, understanding and guidance.

EXPANDED INVOCATION
(optional)

In the Name of God "I AM", I invoke the entire Company of

Heaven and All from the Realms of Illumined Truth to guide, teach and Protect me. I ask You now, Blessed Ones, to receive the Love I send forth to You, and I ask that you assist me in my endeavor to find and manifest God's Will in my Life.

Proceed gently to the final step.

LISTEN

This is the point of opening up all your receiver circuits and Listening. Remind yourself that you are not going to fall asleep. Still your mind. Maintain the strength to receive any spiritual clarity.

Close out the world, and Listen to the rhythm of your Heartbeat. Experience the Harmony as it blends with the rhythm of the Universe. Remember, telepathy is a passive detection of a thought. You are not concentrating on receiving; you are not thinking; you are passive, peaceful, receptive. YOU ARE LISTENING.

"BE STILL AND KNOW THAT 'I AM' GOD"

INVOCATIONS AND AFFIRMATIONS
TO MAGNETIZE THE WILL OF GOD
INTO THE PHYSICAL PLANE OF EARTH

THE CALL FOR ASSISTANCE MUST COME FROM THE REALM WHERE THE ASSISTANCE IS NEEDED. "ASK AND YOU SHALL RECEIVE."

The Invocation of the Qualities of God is a True Science. We must practice it carefully and rhythmically. As our primal Life Essence flows into our Hearts, we each qualify that Gift of Life with our thoughts and feelings. If we are in Communion with our God Presence, the Life force is charged with the Power to do God's Will, the Wisdom to use the Light effectively, and the Love to bless all Life.

We have the ability to Invoke the Light of God into every one of our Life experiences. When we Invoke God's Light which is *always* Victorious, It will pass through our four lower bodies raising the vibration of each of our vehicles out of the conflict and chaos around them. That FREES us from tying into the negativity and enables us to objectively observe the possible solutions with greater clarity. From this place of detachment we can Harmoniously communicate with our God Presence and ask for guidance. If we practice this discipline consistently, we will remain in the continual flow of guidance from our God Presence, and we will remain detached from all the negativity around us.

Remember, the need of the hour is not that we do battle with, resist, and fight everything that is causing a problem in our Lives, but rather that we Invoke the Light of God effectively, thus lifting ourselves up out of the confusion. Then, from our new perspective we can see viable solutions and Transmute the negative situation back into Light.

The following Affirmations and Invocations are designed to specifically draw the qualities of the First Ray of God's Will into our Lives. If we daily energize these thoughtforms, through the Power of the spoken word, they will soon begin to reflect on the material plane around us. Then, we will see very definite changes occurring in our Lives.

Center yourself within the Presence of God pulsating in your Heart and recite these Affirmations and Invocations with DEEP FEELING.

GIVING YOUR GOD PRESENCE DOMINION

Mighty "I AM" Presence, take command of my outer self this day. Take command of my every thought, feeling, spoken word, action and reaction. Produce Your Perfection and hold Your dominion within me. Put and keep me always in my right and perfect place. Show me the perfect thing to do and through me, do it perfectly. So be it, Beloved "I AM".

A PREPARED VEHICLE

In the Name of the Cosmic Law of Love, Forgiveness and God's Holy Will which I now Invoke:

"I AM" Transmuting my human consciousness by God's Sacred Light. (3 times)

Oh Sacred Light, blazing as a radiant, spiraling Flame within my Heart:

Charge my physical vehicle into a higher physical consciousness. (3 times)

Charge my etheric vehicle into a higher etheric consciousness. (3 times)

Charge my mental vehicle into a higher mental consciousness. (3 times)

Charge my emotional vehicle into a higher emotional consciousness. (3 times)

and grateful for this Sacred Light . . . "I AM" now sublimated, refined, accelerated and Transformed by the currents of God's Light and a prepared vehicle for the expression of my God Self on this Planet. So be it. Beloved "I AM".

GREATER PRESENCE IN ACTION

(To be used regularly and/or for specific problems in your Life or service, especially if you have been thrown off center by a problem.)

In the Name of the Magnificent Flame of Life "I AM" . . . I do now affirm that in all areas of Life and Service: "I AM" relinquishing self and human will. (3 times)

As the embodied Flame "I AM" . . .

I KNOW there is a greater Power than myself in action here. (3 times)

I KNOW there is a greater Wisdom than myself in action here. (3 times)

I KNOW there is a greater Love than myself in action here. (3 times)

I know this is the Victory of the Light in Action through me! I accept this as the Truth in all areas of my Life and Service. "I AM" that Greater Presence here in action... "I AM" that "I AM". SO BE IT!

RESTORATION OF MY LIFE

My Divine Essence . . . I Love and adore you. Shine through my every effort at becoming ONE WITH THEE. Oh, Flaming Presence of Light, let the gift of Divine Love, which is Yours alone to give, flow through me to set Life FREE. I ask that I might be Love's open door.

And as I accelerate my journey toward Eternal Oneness with you, I consciously draw back to myself all my own energies that I am so desirous of Loving free. Help me, oh Flame in my Heart, to Love myself free . . . all returning energy . . . as I am about my Father's business of LOVING ALL LIFE FREE.

"I AM" reclaiming all my energies back into the Heart of Love. (3 times)

"I AM" the Light of God in action, Loving me FREE, (3 times)

"I AM" grateful to the Sacred Fire, the most powerful aspect of Love that instantly Transmutes all outstanding energy back into Perfection. "I AM" again made Whole with Thee! As God's Most Holy Name… "I AM".

TO THE COSMIC SPIRIT OF GOD'S HOLY WILL

Blessings for Your Presence in this Universe. Gratitude for Your motivating Power which directs the Cosmic Beings, Ascended Masters, Archangels and Archaii, Seraphim, Cherubim, Angelic Host, and the God Presence of all Humanity.

We invoke, consciously, the descent of the full gathered Cosmic Momentum of the Divine Will of the Universal "I AM" Presence into the emotional, mental, etheric and physical strata wherein mankind presently abide! LET the inherent desire to do God's Will expand through every unascended being! LET the Joy that is the reward of such service expand through their auras! LET the outer mind of Humanity accept that God's Will is the fullness of all good and perfect experiences for all His creations! LET the fallacy that distress and imperfection are God's Will be removed from the consciousness of all people! Remove the lethargic acceptance of imperfection from the people of Earth! Replace it by a keen acceptance and awareness of the all-encompassing Love of the Creator for his creations!

We accept, upon behalf of all Humanity, the Presence of God's Will externalized through every beating Heart! So shall there be established on Earth the glory of God and the fulfillment of Beloved Jesus' Promise: "Eye hath not seen nor ear heard, nor has it entered into the minds of men, the glory that the Father hath prepared for those who Love Him." So be it!

FORCEFIELD OF PROTECTION

Beloved Presence of God "I AM" in me . . . I gratefully acknowledge in my mind and accept in my feelings the Living Reality of Your Mantle of Electronic Light Substance enfolding me in a blazing aura of ever-expanding protection.

From within Thy Cosmic Heart I feel the pulsation of the Flame of Divinity, the Presence of God, radiating through my consciousness . . . through which flows at all times, the virtues, qualities, and blessings from God—and His Messengers—to me and through me to all Life everywhere.

I also acknowledge and accept the mighty armor of Light and invincible momentum of Faith so Lovingly offered to me by my own Angel of Protection, and with Loving conviction I decree:

> The Light of God is Always Victorious (3 times)
> I Live this day in God Light. (3 times)
> God is in control wherever "I AM". (3 times)
> THE HARMONY OF MY TRUE BEING
> IS MY ULTIMATE PROTECTION

I do now invoke the added assistance of God's magnificent First Ray to keep this ACTIVITY OF LIGHT sustained around me and my world so that only the WILL OF GOD may manifest in all my activities, in all places and at all times.

I make this call . . . As God's Most Holy Name "I AM".

INVOKING DIVINE ORDER

In the Full Power and Authority of the Beloved Presence of God "I AM" . . . I invoke the Power of Divine Order into my Life! . . . COME FORTH NOW!!! . . . and ASSIST ME in having DIVINE ORDER in my HOME, BUSINESS AFFAIRS, and SPIRITUAL SERVICE, and in all homes, businesses and outer activities of Humanity.

Keep this Eternally sustained, all powerfully active, ever-expanding and world encompassing, until all know the Divine Order within God Consciousness.

I THANK YOU!...and ACCEPT
THIS CALL FULFILLED.
AS GOD'S MOST HOLY NAME . . . "I AM"!!!

A DECLARATION OF FAITH

In the Name of God, I AFFIRM my Faith that GOD'S FIRST CAUSE *IS* PERFECTION FOR ALL THINGS!

By Living, moving and breathing the Reality of that FIRST CAUSE, I CREATE THE OPPORTUNITY FOR THE COSMIC FAITH OF GOD TO HAVE ITS NATURAL EFFECT THROUGH MY LIFESTREAM.

"I AM" consecrated to projecting my deep inner conviction of "GOD REALITY" onto the screen of Life around me, until It stands forth as a Living example of God's Faith in Humanity . . . and until all people choose to return their Faith to God.

"I AM" an open door for God's Limitless Faith in Humanity and Humanity's returning Faith in God.

SO BE IT, BELOVED "I AM".

BLAZING GOD'S WILL

In the Full Power and Authority of the Beloved Presence of God "I AM" . . . Legions of God's Will . . .

COME NOW!!!   COME NOW!!!   COME NOW!!!
and BLAZE!!! and BLAZE!!! and BLAZE!!!

the Cosmic Flame of God's Will through *me and clear

away any destructive activity of *my own free will which might rush in to impede *my conscious desire to do GOD'S WILL.

Help* me to become and remain obedient to the LAW of HARMONY and BE God in Action . . .

I ACCEPT this Call FULFILLED . . . AS GOD'S MOST HOLY NAME "I AM" . . .

* Examples of inserts:
1. Me
2. All Governments and Governmental Leaders
3. All Religions and Religious Leaders
4. All Military and Military Leaders
5. All Children and Young People
6. All Light Workers
7. All Humanity
8. All Life on Earth

DECREE FOR THE EARTH AND HER NATIONS

In the Full Power and Authority of the Beloved Presence of God "I AM"

We, the Children of Earth, humbly come to the Throne of our Father-Mother God to invoke into the physical plane of Earth the most intensified activity of GOD'S WILL ever manifested in the history of time.

We ask the Legions of Light serving this Sweet Earth to absorb this Divine Essence into every fiber of Their Beings and project it into the Heart Flame and conscious mind of every person associated with the governments of this Planet in any way shape or form.

Blaze the Cosmic Flame of God's Will through each of these souls, and clear away any destructive activity of their own free will which might rush in to impede their conscious desire to do God's Will.

Seal all governmental positions, individually and collectively, in the radiance of God's Will.

Reveal through Illumination's Flame, the Divine Purpose and Plan for each office and individual, and give to each person the Spiritual Courage to fulfill that plan perfectly.

Let the Will of God be MANIFEST in, through and around all the governments of the world NOW and FOREVER.

Let the LIGHT OF GOD THAT IS ETERNALLY VIC-TORIOUS Illumine and lead all Humanity everywhere.

We Consciously ACCEPT this MANIFESTING NOW... even as we call!

SO BE IT!   BELOVED "I AM".

These Invocations and Affirmations are from:
   The "Book Of Invocation"
   Group Avatar
   P.O. Box 41505
   Tucson, Arizona 85717

Available Tapes Associated With This Chapter Are:
   A. GOD'S WILL
   B. THE WORLD HEALING MEDITATION
See page *xxiv* for more information and order blanks.

CHAPTER 2

THE SECOND ASPECT OF DEITY IS ENLIGHTENMENT

COLOR – SUNSHINE YELLOW SECOND RAY

THE SECOND UNIVERSAL LAW OF "AS ABOVE, SO BELOW"

THE ATTRIBUTES OF THE SECOND ASPECT OF DEITY ARE:

GOD ILLUMINATION
WISDOM
UNDERSTANDING
CONSTANCY
STIMULATION AND INTENSIFICATION
OF SPIRITUAL GROWTH
A MOMENTUM OF PROGRESS
PRECIPITATION
CHRIST CONSCIOUSNESS

"YE ARE GODS"

Jesus answered them, "Is it not written in your law, I said, "YE ARE GODS?"

PsalmJOHN 10:34

"YE ARE GODS; and all of you ARE children of the most High."

PSALM 82:1-6

"Verily, verily, I say unto you, he that believeth in me the works that I do shall he do also, AND EVEN GREATER WORKS THAN THESE SHALL HE DO..."

JOHN 14:12

For as many as are led by the Spirit of God, they are the sons of God—the spirit itself beareth witness with our spirit, that we are the children of God; and if children, then heirs, heirs of God, JOINT HEIRS WITH CHRIST..."

ROMANS 8:14, 16, 17

When I consider Thy heavens, the work of Thy fingers, the moon and the stars, which Thou hast ordained; what is man, that Thou art mindful of him and the son of man, that Thou visitest him? For Thou hast made him a little lower than the angels, and has crowned him with glory and honor. Thou madest him TO HAVE DOMINION OVER THE WORKS OF THY HANDS; THOU HAST PUT ALL THINGS UNDER HIS FEET."

PSALMS 8:3-6

Continually throughout the Holy Bible and most other Spiritual writings, it is clearly stated that we are the Children of God. WE ARE THE SONS AND DAUGHTERS OF GOD! The magnitude of that Reality has eluded us. In fact, we have created such a schism between our outer personality and our God Self that I have actually heard religious leaders state "mankind is innately evil." They have gone so far as to declare it blasphemous for us to profess that God is within our Hearts.

That consciousness always reminds me of a story I once heard:

When God was in the process of creating His Children, He was contemplating where to anchor His Divine Spark so It would be in a safe place. One Angel suggested, "Let's put the Spark of Divinity on the top of the highest mountain. No one will look for It there."

Another Angel recommended, "Let's put mankind's Divine Spark in the center of the Earth. No one will bother It there."

A third Angel said, "I think we should hide It at the bottom of the deepest ocean where It will never be found."

After a while, God spoke and said, "I know where I will place My Divine Spark. I will place It in My Children's Heart. They will never think to look for It there." And so He did . . .

This is the Dawn of the Age of Enlightenment. As prophetized since ancient times, it is the Age when *"the mystery of God will be fulfilled."*

In St. John's Revelation, this Truth is clearly stated:

Chapter 10

1.   *"And I saw another mighty angel coming down from heaven, clothed with a cloud; and the rainbow of the cloud was upon his head, and his face was as though it were the sun, and his legs as pillars of fire;*

2.   *"And he had in his hand a little book open; and he set his right foot upon the sea, and his left foot on the land.*

3.   *"And cried with a loud voice as when a lion roars, and when he had cried, seven thunders sounded their voices.*

4.   *"And when the seven thunders had spoken, I was about to write; but I heard a voice from heaven saying, 'Seal up those things which the seven thunders uttered, and do not write them.'*

5.   *"And the angel which I saw standing upon the sea and on the land raised his right hand to heaven, and*

6.   *"Swore by him who lives for ever and ever, who created heaven and the things which are therein, and the earth and the things which are therein, and the sea and the things which are therein, that there should be no more reckoning of time;*

7.   *"But in the days of the voice of the seventh angel, when he shall*

begin to sound, the mystery of God will be fulfilled, as he has pro-claimed to his servants, the prophets."

This passage indicates there definitely was additional in-formation given to St. John that he was not allowed to give to Humanity at the time. But, in the future Age, "in the days of the voice of the Seventh Angel, when He shall begin to sound, the mystery of God will be fulfilled . . ." In other words, the information will be revealed.

In my book "Take Charge of Your Life" I have explained in some detail the Ages and their influence on the Planet and Humanity, but for our purposes here, I will briefly reiterate that an age is a span of time that lasts approximately 2,000 years. The coming of Jesus signaled the inception of the last Age (2,000 years ago) and the beginning of the Christian Dis-pensation. That Age reflected both the Sixth Ray influence which is Peace, Ministration, Healing and Devotional Wor-ship, as well as the forcefield of Pisces, the constellation in the natural zodiac surrounding the Earth which had pre-dominant influence at the time.

Jesus used the Power of these two forces continually throughout His Lifetime to help Him fulfill His Divine Mis-sion. He was known as the Prince of Peace (Sixth Ray) and His symbol was the fish (Pisces).

Jesus stated often that our time was at hand, and yet He professed it was not that moment in time, but in the time to come that the Lord's Prayer would be fulfilled and Heaven would manifest on Earth–the time of "His Second Coming."

It is the end of the Age of Pisces and the Sixth Ray; the beginning of the next 2,000-year cycle. We are moving into the forcefield of Aquarius and the influence of the Seventh Ray which is Freedom, Mercy, Compassion, Forgiveness and the Violet Transmuting Flame of Love. It is the time of the Seventh Angel, and He is beginning to sound. The Light of Truth is pouring into the Planet, and the mystery of God is being fulfilled.

As is always the case when higher vibrations of Illumined Truth begin filtering into people's consciousness, confusion results. Our present belief system begins to crumble, and we feel very vulnerable and afraid. We grasp onto our crum-bling beliefs and cling for dear Life. We often refuse to accept the new concepts, and we stubbornly insist our limited perception is accurate and all that exists. We feverishly read the Holy Books and try to confirm our beliefs by *literally* interpreting the message to fit our distorted material senses. Hence, our confusion and fear deepens. We then begin denying and rejecting the Light of Truth so completely that we fall even deeper into the chasm of ignorance.

This is occurring at the present time on the Planet just as it did in the inception of the last age. In the last age the world religions were expecting the coming of the Messiah just as we are expecting the Second Coming of the Christ now. The religious leaders of that day felt very confident in their *literal* interpretation of what was going to transpire when the Messiah came. But when in fact it occurred in a way far more subtle and natural than their phenomenal expectations, they refused to acknowlege it and missed the whole event. Many are still waiting.

As I have mentioned before, we are multi-dimensional beings. When we try to gather the infinity of Heaven and reduce It down to finite third dimensional reality, we totally and completely misconstrue the Truth.

Many of the religious leaders are vehemently resisting the Truth now pouring into the Planet and the frequencies of the New Age of Enlightenment. Resisting a new age is futile. It is like resisting a new year; we can resist all we want, but *nothing* will stop its progress.

As we progress from Age to Age, God and the Legions of Light that abide in Heaven to do His Will evaluate the status of Humanity and project forth the highest vibrations and clearest guidance possible to assist us on our journey Home. In ancient times the Legions of Light, the Spiritual Hierarchy, used to reside on Earth to guide Humanity through Their example and the effective utilization of God's precious Gift of Life. At that time, Humanity had fallen far from grace, and we had lost the knowledge of our Oneness with God. Unfortunately, we began to misunderstand who these Beings of Light were. Instead of realizing They were merely our sisters and brothers who had evolved to a higher state of evolution, we began to Deify and worship Them. Historically, Greek mythology reflects that time, when the so-called

Gods and Goddesses walked and talked with mankind.

Since we began to focus our attention on the Beings of Light around us instead of on God, the presence of the Spiritual Hierarchy became a distraction rather than a benefit. When this was realized by all concerned, it was decided that the Spiritual Hierarchy would accelerate in vibration, lifting up beyond the physical sight of Humanity. When this occurred, we could no longer see these evolved Beings, and we became confused and afraid. Instead of turning our attention to God, we began creating false idols and objects to worship.

The Godhead then realized that it was necessary to lift Humanity's consciousness up so we could remember the higher Octaves of Truth. Radiant Beings known as Avatars and Buddhas volunteered to come to Earth. Through their concentrated efforts, they raised their consciousness up from the third dimensional plane into the Realms of Light known as "Nirvana" or the Fourth Dimension. They accomplished this through a process of obtaining Enlightenment. Thus, they created a blazing path of Light over which the Truth of the Realm of Perfection could flow into the consciousness of Humanity.

The stage was then set for the entrance of the Fifth Ray. The Fifth Ray pulsates with Illumined Truth, Concentration, Consecration and Inner Vision. It was determined by the Godhead that the greatest need of the hour was for Humanity to again know of the One God. Therefore, the full gathered momentum of the knowledge of monotheism appeared on the screen of Life through the Sacred Doctrine of Judaism.

When the Sixth Ray dawned 2,000 years later, it was clear that Humanity had begun to return our attention to the One God. But even so, we considered ourselves very separate from God. We were functioning with the notion that "man is a worm in the dust," and God is a vengeful, Powerful Being to be feared. It was obviously time for the next step of our journey back to God. Humanity needed to experience God on a tangible, personal level.

A Radiant Being of Light volunteered to come to Earth to show Humanity the *Love* of God. Through the perfect application of the Natural Laws of the Universe, Beloved Jesus showed us by His own example our potential Victory. Throughout His ministry, Jesus taught us of the Father within. He brought to us the knowledge of the Christ, the level of consciousness we must attain in order to return to the Father. He showed us how to cooperate with the Blessed Elemental Kingdom, and how, by projecting forth the perfection of the Christ within, we can Transform our environment; Heal the sick, the lame, the blind; control the Earth, the Air, the Water and the Fire; multiply our supply of food and whatever else we need; and attain our Eternal Victory over death through the Power of the Ascension.

Jesus taught us that we ARE the Children of God, and all that the Father has is ours. He also brought with Him to Earth a Cosmic Dispensation. This Dispensation was the "Law of Forgiveness." That is why it is said that "He Forgave the sins of the World." Through the successful accomplishment of Jesus's Divine Plan, including His Resurrection and His Ascension, He Transmuted, through the Power of Forgiveness, the sea of negativity surrounding the Planet. This formed the blueprint for the New Age, the Christian Dispensation. A new order was established on Earth, and for the first time Humanity could ask to be Forgiven, and it would be done. Prior to this merciful gift, we Lived under the Law of Judaism which was "an eye for an eye, a tooth for a tooth." Because we didn't understand how to correctly apply the Law of Forgiveness, we didn't use it as effectively as possible. Consequently, much of the veil of maya has been re-created by a recalcitrant Humanity.

Jesus blazed a path of Light into Christ Consciousness for all of us to follow. Unfortunately, as has been the case in past Ages, we misunderstood a great deal of His message. He stated clearly "These things I do, you shall do and greater things shall you do." He came to show us what we *must* learn to do for ourselves. But instead of aspiring to follow in His footsteps we again separated ourselves by Deifying Him and worshipping Him.

He is called the Savior and truly the Truth of the Christ He revealed to us and the Gift of Forgiveness He brought to Earth can save each of us and the Planet as well. The misunderstanding is that we are not "saved" merely because Jesus was here or because we declare our Love for Him and say the words, "I accept Jesus as my personal Savior." We are only "saved" if we absorb His Truth, apply it to our Lives and become the Christ ourselves as He so aptly demonstrated to us.

KNOW THE TRUTH AND THE TRUTH WILL SET YOU FREE!!!

In the New Age now dawning Humanity is being given access to the Realms of Illumined Truth. Because of the urgency of the hour and the magnitude of the task at hand, merciful dispensations are being granted by our Father-Mother God.

In Ages past each evolving soul had to climb the mountain of attainment on the evolutionary path back to God through tremendous struggle and anguish. One of my favorite poems reflecting that quest is "The Ancient Path Reclaimed" by Annalee Skarin.

THE ANCIENT PATH RECLAIMED!

Up perpendicular ledges and towering granite cliffs
We've snatched at jutting projections and clung to cloud-
    wrapped rifts!
Souls despairing in anguish, we've struggled in hopeless
    dismay,
Seeking His trail to follow as we've climbed our rugged way!
Never were crags so awesome! Nor ever a mountain so steep!
Nor ever a need so urgent a rendezvous to keep!
Of't with torn, bleeding bodies we've clung to some swaying
    ledge,
Or only held on blindly to some crumbling, precarious edge!
We've snatched at roots or gravel to feel them give way at our
    touch!
We've asked so very little! And needed that "little" so much!
Once, hurled back by a landslide, we lay bruised against a tree,
While above, on the top of that mountain, awaited a destiny!
A thousand times we were hurled back in a broken, anguished
    heap!
A thousand pit-falls overcome, our rendezvous to keep!
A million hazardous testings we faced in that upward climb!

A million sobbing heartbreaks, etched deep on the face of
"time!"
The top of the mountain was cloud-banked, the goal obscure,
unclear—
It was only a dream, seen vaguely, as we climbed those crags
in fear!
"Twas only a vision beckoned, above the dreary world—
Only a vision of glory that ever its promise unfurled!
At last! Aft'r years of struggle! A seeming eternity!
Our goal loomed high above us! Our rendezvoused destiny!
Inch by inch! Slowly! Soul-searing! We grappled with ele-
ments wild!
Exiled! Cast out in discredit like destiny's orphaned child!
So many times, on that last cliff, we were hurled to the ledge
below!
But somewhere along that upward climb our "faith" had
advanced to "KNOW!"
Up that ledge we dug our way! Up! Up the mountain so steep!
Up! Up through those exiled years of Life, our destiny to keep!
Our strength increased with our progress! Joy became mighty
and strong!
In danger, or heart-rending setbacks, we'd lift up our hearts
in song!
When we'd finally reached the top, place of our noble, destined
tryst,
We breathed in humbled, breathless awe as we kneeled at the
feet of The Christ!
"You've traveled the road I mapped for man, the way to
overcome!
You've learned to hear the voice of God! And let His Will
be done!
The road I left the map for, that age-dimmed, forgotten Way
You have blazed anew in power more brilliant than the day!
Turn! And look back where you've traveled! Look back where
the mountain has been!
There's My open highway of glory you've rebuilt for the race
of men!"

That beautiful poem expresses the challenge of returning
to the Christ during the Piscean-Sixth Ray Age now ending.

Fortunately for all Life, the New Age of Enlightenment blends the Seventh Ray of Spiritual Freedom with the Aquarian frequencies of Intensified Spiritual Growth. The pure God Qualities pouring into Earth at this time are Merciful beyond our comprehension. They vibrate with the essence of Forgiveness, Mercy, Compassion, Transmutation, Freedom and Progress in Spiritual Growth. Through this Merciful activity of Light, Cosmic dispensations have been granted that give the Legions of Light serving Humanity from the Heavenly Realms permission to come through the veil to meet us half way. For the first time in aeons, the Spiritual Hierarchy, our Illumined sisters and brothers guiding us Home, are accessible to ALL Humanity. Each one of us now has the opportunity to lift up our consciousness and touch the Realms of Truth. When we begin to do this constantly and rhythmically, the Wisdom and Understanding of our true God Reality pours into our conscious mind, and we experience the wealth of knowledge available to us through the Grace of God.

The Godhead and the Legions of Light serving Earth at the present time have again evaluated the status of Humanity and perceived our greatest need for this Age. It has been determined that the need of the hour is to bring to the mankind of Earth the realization of our own Divinity. The clarion call for remembrance is reverberating through the Universe at both Inner and Outer levels. The Cosmic Tones are awakening the God within.

As we reach up and tap the knowledge of the ages, we can perceive clearly our origin and our involutionary and evolutionary progress. This Enlightenment clears away the cobwebs of confusion, doubt and fear. The Light of Truth solves what we have accepted as mysteries. The prophecies of old are brought to fruition as "the Mystery of God is fulfilled."

I would like to share with you now some of the Illumination pouring forth from the Realms of Truth. This knowledge is given to us as a gift for our greater Understanding. The Wisdom of God transcribed here is not for the entertainment of our curiosity or our outer minds, but rather a *jewel* to inspire us ever inward and upward on our return journey to our Father-Mother God. This Truth is not to be accepted on blind Faith. It is to be accepted only after each of us has individually reached into the Octaves of Truth and confirmed it through the Presence of God blazing in our Hearts.

While the attention of the Spiritual Hierarchy and Humanity is upon the Presence of Truth in this Universe, we invoke the Holy Christ Self in every human Heart to magnetize and radiate Cosmic Christ Truth to and through the individual and the mass mind as well.

LET TRUTH NOW BE KNOWN AND APPLIED
IN THIS PHYSICAL APPEARANCE WORLD AND
IN THAT APPLICATION GOD'S WILL SHALL BE DONE
ON EARTH AS IT IS IN HEAVEN!   SO BE IT!

IN THE BEGINNING . . . "I AM"

"So God created man in His Own Image, in the Image of God created He him, male and female created He them."

GENESIS 1:27

Our Father-Mother God is represented by what is known as the Glorious Immortal Three-fold Flame. This Sacred Flame expresses the three-fold activity of Life as exemplified in the Holy Trinity–the Divine Balance of Love, Wisdom and Power; the Father, Son/Daughter (Christ) and Holy Spirit (Mother).

In the Beginning our Father-Mother God drew forth from Their Heart Centers the Spirit Sparks (Their Children) that would be sent forth to expand the borders of the Father's Kingdom. On completion of that Sacred Activity, it was necessary to create "garments" for Their children, so each Spirit Spark could function and be protected in their involutionary and evolutionary process.

Each Spirit Spark was directed into Universal Light where our God Parents clothed us in the Immortal Three-fold Flame of Their Beings and projected around that Flame a great White Fire Being. Within the blazing Sun of our White Fire Being our Spirit Spark expressed the dual nature of the Masculine and Feminine Polarity of God. Each of these aspects manifested as a radiant Being of Light, one male and one female. These individual Beings, residing in the White Fire Being, are known as Divine Complements or Twin Flames. They are our "I AM" Presences. This was our first individualization, a radiant Spirit Spark clothed in the Immortal Three-fold Flame of God, enveloped in a blazing White Fire Being expressing the duality of the Feminine and Masculine Nature of God "I AM". This was our first manifest form as we stood before God "created in His own Image."

After we obtained our Garments of Light it was time for us to proceed with our *involutionary* process. At that point we had the free will choice to remain in the Realms of Perfection experiencing the Octaves of Bliss, or we could choose to accept the responsibility of passing through the Seven Spheres of Learning (also known as the Seven Rays) into the physical world of form. We obviously chose the latter.

Both "I AM" Presences, our Masculine and the Feminine Presence, had the free will to decide Their own individual progress. The two Divine Complements decided Their next step and proceeded forth from the White Fire Being as two individual "I AM" Presences. Sometimes we choose the same path as our Twin Flame, but sometimes we don't.

We chose to accept the responsibility of passing through the Seven Spheres of Learning into the physical world of form and stepped forth from our White Fire Being individualized as "I AM".

"I", ALPHA (the beginning), signifying the ONE, the Source, the Father.

"AM", OMEGA (the ending), signifying the Mother.

The Masculine and Feminine Polarity of God "I AM" are the beginning and the ending, the ALPHA and OMEGA of all that is.

We were now ready to begin our Cosmic Education, ready to enter the Seven Spheres of Learning from where, after sufficient study and discipline, we would be able and qualified to proceed to our next stage of education, our entrance into the schoolroom of Earth, the world of form.

Visualizing God as a Sun, there are, surrounding and enfolding this Sacred Central Focus of Intelligence, Twelve Mighty Spheres of Consciousness. Each one of these

Spheres is separated from the other by its own periphery line which forms a natural boundary. These Spheres are the Causal Body of God. Seven of these Spheres are directly associated with the third dimensional Realm of Earth. Humanity utilizes each of the Seven Spheres of Learning as we evolve into a completed Seven-fold Planetary Being. When it is time to move into the Fourth Dimension, the additional five Spheres are activated as we evolve into the Twelve-fold Aspect of Deity becoming a Solar Being.

God develops and expands His Kingdom by releasing pulsating waves of Divine consciousness. As these Divine Ideas from the Mind of God vibrate from Sphere to Sphere, they are absorbed by the "I AM" Presences abiding there. A constant modification of God Light, an expansion of God Consciousness, is achieved in each Sphere so that God's Ideas become embodied in the substance of that Sphere in orderly sequence and eventually reach the Seventh Sphere where they await precipitation into the third dimensional plane of Earth.

After the decision had been made by our "I AM" Presence to accept the responsibility of descent into the world of form, our "I AM" Presence entered the First Sphere.

As our "I AM" Presence passed through the Seven Spheres, we were given many opportunities to learn and grow, but the most important thing that occurred during that process was the formation of our Causal Body. This consisted of the accumulated good which we derived by going from Sphere to Sphere absorbing and expanding the Divine Consciousness of God.

The First Sphere represents the Heart of Creation itself. It is the initial impulse from the Mind of God and represents the First Cause of Perfection. As our "I AM" Presence bathed in this Realm of Light, the totality of God's Will became known. A Forcefield of Sapphire Blue Light began forming around our "I AM" Presence, and the first band of our Causal Body was created.

We had the free will to remain in the First Sphere as long as we liked before proceeding on to the next step of experience. When we felt a sense of completion, we moved on to the Second Sphere. Remember, we were then proceeding as an individual "I AM" Presence, so our Divine Complement may have chosen to remain longer in the First Sphere than we did, or may have moved forward into the Second Sphere sooner than we did. It matters not.

In the Second Sphere we built the Sunshine Yellow Flame of Wisdom into our Causal Body. In this Realm the Divine Ideas and Patterns of future greatness are molded into form through the creative power of Higher Mind Force. Thus, the seed of the Father falls on fertile ground and begins to take form in the world of Divine Thought.

After completing our experiences in the Second Sphere we proceeded to the Third. In this Realm the Divine Ideas are ensouled with Life and become Living, pulsating foci of things to come. Thought is clothed with Life through the feeling nature. This Third Sphere vitalizes all manifestation which will ever externalize on Earth. Here we added the crystalline Pink Band of Divine Love to our Causal Body.

In perfect timing we proceeded on to the Fourth Sphere where the Divine Living Ideas of God pulsate through the electronic substance and are absorbed by the receptive consciousness there. The Qualities of Hope, Purity, Resurrection and Ascension were acquired in this Realm, as the pure White Band of our Causal Body was formed.

Next our experience carried us into the Fifth Sphere. This is the Realm where the seed Ideas of God are ensouled with Truth and consecrated as they are nurtured into form. The Emerald Green Band of our Causal Body was created here.

We then continued our adventure into the Sixth Sphere. This is where we learned how to carry the Nature of God into the world of form. Devotional and emotional worship are the vehicles through which spiritual energies are released to the physical plane from this dimension. Through this experience a Ruby Band of color was added to our Causal Body.

Finally, we moved into the Seventh Sphere, which holds within Itself the etheric pattern of every manifestation of God's Plan which is lowered rhythmically through the six preceding Spheres and which awaits expression in physical form. In this Sphere the Violet Band was added to our Causal Body.

Only those "I AM" Presences who have proceeded

through the Seven Spheres and have self-consciously created a Causal Body around themselves with Seven Bands of color, are qualified to apply for physical embodiment on Earth. We can clearly see that even Lifestreams being born on Earth for the very first time have already had tremendous training at Inner levels prior to birth.

With the fulfillment of our journey through the Seven Spheres of Learning we were ready to take the final step for the *involutionary* process. We were ready to embody in the physical plane of Earth to begin the process of evolution, our return journey Home to the Heart of our Father-Mother God.

The purpose of our embodiment on Earth IS TO ALLOW OUR "I AM" PRESENCE THE OPPORTUNITY TO UN-FOLD A SPIRITUAL NATURE AND BECOME MASTER OF ENERGY AND VIBRATION THROUGH THE CON-SCIOUS CONTROL AND USE OF OUR OWN CREATIVE FACULTIES OF THOUGHT AND FEELING.

Our Individualized God Presence is truly a Son or Daughter of God and Heir to all that the Father has. We have the free will to create, through our thoughts and feelings, the Beauty and Perfection of our Father-Mother God. Our "I AM" Presence contains within Itself all of the Light, Love, Wisdom, Power, Beauty, Opulence, Purity and Harmony of God.

As has been explained previously in this book, the original Divine Plan for the Planet Earth and Humanity has gone awry. But that Divine Plan contained within Itself the perfect blueprint for our evolutionary journey back to God. If we understand the original Plan and perceive where we now stand in the scheme of things, it will help us to regain our direction and correct our course.

THE ORIGINAL DIVINE PLAN . . .

When our Father-Mother God were ready to create our Solar System, the Divine pattern and plan for every particle of Life that would exist within It began forming in the Universal Mind. They pictured and held the perfect blueprint in Their minds and feelings, expanding It from the Heart Center of Their Beings into a great sphere of influence. The periphery of that sphere was the boundary of the Universe within which the Planets, the Suns, the Stars, and all belonging to this Universe would abide. In the Fiat of "Let there be Light," our Father-Mother God spun out of Their very Selves the Universal Light Substance that would be used to create all manifest form.

When the design was complete, a Majestic Being was summoned from the Great Silence known as the Cosmic Silent Watcher. Our God Parents projected into Her consciousness the Immaculate Concept (Divine Blueprint) for this System of Worlds. This Mighty Being absorbed the Plan for this Universe into Her Heart and accepted the responsibility of holding the Immaculate Concept for every electron of precious Life energy evolving in this Solar System until the involutionary and evolutionary process was complete, and ALL had evolved back to the Heart of God. The Cosmic Silent Watcher expanded her Causal Body out to the periphery of our God Parents sphere of influence, the boundary of our Universe. Her Causal Body was comprised of the seven bands of color from the Spheres of Learning, and It created a cradle in which our Solar System would rest.

In due time another Great Being was summoned from the Great Silence. This was the Planetary Silent Watcher. The Cosmic Silent Watcher holds the Immaculate Concept for the entire Solar System; the Planetary Silent Watcher holds the Immaculate Concept for a particular planet.

When the Planetary Silent Watcher for Earth was called forth, She accepted into Her keeping the Divine Blueprint for the Earth and all Life evolving here. She accepted the responsibility of holding the Immaculate Concept for Earth until the Divine Plan is fulfilled in every detail. She too expanded Her Causal Body to form a cradle which would hold this Blessed Planet.

At last the Cosmic Moment had arrived for the birth of Planet Earth. The Silent Watchers stood in readiness, and the Seven Mighty Elohim, the Cosmic Builders of Form, were summoned.

The Seven Elohim answered the call of our God Parents and gathered around the Causal Body of the Planetary Silent Watcher to study intently the Divine Plan for the Planet Earth. It was Their joy, service and opportunity to bring the

Divine Plan for Earth into form.

Each of the Seven Elohim represents one of the Seven Spheres of Learning. They individually studied the part of the Divine Plan in the Causal Body of the Silent Watcher that corresponded to Their specific Sphere. Then in one Unified effort, They projected Seven Mighty Light Rays from Their Heart Centers which formed the matrix for the Planet.

When this was accomplished, the Elohim summoned the Directors of the Forces of the Elements and the lesser Builders of Form, the Devas and Elemental Beings. These Beings began magnetizing the Electronic Light Substance to create the physical plane of Earth according to the instructions given Them by the Elohim. The Directors of the Water Element drew forth the Elemental Beings of the water, the Undines, and together They drew the unformed Light Substance to create the beautiful lakes, the great rivers, the giant waterfalls and the crystal seas.

The Directors of the Earth Element called forth the Blessed Gnomes, the Nature Spirits and the Mighty Devas. These Beings worked together to create magnificent mountains that pointed their fingers toward God. They created the physical Earth itself, the flowers, trees, fruits, nuts, every blade of grass. They created every herb bearing seed necessary to sustain Humanity in perfect Harmony.

The Directors of the Air Element invoked the Sylphs of the Air, and these Beings drew forth the Breath of the Holy Spirit to form the atmosphere of Earth. They directed the North Winds, the South Winds, the East Winds and the West Winds into the third dimensional plane to assist Humanity and the other Elemental Beings.

The Directors of the Fire Element called forth the Elemental Beings of Fire, the Salamanders. Our Father-Mother God projected forth the Masculine Ray of God which entered Earth as a tremendous shaft of blue Light in the Himalaya Mountains in Tibet. They then projected forth the Feminine Ray of God which entered the Earth as a tremendous shaft of pink Light in Mt. Muru in the Andes Mountains in South America. Where the Masculine and Feminine Rays met in the center of the Earth, the permanent atom, the Immortal Three-fold Flame of God was formed. This Sacred Fire in the center of the Earth, also called the Eternal Sun of Even Pressure, contains within Itself the magnetic power by which the Universal Light Substance is drawn into the spherical form of Earth. This Cosmic Fire interpenetrates all Life.

The Elemental Kingdom was given the Fiat to OBEY every direction of Humanity. These selfless servants of God were prepared to create for mankind a "coat of flesh," and They were trained to keep these physical vehicles of ours in repair. They learned to materialize out of primal Light the nourishment for replenishing these bodies and the necessities which would make our exile on Earth Harmonious and Happy.

Then one Cosmic Day, the work of creation was complete, and the Mighty Elohim signified to the God Parents that the Planet Earth was ready for habitation.

Three distinct types of Intelligent Life–Angels, Humanity and Elementals–were given the opportunity to unfold their God natures on this small Star, each contributing in some manner to the well-being and progress of the other. Their combined Life Force was ordained to weave the spiritual bridge that would tie the Earth to the Heart of God.

To guard and nourish the Spiritual Nature of mankind and to help develop the inner Spark of Divinity into the Flame of Conscious Mastery, the Angelic Host was sent Earthward to stand by Humanity, radiating the Love, Wisdom, Faith, Power and Will of God into the atmosphere and aura of the evolving God Consciousness of every man, woman and child. The Angelic Host accomplished this under the direction of the Seven Great Archangels.

When the Elemental Kingdom had made the Earth verdant with splendor, and the Angelic Kingdom had filled the atmosphere with the Essence of Godliness, the Planet was ready to welcome Humanity into a new experience of evolution with opportunity, promise, beauty and plenty. The first Lifestreams to take embodiment on Earth were known as the Holy Innocents.

DESCENT OF THE HOLY INNOCENTS

Once the "I Am" Presence had completed Its sojourn through the Seven Spheres of Learning developing Its Causal Body, It was ready to proceed into the physical dimensions of Earth. When the moment was right, the "I Am" Presence projected a replica of Itself into the world of form. This replica was known as the Holy Christ Self, and It was stepped down in vibration from the "I Am" Presence to enable It to function effectively in the denser vibrations of the third dimensional plane.

The Holy Christ Self was a shining Being of Light clothed in the Immortal Three-fold Flame. It was in constant communion with the "I Am" Presence and continually manifested the Will of God on Earth. This replica of the "I Am" Presence was the cohesive Power around which the Builders of Form created the four lower bodies necessary for the Earthly experience of each human being.

The four lower bodies, used as the vehicles of the Holy Christ Self on Earth, consist of the Emotional Body, the Mental Body, the Etheric Body and the Physical Body. The Emotional Body is the feeling world. It is the largest of the four and is designed by the Builders of Form to act as a cradle in which the other lower bodies are held. Its correct service is to nourish the Divine Ideas that pour forth to the Holy Christ Self from the "I Am" Presence, Who in turn receives them from God.

The Mental Body is the mind as we understand it, the vehicle of consciousness. It interpenetrates both the Emotional and Physical Bodies and conveys thought in the mental plane through color, sound and form.

The Etheric Body extends a little beyond the Physical Body and interpenetrates every cell and organ. It is composed of very sensitive chemical ethers that record every thought, word, action or feeling we experience in our Earthly sojourn. It is known as the Seat of all Memory.

The Physical Body is the vehicle that we are most aware of and is the anchorage point of the Holy Christ Self on Earth.

Prior to the "fall of man" the four lower bodies of Humanity were radiant and beautiful beyond anything we see today. These vehicles continually outpictured the perfect form of our Holy Christ Self. In the original Divine Plan our Holy Christ Self was the Master of our four lower bodies, and these vehicles obeyed every command of this radiant Presence. Our faculties of thought and feeling were used only to create Perfection. The Holy Christ Self became Master of energy and vibration, consciously projecting onto physical matter the perfect thoughtforms It drew from the Causal Body and the "I Am" Presence.

As I mentioned earlier, the purpose of our Earthly existence in the dense third dimensional plane is to give us the opportunity to use our creative centers of thought and feeling to manifest the Perfection of the Heavenly Realms in physical form, thus enabling us to be co-creators with God, ever expanding the borders of our Father's Kingdom.

Our Life on Earth is cyclic, and every 2,000 years one of the Seven Spheres of Learning, or the Seven Rays, has a predominant influence on the Planet. In the original plan the "I Am" Presence would project the Holy Christ Self into the third dimension for the first time when the First Ray or Sphere was predominant on Earth. The Holy Christ Self would magnetize the Elemental Substance around Itself, creating either a male or female physical body. Then, the Holy Christ Self would set about learning all It possibly could about the God Qualities of the First Ray. It would draw the accumulated knowledge from the first band of Its Causal Body and project it through the four lower bodies creating a vortex that would continually allow the God Qualities of the First Ray entrance into the physical plane. This vortex is located in the area of the throat and is known as the Throat Chakra.

The Qualities of the First Ray are God's Will, Illumined Faith, Power and Protection. During this first Earthly experience, the Holy Christ Self would draw the Divine Ideas of the First Ray from the "I Am" Presence and experiment with creating every conceivable aspect of the First Ray on Earth. If the Holy Christ Self had created a female physical body, then It would develop the feminine nature of every aspect. If the physical body was male, then the masculine nature of every aspect of the First Ray was developed. Upon completion of the experience, the Holy Christ Self would leave the physical plane and return to the Heavenly Realms to await Its next opportunity.

After a period of rest the Holy Christ Self again entered the physical plane, still under the influence of the First Ray, but this time It created the opposite gender in the physical body, so It could complete the total experience of learning both the masculine and feminine nature of the qualities of the First Ray.

At the culmination of the 2,000-year cycle of the First Ray the Holy Christ Self had experienced two embodiments, one as a male and one as a female. Each Lifetime often lasted 700 or 800 years, and during that time, the Throat Chakra was completely developed.

Originally, this exact same pattern was continued in the next 2,000-year cycle when the Second Ray was predominant on Earth. The Holy Christ Self had two embodiments during that time, one as a male and one as a female. The qualities of the Second Ray, which are Illumination, Wisdom, Understanding and Enlightenment were experienced and projected into the physical plane through a second vortex that was developed at the top of the head. This center is the Crown Chakra.

In the third 2,000-year cycle the Heart Chakra was developed as the masculine and feminine natures of Divine Love were experienced in the physical plane.

The fourth 2,000-year cycle enabled the Root Chakra to develop through the physical manifestation of the Fourth Ray of Purity, Restoration, Resurrection and Ascension.

The pattern continued in the fifth 2,000-year cycle, and through one masculine and one feminine embodiment, the Fifth Ray of Truth, Concentration, Consecration and Healing was expressed in physical form through the development of the Third Eye Chakra.

Next, the sixth 2,000-year cycle offered the opportunity for Peace, Devotional Worship and Ministration to be expanded into the third dimension through the development of the Solar Plexus Chakra.

Finally, the seventh 2,000-year cycle completed the experience as the Central Chakra was developed. The Seventh Ray of Spiritual Freedom, Mercy, Compassion, Forgiveness and Transmutation brought to fruition the physical experience of the Seven Spheres of Learning. When this final chakra was developed, the Earthly experience was finished, and the Holy Christ Self Ascended into the Higher Octaves of Light to continue Its evolutionary journey Home to the Father.

Originally, the Divine Blueprint for our Earthly experience was very simple. We would enter the physical plane only twice in every 2,000-year cycle—once as a male and once as a female—a total of fourteen embodiments over a 14,000-year period. In each 2,000-year cycle we would develop the masculine and feminine polarities of one of our major chakra centers. By the end of the 14,000-year cycle we were Masters of the Seven Spheres of Learning and a completed Seven-fold Planetary Being.

This Divine Plan was fulfilled by several of the original evolutions of the human race. For millions of years the Earth knew only Perfection. Not one electron of precious Life energy was released into the physical plane of Earth that was less than Harmonious. Humanity was consciously aware of our purpose and reason for being. We remembered all we had learned from one Lifetime to another. We grew between embodiments, and our progress was swift and sure. Our accumulated knowledge was continuously available for us to draw on to assist us in our forward progress. We were in constant communion with our "I Am" Presence and realized our own Divinity. We *Lived* the Truth, *"All* that the Father has is mine."* We revered the Oneness of all Life, and we walked and talked with the other evolutions on Earth—the Angels and the Elemental Beings. This was the time allegorically referred to as the Garden of Eden—Paradise on Earth.

Then, at a particular moment in the Earth's Evolution, Humanity became curious and began experimenting with our creative centers of thought and feeling in ways that were less than Harmonious. At first, these discordant thought-forms would send little fragmented currents of energy through the atmosphere of Earth. With no other discord in the atmosphere the fragmented currents would return with very little ramification. Since the energy was discordant, it could not pass through our Heart Center on its return to the Source, so it remained around the Earth Plane. Slowly but surely, this energy accumulated, and Humanity experimented with more and more energy creating greater and greater amounts of discord. Gradually, this negative energy began forming a veil around the Earth. As the negative energy returned to Humanity, we experienced discomfort and pain for the first time. We were confused and often didn't handle the experience well. Consequently, we created more negative thoughts and feelings.

During this time, the Holy Christ Self realized that our four lower bodies were getting out of control. Instead of just obeying the Divine thoughts projected from the "I Am" Presence, the Mental Body and the Emotional Body were expressing thoughts and feelings apart from the Holy Christ Self. Our Holy Christ Self could not interfere with our gift of FREE WILL, but, as a merciful activity to Life, began withdrawing the amount of energy It was releasing through the four lower bodies so that we would not completely overwhelm ourselves with misqualified energy. What at one time was a tremendous shaft of Light began to shrink until it became a mere sixteenth of an inch in diameter. The pillar of Light that used to surround us is now referred to as a silver cord. The Holy Christ Self that used to engulf our four lower bodies is now only a fraction of an inch in size and resides in the "airless chamber" of our Heart.

As our four lower bodies began creating thoughtforms and feelings apart from the Holy Christ Self, these vehicles started to believe they were separate identities. This was the beginning of the creation of the ego or the human personality. This was the beginning of our separation from God.

As the veil of maya became thicker and thicker, we lost the awareness of our Oneness with God. We began coming back to Earth, not only to develop our chakras and manifest the Seven Spheres of Learning physically, but also to Transmute the energy we had misqualified in the previous Life. Unfortunately, in each Lifetime we created more negative thoughts and feelings, thus compounding the problem and manifesting a snowball effect that eventually resulted in our utter "fall." At that point in time we were buried in darkness, and the original Divine Plan was totally lost to our conscious minds. We began coming back to Earth much more frequently, but once we were immersed in the dense veil of maya on the physical plane, we forgot why we were here. We went through literally thousands of Lifetimes with hardly any progress at all. Many times we even ended up worse off than before. This is the time referred to, allegorically, as "the fall of man." At that moment Earth was truly the dark star.

EARTH'S RETURN JOURNEY HOME . . .

The Law of the Universe is Balance. When a planet and the evolutions evolving on the planet utilize the Gift of Life from God, they are responsible for how they use every electron. It is a Cosmic Law that in order for God to continue breathing Life into a planetary system, the Lifestreams using that Gift of Life must expand the gift adding to the Light of the World as It returns to the Father. This is the balance of the Inbreath and the Outbreath of all Life.

When the Earth had fallen to its darkest ebb, It was not emanating the necessary balance of Light to warrant Its Gift of Life. At that point the Godhead determined that the Gift of Life must be withdrawn from the Planet, thereby allowing all the Lifeforms on Earth to disintegrate and return to unformed primal substance. When the knowledge of this decision reached the Spiritual Hierarchy, Who selflessly serve the Planet Earth, an urgent plea and clarion call rang through the Universe. The Spiritual Hierarchy pleaded with the Godhead and all the Legions of Light throughout this System of Worlds to allow Divine Intervention in the salvation of this fallen star. Through that plea a Cosmic Dispensation was granted and a span of time allotted to see if Earth could regain Its path. The Spiritual Hierarchy invoked the assistance of the entire Universe, and from Galaxies beyond Galaxies and Suns beyond Suns, the greatest Unified effort of Divine Love ever manifested in the history of time was projected forth into this small dark star.

A tremendous Being of Light from the Octaves of Perfection volunteered to come and envelop the Earth in His Causal Body giving off the Balance of Light and Love that Humanity was not able to emit. With His own efforts, He volunteered to balance God's Gift of Life for all evolving on Planet Earth. In the Bible this savior of the Planet Earth is referred to as The Ancient of Days.

Whenever there is a significant amount of energy released for a particular purpose, God evaluates the situation and decides if additional grants of energy or assistance can be allowed. In this case it was evident that there was enough desire from the Universe, if not Humanity, to save this precious Planet. Again a Cosmic Dispensation was granted, and it was agreed that the Planet Earth would survive and additional assistance would be permitted to awaken the Divinity within Humanity and Heal our separation from God.

For aeons of time great Avatars from the Realms of Truth have been allowed to embody on Earth to show Humanity the pathway Home, but mankind is recalcitrant and progress has been painfully slow. Now, during this Cosmic Moment, the assistance being given Planet Earth is unprecedented. Instead of one Avatar being allowed entrance into the physical realm, literally millions of very Illumined souls are volunteering to come to Earth to help usher in the Permanent Golden Age. These souls are infiltrating every conceivable walk of Life. They are reaching up into the Realms of Truth and absorbing the Divine Ideas from the Mind of God that will enable Humanity to Love this Blessed Planet FREE. These Illumined Ones are offering themselves as a "cup," a Holy Grail, through which the Light of God will pour into the physical realm of Earth, thus activating the Flame of Divinity in the Heart of every man, woman and child. As each Heart Flame is awakened, the Holy Christ Self of each one will burst the chains of human consciousness, and as Humanity's attention is focused on the Christ within, the Christ will grow to full stature once again, taking command of the four lower bodies and becoming One with the "I Am" Presence. *This, in Truth, is the Second Coming of the Christ.* This sacred Activity is occurring NOW under the direction of the all-encompassing Presence of Christ Who's Luminious Presence is at this moment, embracing every particle of Life on Earth.

Become now the Transcendent Being of your Holy Christ Self. This is your Sacred Trust.

On The Doctrine Of Transcendent Being

To feel oneself or to realize oneself as the Keeper of a Sacred Trust is a great experience in consciousness. In some ways it adds to one's dignity, at the same time keeping one very gentle and humble. It is thus that each becomes his own high priest; his Heart the altar; the Transcendent Being, the God that dwells in the Holy Place. Religion becomes an intensely intimate and personal matter when the Transcendent Being is the direct object of all religious experience.

It is the God which abides with man. It is not an idol god, but a Ray of God, the Principle, the Truth. It mingles through a mysterious alchemy with the mortal parts of man, though it is never limited or destroyed by man.

It stands, has stood, and shall stand. It remains the Silent Watcher of one's Being. It is not the voice of conscience for it never criticizes, never blames, never doubts, never questions.

Like the passionless face of the meditating Buddha, it sits in the Heart and waits; waits through the ages during the hundreds of Lives, unmoved and unchanged, with ever-closed eyes and imperturbable, passive features. It waits for the day of liberation. There is no hurry, for there is no time. There is no delay. There is only a timeless Mystery waiting for liberation—waiting and yet not waiting, for here waiting has no reference to time. Timeless waiting is a mystery that is wound up in realization; in the sublime secret of personal awareness.

Of all the mysteries of metaphysics, none is more sublime in its concept than the Doctrine of Transcendent Being, the ever-coming Self. While man builds his own soul, he is really building the Universal Soul with virtues not his own; he is building virtues with Wisdom that rises not in himself; and he is perfecting a Wisdom apart from himself—and of himself!

All the constructive and creative powers which man expresses flow into his personality from some deep and hidden source. Their purpose is not to build his personality, but to perfect the Transcendental Being, which, born in the manger, a symbol of its material environment, under the true indwelling Light, unfolds and develops until it becomes a World Savior, truly the savior of each man's world, and the time of Resurrection and Ascension become the timeless Reality of Man's Being!

Beloved Ones, PIERCE THE FORM! Learn to recognize all ideas as essentially formless, but perceptible inwardly as manifestations of the Law.

When you read books, when you listen to teachings, when you contemplate the old wisdom, pierce the form. Ponder the words of Maimonides: "Beneath the body of the Law is the soul of the Law; and beneath the soul of the Law is the Spirit of the Law." Search for the spirit of the doctrine. Accept nothing less.

In everything which occurs to you as incident or circumstance, recognize symbols of the formless. Realize that all visible physical bodies and all tangible, conceivable forms of knowledge are indeed the multi-colored fringe on the robes of the Infinite.

Remember the inscription on the Temple of Sais in Egypt: "I, Isis, am all that has been, that is or shall be; no mortal man hath ever me unveiled." Recognize the world as the veil, and realize that he who is entering into the hidden place must rend the veil of the temple from the top to the bottom. With the sword of insight, PIERCE THE VEIL AND FIND THE LAW.

Group Avatar

Available Tape Associated With This Chapter Is:
C. ENLIGHTENMENT
See page *xxiv* for more information and order blanks.

CHAPTER 3

THE THIRD ASPECT OF DEITY IS DIVINE LOVE

COLOR–PINK
THIRD RAY

THE THIRD UNIVERSAL LAW OF DIVINE LOVE

THE COHESIVE POWER OF THE UNIVERSE

THE ATTRIBUTES OF THE THIRD RAY ARE:

ADORATION
TOLERANCE
HUMANITARIANISM
REVERENCE FOR ALL LIFE
BALANCING THE EMOTIONAL BODY
SACRED SUBSTANCE OF
THE FEELING NATURE OF HUMANITY

The Power of Divine Love

Oh, Supreme Presence of God within all Life, into your Eternal Heart of Love do I immerse myself now and forever. I consciously surrender my vehicles to be merged with the Love Nature of Your Being until "I AM" a pure Focus of Love—a Living jewel in Your Crown of Adoration.

The path I walk in Life leads only to Love. My physical body filled with Love becomes shining and invincible. My etheric vehicle radiating Love Transmutes the past. Love in my mind insures expression of Your Divine Thoughts. Love in my feelings reaffirms that God is the only Power acting.

As "I AM" thinking, feeling and remembering only Love, I know that God is working through me—radiating forth all the children of Love—Peace, Contentment, Tenderness, Happiness, Security, Health and Opulence—to Life which I have promised to Love Free.

In this awakened consciousness of Love, my spirit becomes Holy Spirit, and "I AM" the Love of God reaching out to claim Its Own! In Love I magnetize all God's Blessings to me, and in Love I radiate these Blessings forth to Life around me. "I AM" the Spirit of Love permeating form until all is drawn back into the indivisible Whole.

I feel the pulse beat of Love in all Life and the continuity of Love in all experiences I have ever known. It is all Love.

I was born out of Love. "I AM" evolving through Love. I shall Ascend back into Love.

"I AM" ALL LOVE, and "I AM" grateful. So be it! "I AM"

Group Avatar

The essence of Divine Love . . . pure, strong, gentle, complete and unconditional... is the vibration from which we were born out of the Heart of God and the vibration through which we must evolve and Ascend back to the Heart of God. This frequency of Love has no bonds, no barriers, no conditions. Within the Infinite Power of Divine Love there is no pain or sorrow, no lack or limitation. It contains within Its essence our full potential to rise above all human conditions, all self-inflicted suffering, all manner of chaos, confusion, hopelessness and despair. Divine Love heals the illusion of separation. It rejuvenates, revitalizes and makes whole all It embraces. Divine Love is the single greatest source of Forgiveness. It is the full gathered momentum of our Eternal FREEDOM.

Through Divine Love, we will each be drawn up into the realization and acceptance of our own Divinity. Within the Wisdom of Divine Love is revealed the knowledge that each and every one of us holds a unique silken thread to the Tapestry of Life. Every single thread is necessary and critical to the perfect fulfillment of the Immaculate Concept of the Divine Plan for the Earth. As we tap the frequencies of Divine Love, we begin to experience Gratitude for all of the blessings of God that contribute so generously to our Earthly pilgrimage. Within the flow of this mighty force our Faith in ourselves is renewed, and we once again perceive ourselves as valuable human beings. Never again will we say, "What good could I possibly achieve? What value am I? What difference will one soul possibly make?" We will recognize those thoughts to be a sacrilege before the Universe. We will know that we were created and sustained by God because He has chosen to express some beautiful manifestation through us. He has chosen us to fulfill a portion of the glorious Divine Plan, and asked that we release the unique perfume and music of our Being to bless all Life. The Purity of our individual fragrance and tone is unlike any other ever released by the evolving Lifestreams on this sweet Earth. Something Sacred is hidden in each of our souls that has never been known by another, some beautiful manifestation of Life which God and our "I AM" Presence alone can externalize. It is time for all Humanity to accept this Truth and stand revealed as the Christ grown to full stature. The Holy Christ Self is waiting in our Hearts today for the summons to burst the tomb of matter. When this occurs, the fullness of Its vital Life will be released Transfiguring our flesh, vitalizing our Spirit and externalizing the Kingdom of Heaven to the periphery of our spiritual influence.

There has been so much written about Love it has almost become a platitude, but Love in Its Purity is the mightiest force in the Universe. Love is a principle–a consciously maintained attitude of radiation. Love is the fulfillment of the Law because there is no Power that can deny It or fail to respond to Its call. If we tap the Heart of our God Self and magnetize forth the peaceful radiation of impersonal Divine Love, though we never move from our place of meditation, all the good of the Universe will be deposited at our doorstep. THAT is the power of Divine Love. As incredible as it seems—*that is the Law.*

When we truly experience the pure vibration of Divine Love, we will recognize it as the most priceless element in all existence; we will perceive it as a dynamic Living force. Love is the vehicle upon which all Light is carried into form. It transcends time and space. It is Spiritual and all Powerful.

As Divine Love is breathed into the world of form, It carries through the Heart Center of each soul the Christ Light that dispels all gloom and darkness. It banishes decay, misery and evil. It overcomes fear and separation. Negativity and discord cannot abide in the Presence of Divine Love for this Sacred essence is a force of unlimited and unspeakable Power. Divine Love is a creative force that is ALWAYS constructive and beneficial. It exalts and glorifies.

This gift of Love from God is endowed with a deeper vision that peers beyond the scars and blemishes on the surface. Its Healing tenderness penetrates all exteriors to behold the Truth of each soul, the reality of each experience. Divine Love pierces beyond the visible into the innermost depths of Perfection and finds Its resting place there.

Our purpose and reason for being is to be the bearers and transmitters of Divine Love. This Sacred Essence which renews all to everlasting Life is the key to EVERY door.

Love is the cohesive power of the Universe binding into form all physical matter, every atom and particle of Life. It holds families together—the world and the entire Universe. Without Love all physical substance would disintegrate into unformed, primal energy. When we eliminate Love from our lives, we, too, begin to disintegrate and fall apart. When we incorporate Divine Love into every aspect of our Lives, we experience cohesiveness and success beyond the comprehension of our finite minds.

With the fully developed God-given faculty of Love, we have the Power to create whatever our Spiritual vision of Love beholds. As we command "LET THERE BE LIGHT,"

Eternity itself stands still in the wonder of that Presence. Through Love, great Light is released, and through Love, the Light fulfills Its Glory, becoming the exalted essence of understanding, comprehension and knowledge. We then experience knowing the God within. It is through Love alone that our Divine Self can be contacted and developed.

As we begin to develop the Divine Self through Love, we will change and be Transformed into a new, vibrant Being of radiant Light, expressing poise and power. We will become increasingly attractive to our fellow Beings as we automatically begin to magnetize others into our Lives. Those Life-streams in our sphere of influence will experience comfort and peace in our Presence as our Love pours forth from our Hearts and fills the electromagnetic energy field which surrounds us.

Our Love will amplify the Love in the people drawn to us, and they will begin to experience the Glory of God as the Light expands within their Hearts. This Celestial Song of Love reverberating through every Heart is the greatest gift from God available to us on Earth.

As Love and Light are intermingled and brought forth through praise and gratitude, we begin to realize that nothing is impossible. We then "Speak only with the voice of Love, see only with the eyes of Love, and hear only with the ears of Love."

As we develop this perfect gift of Divine Love, our old stagnant beliefs and patterns begin to crumble and the Divine Ideas from the Mind of God fill our consciousness. Our whole Being assumes a new vitality, beauty, purpose and meaning. Compassion replaces condemnation, Forgiveness replaces accusation, Healing replaces disease, Abundance replaces limitation, and Love replaces loneliness. As we are filled to overflowing with the essence of Divine Love, It begins to radiate out through every cell of our physical bodies, and we become vibrantly beautiful. Our hands radiating forth Love, bless all they touch; our eyes, seeing through Love, perceive only Perfection in all Life; our ears, filled with Love, hear the Music of the Spheres; and our nostrils, breathing Love, inhale the fragrance of the Holy Spirit. Thus, we become renewed and Divine. In this exalted state of Divine

Love we speak with Wisdom, Compassion, Tenderness and Understanding. Each Loving word will wing Its way across the face of the Earth blessing all Life.

Then we will know as never before: "Though I speak with the tongues of men and of Angels and have not Love, I am become as a sounding brass or a clanging cymbal. And though I have the gift of prophecy and understand all mysteries and all knowledge and have all faith so I could remove mountains and have not Love, I am nothing."

Now, with great insight and a new level of awareness, we realize Divine Love is the highest attribute of the human soul. It is the most vital energy required for our Spiritual attainment, and the further we have advanced on the ladder of evolution, the more spontaneous and far-reaching will be our expression of Love.

In our time of need Love is available to assist us as a positive, concentrated action. We receive It, according to our capacity to accept It, at the time of our call. Without Love the clearest vision remains but a cloudy vapor.

Through Love, we will have constancy in the most trying of circumstances, and we will be able to respond at the moment when it is needed most.

As we master this Divine Gift, we will continually pour forth our full gathered momentum of Love for the good of ALL. We will experience, through higher levels of awareness, our Oneness with all Life. Then the separation will be no more, and Reverence for all Life will be THE ORDER OF THE NEW COSMIC DAY.

Magnetizing Divine Love
Into Our Daily Experience

The Spark of Divinity anchored in every human Heart is referred to as a Three-fold Flame. This Flame represents the Divine Balance of Love, Wisdom and Power. It vibrates with the colors pink, gold and blue.

The balanced pulsations of this Flame of Divinity are dual in nature. One pulsation is the Inbreath–Assimilation and Absorption. The second pulsation is the Out-breath–Expansion and Radiation. On the Inbreath, the Flame extends in consciousness into Infinity, reaching up to the Source of never-ending Perfection. On the Outbreath, the Flame radiates Its full blessings, eventually extending Its Light throughout the Planet and into the Universe. As each Outbreath becomes a stronger pulsation of blessings, each inbreath is further energized to new heights of Divinity.

Because of this dual activity, the Heart Flame is described as both a Portal to the Pure Land of Boundless Splendor and Infinite Light within, as well as the Source of all Divine Blessings for Humanity and the Planet. Our Three-fold Flame is both our inward Portal to our "I AM" Presence, our God-Self, and the Source of all God good radiating outward into our Lives. Through this Flame, our inner journey and our outer service to Life are balanced. It is in this balance that we will find our True Self, the Master within . . . the "Lord of the Flame." It is in this balance that we will enter the flow of Pure Divine Love. The Three-fold Flame in every human Heart is a point of "I AM" Consciousness directed downward (into denser vibration) from the "I AM" Presence. The Three-fold Flame in the center of our Being contains all the basic elements of Creation in the Light: energy, matter and intelligence or Power, Love and Wisdom.

The Holy Breath should be the vehicle of the Assimilation and Expansion of our Three-fold Flame, continuously assimilating the nature of Divine Love into the Flame on the Inbreath and expanding the Blessings of the Divine Self into the world around us on the Outbreath. For most of Humanity the endpoint of the In-breath is simply survival of the physical body and brain consciousness, receiving from God barely enough of the Heavenly Blessings to sustain Life. The goal should be that with every Inbreath we proceed up into the Divine Consciousness within the Three-fold Flame, tapping the Realms of Divine Love and with every Out-breath, the Blessings are ever-expanding, projected out with ever-increasing intensity and Divine Force to all our known world. Thus, we build our Spiritual Aura through which can proceed the "miracles" of the Realms of "I AM" Consciousness.

It is time to begin assimilating the entire nature of Divine Love into the Flame on every Inbreath as we rise up endlessly toward the Supreme Source while simultaneously expanding out to our world the Divine Essence we receive with the vehicle of our Causal Body enfolding it. We then interconnect by Light Rays with all other persons around us. That is a "Lord of the Flame." If we can perceive this, we will see the vision of Group Avatar—interconnected Light Rays between Foci of the Three-fold Flame, each a source of specific Divine Blessings into the overall matrix: One Energy, One Body, One Vibration of Divine Love. Imagine the entire Family of Humanity expressing this Divine Pattern, each and every one a Lord of their own Flame, assimilating their Divine nature into that Flame, dispensing more and more profound Gifts of Its Blessings outward, interconnected by Light Rays with each and every other person in a planetary matrix of Light. This is the Light Pattern of the race as held in the Heart of God.

Love . . . And Let It Begin With Me

Think lovingly, speak lovingly, act lovingly, and your every need shall be supplied. You shall not walk in desert places . . . no danger shall overtake you. Love sees with faultless vision, judges true judgment, acts in wisdom. Look through the eyes of Love, and you shall see everywhere the beautiful and true. Judge with the mind of Love, and you shall not err, shall wake no wail or sorrow. Act in the Spirit of Love, and you shall strike undying Harmonies upon the Harp of Life.

(author unknown)

It is an immutable natural Law that in order for us to be capable of Loving any other part of Life—any person, place, condition or thing—WE MUST FIRST LOVE OURSELVES. In my perception the overwhelming, underlying factor in every failure, every challenge, every painful experience we are enduring is a deep-seated, ingrained belief of unworthiness and low self-esteem. Most of us on many levels do not feel valuable or deserving of the Joy of Life. We may intellectually desire it, but deep inside we don't really believe we will ever experience it.

It is time for us to release these distorted beliefs, these lies about ourselves we have fabricated, which prevent us from reaching our highest potential and block our natural God-given heritage of Happiness, Prosperity, Health, Loving Relationships, Fulfilling Jobs and Abounding Joy.

As we move forward into the Realms of Illumined Truth, we are perceiving with greater Clarity just how these distorted belief systems about ourselves were formed. There are several factors involved, and as we truly begin to understand them, we will willingly and gladly let go of our erroneous concepts and accept our Reality as Sons and Daughters of God.

Our Lives, at any given moment, are reflections of our behavior patterns; our thoughts, words, actions, feelings and beliefs. We are always a sum total of everything we have ever experienced since our inception. As we sojourn through Life's challenges, we accumulate a variety of emotions and feelings. Each of us has, at one time or another, undergone the gamut of emotions from bliss to despair. When these emotions are named–Happiness, Love, Comfort, Joy, anger, pain, humiliation, rejection, etc.–we can often recall the incident and the person whom we consider responsible for evoking such feelings in our Lives. We can easily remember because the occurrence is recorded clearly in our Etheric Body where it continually pulsates at a subconscious level.

Our Etheric Body is one of the most important, but probably the least understood, of our four lower bodies. It is known as the "seat of all memory", and all of our experiences are recorded within the etheric substance of this vehicle. The Etheric Body is an energy field that interpenetrates every cell and organ of our Physical Body, and it extends a little beyond our body's perimeter. It is comprised of various chemical ethers, and the radiance of this vehicle is often referred to as the aura. Every thought, word, action or feeling we send forth passes through the Etheric Body on an electromagnetic current of energy very similar to a television or radio wave. The frequency of vibration of these currents of energy is continually being recorded in the very sensitive chemical ethers of this vehicle.

The records and memories of everything we have ever experienced resonates at a sub-conscious level in our Etheric Body, and as we sojourn through Life, our day-to-day activities periodically activate these memories and bring them to the surface of our conscious mind. It is important that we clearly understand this process because it will reveal to us how our previous experiences and attitudes keep interjecting themselves onto our present Life situations, confusing the present issues, thus keeping us stuck in the past and preventing us from moving forward.

As an example, when we are born we are very self-centered, and from our perception as an infant, we believe the world revolves around us. Babies are like little sponges, and they absorb everything that is going on in their environments. They are constantly forming opinions about what the world is like, according to the way they are treated. If they are Loved and nurtured, they observe the world to be safe and friendly. If babies are abused and neglected, they observe the world to be hostile and cruel. Each day children go through a multitude of emotions and feelings, and each and every one of these feelings is recorded in the Etheric Body. As this process continues day after day, the accumulated experiences begin to form a pattern. For instance, if a child is continually abused, he will interpret that experience according to his wisdom and understanding at the time of the incident. From a child's frame of mind adults appear "all knowing" and rather God-like. Consequently, if an adult is abusing the child, the child will think that there must be something very wrong with himself. He believes that he is bad, no good, worthless. These feelings are very painful, and they leave a powerful vibration of worthlessness in the child's Etheric Body. As the abused child continues his journey through Life, he may experience other situations that he interprets as rejection, failure, or an indication of his lack of value as a human being. As these feelings pass through his Etheric Body, they amplify the vibrations of worthlessness recorded there and gradually, day in and day out, as these destructive, distorted beliefs build in momentum, the child starts forming a sense of identity and begins accepting these erroneous concepts as Truth. This self-destructive belief of worthlessness becomes an ingrained pattern, and the child then begins to behave in a manner that will confirm his belief system.

Whatever we believe about ourselves at a deep inner level, we will continually manifest in our Lives. If we believe we are worthless, no matter what opportunities are presented to us in the way of successful education, Loving relationships, fulfilling jobs, etc., we will find a way to sabotage ourselves and fail, because to succeed would be in conflict with who we believe we are. Once we accept an identity, regardless of how distorted it may be, we hold on to it for dear Life because the fear of finding out who we really are is too great.

If we will each think back as far as we can remember and just observe, in a detached manner, the number of times we didn't feel good about ourselves, we can easily see how our low self-esteem was formed. Even children raised in fairly harmonious family situations have all kinds of distorted programming because children don't always interpret situations accurately. We all have records of past hurt, resentment, anger, fear, jealousy, doubt, pain and sadness. We have memories of things that made us feel bad about ourselves, not valuable, unimportant—experiences that robbed us of our dignity, our self-respect, our self-esteem. As we reflect over our past, it is easy for us to see that we all have extensive misqualified feelings and thoughts recorded in our etheric memories. Now, as adults, we can review our past and with greater awareness, perceive the error of our childhood perception. We can intellectualize that our abuser was wrong, or that the situation did not mean we were "no good" or worthless, but that mental activity doesn't do anything to change the vibrations or the patterns and beliefs recorded in our Etheric Body.

Therefore, through sheer mindforce, we can convince ourselves for awhile that we are "OK," but as soon as a difficult circumstance challenges our confidence, those old records are activated, and our failure consciousness of unworthiness is catapulted forth onto the present situation. We thus travel through Life dragging the excess baggage of our past with us. We hold onto the distorted belief patterns of who we think we are, and proceed to magnetize people and situations into our Lives that will confirm for us our belief that we are not valuable or worthy. This vicious circle has been a normal mode of operation literally for centuries. It is a mode of operation that must cease now and forever.

In order for us to be truly FREE to fulfill our Divine Plan, our purpose and reason for being, we must Transmute our distorted concepts and accept the Reality of our God Self. In Truth, all feelings of low self-esteem, unworthiness, failure, loneliness, rejection, etc., are nothing more than separation from God. When we lift up and reunite with the Presence of God, all feelings of unworthiness drop away. Failure consciousness cannot be sustained in the Presence of God's abundant Light.

The following breathing exercise is a very easy but incredibly Powerful way to begin lifting up into alignment with our God Presence. If we will daily practice this simple breath, we will begin to quickly experience its Transforming Power. When we are lifted up into our God Presence on the Holy Breath, the distorted belief of unworthiness will be Transmuted by the radiant Sun of "I AM".

Projecting Your God Reality Into Your Physical Heart Flame On The Holy Breath

Begin by breathing in and out slowly three times. *FEEL THE HOLY BREATH*.

Enter now the Sacred Presence of the Three-fold Flame within your Heart.

A.   Take a slow, deep inbreath, contemplating your Higher Self, your God Presence. Hold the breath in for a moment and become your God Presence.

B.   On the slow, controlled outbreath affirm positively: "I AM" consciously breathing into my Heart Flame the Divine

Pattern of my True God Reality. (Repeat 3 times.)

A.   Take a slow, deep inbreath, contemplating your Causal Body. Hold the breath in for a moment and become your Causal Body.

B.   On the slow, controlled outbreath affirm positively: "I AM" consciously breathing into my Heart Flame the full gathered momentum of my Causal Body. (Repeat 3 times.)

A.   Take a slow, deep inbreath contemplating your higher mental body, your Holy Christ Self. Hold it in for a moment and become your Holy Christ Self.

B.   On the slow, controlled outbreath affirm positively: "I AM" consciously breathing into my Heart Flame the Love Nature of my Holy Christ Self. (Repeat 3 times.)

Repeat the exercise two more times as the Heart Flame becomes more of the Reality of your Permanent God Nature.

Group Avatar

The Children of Divine Love; Tolerance, Patience, Kindness, Humanitarianism, Reverence, Balance

There is no difficulty that enough Love will not conquer—
No disease that enough Love will not heal—
No door that enough Love will not open—
No gulf that enough Love will not bridge—
No wall that enough Love will not throw down—
No sin that enough Love will not redeem—
It makes no difference how deeply seated may be the troubles,
how hopeless the outlook, how muddled the tangle,
how great the mistake.
A sufficient realization of Love will dissolve it all—
If only you could Love enough you would be the happiest
and most powerful being in the World.

Emmett Fox

Our relationships are mirror reflections of our consciousness. Whether they are wonderful or destructive or a combination of both, at any given moment they are reflecting what we are sending out through our thoughts, words, actions, feelings and beliefs. I know this is one of the most difficult concepts to accept, but as we learn more about the complexity of our Beings, we begin to clearly perceive the Truth of that statement.

We Live, move and breathe within an electromagnetic forcefield of energy. Daily, this forcefield is created and sustained by our thoughts, attitudes, emotions, actions, frame of mind, beliefs, etc. All four of our lower bodies contribute to this forcefield that surrounds us: physical, etheric, mental and emotional. This electromagnetic forcefield is just as the name implies–MAGNETIC. Consequently, it magnetizes energy to itself that is vibrating at the same frequency.

Every single person on the Planet is evolving within their own self-created electromagnetic forcefield. Once we understand this Reality, it makes it easier for us to recognize how our relationships reflect our consciousness. For example, if we are suffering from ingrained beliefs of failure consciousness or unworthiness, those distorted vibrations will fill our forcefield and magnetize to us other people whose forcefields are also vibrating with failure consciousness and unworthiness. When our forcefield enters the forcefield of the other person, the discordant vibrations are amplified for both of us. This makes us very uncomfortable, and we begin to feel that we don't like each other. We may even argue or attack the other person verbally.

If we are feeling good about ourselves and our forcefield is filled with Love, we will magnetize to ourselves someone that is also content with who they are. As we enter each other's forcefield, these positive feelings are amplified, and we feel very comfortable in each other's presence.

Now, in these two examples I have greatly simplified the process, but that is the essence of what occurs.

We must realize that every person on the Planet has myriad frequencies pulsating in their forcefield from all of their Earthly experiences. Therefore, our relationships are very complex. Sometimes the same person can amplify within us positive and negative frequencies at the same time, thus creating a Love-Hate relationship.

The advantage of having this knowledge is that we can now use our relationships as wonderful tools and opportunities for growth. By observing how we feel about the people in our Lives, we can determine what we are feeling about ourselves. Often, we are oblivious to our true feelings because Life was so painful we numbed ourselves as a means of survival. But, now with greater insight, we can observe every facet of our relationships and know that the way we *feel* about each person is reflecting some aspect of ourselves.

When someone "pushes our buttons" it means they are amplifying a frequency in our own energy field we are not comfortable with. If we didn't have that particular frequency in our forcefield, they could not "push our buttons." I know that is difficult to accept, because when someone is a source of irritation for us, the last thing we want to see is any comparison to ourselves in their behavior. But, the only reason people affect us in an adverse way is because, at some level, we are buying into what they are saying or doing. At some level we are believing them even if we are fighting tooth and nail to deny it. If we really didn't believe what they were saying, it wouldn't have the same effect on us.

With this Wisdom we can evaluate all of our relationships; Parents, Spouses, Children, Relatives, Friends, Lovers, Co-workers, Employers, Associates, Casual Relationships and all of Humanity. We can observe where we are buying into destructive beliefs and where we are giving our Power away. Then, we can begin Transmuting our electromagnetic force-field by reprogramming our self-concept and self-image. As we recognize and accept our true God Reality and release all negative beliefs about ourselves, we will see our feelings and attitudes toward our relationships changing miraculously. *When our forcefield is filled only with Love, our relationships will reflect that LOVE.*

People truly treat us and perceive us the way we perceive ourselves. If we don't like the way people are treating us, we need only to Love ourselves more and our relationships will be Transformed. Experiment with this Truth and create for yourself the Loving relationships you have been longing for.

Naturally, this doesn't mean that every single person we come in contact with will automatically express only Love and Light with every thought and word, but it does mean that we will stop giving our Power away to people, and that they will no longer have the ability to affect us in an adverse way simply because we will no longer buy into their behavior or take it personally. We will be Loving and respecting ourselves and amplifying the Love and respect in them. Hence, they will be lifted up out of their negative feelings, and gradually, they will begin to believe they are valuable also.

Occasionally, we may be in a relationship that is abusive or violent. Sometimes we have such a low opinion of ourselves that we magnetize someone into our Lives who will "punish" us in a way we subconsciously feel we deserve to be punished. This is not an uncommon pattern in people who were abused as children. Needless to say, anyone who abuses another person, either physically or mentally, is not Loving or respecting him/herself. People who are so severely programmed may not be able to start Loving themselves just by experiencing our Love, but as we begin to Love ourselves, we will value ourselves enough to extricate ourselves from abusive situations. We will no longer tolerate violence or abuse of any kind.

Sometimes, the fear of leaving a relationship is greater than the fear of abuse, but I promise you, when you begin Loving yourself, you will magnetize such wonderful people into your Life you will gladly let go of destructive relationships and move forward into Joy.

I am a counselor, and one of the things I have people do to begin Loving themselves more is to write a list of all of the wonderful qualities they possess. Sometimes people feel so bad about themselves, they cannot come up with even one positive trait. In that case I have them look at all of the people they Love and admire and list the qualities they appreciate in those people. The Reality is that our relationships are mirror reflections of ourselves. Consequently, for us to even recognize and appreciate particular wonderful qualities in other people means, at some level, those qualities resonate as Truth within us, regardless of how oblivious we may be to them.

The only reason we believe we are stupid or worthless or

failures is because we affirmed those lies to ourselves over and over again throughout our Lifetime. Now, to reprogram ourselves we must begin daily affirming the TRUTH.

"I AM" VERY SPECIAL

"I Am" special...in all the world there is nobody exactly like me...

Since the beginning of time, there has never been another person exactly like me...nor will there ever be in the future...

No one has my smile, my eyes or nose, my hair, my hands or my voice. Nobody owns my handwriting..."I Am" special...No one can paint my brush strokes. Nobody has my special taste in food or music or drama or for art. No one in the world sees things just exactly as I do...

In all of time there has never been anyone who laughs exactly as I do, or cries, or who thinks exactly like I do...And what makes me laugh or cry or think in precisely my way might elicit a totally different reaction from someone else..."I Am" special. "I Am" different from every other person who has ever lived or will ever live in the history of the Universe.

"I Am" the only one in the whole of creation who has my particular set of abilities...Now, there is always someone who is better than "I Am" at one thing or another because every human being is superior to every other person in at least one regard...But, "I Am" special...And "I Am" superior to each other person in at least one regard...

No one in the Universe can reach the quality of the combination of my talents, my abilities, my feelings, my heart, my head, my hands...Like a room full of musical instruments—some may excel alone—but none can match the symphonic sound made when all are played together..."I Am" a unique symphony...

Through all Eternity, no one will ever look, walk, talk, think or act exactly like I will..."I Am" special..."I Am" rare...And in all of rarity, there is enormous value...Because of my great value I need not imitate any other person...I will accept, verily, celebrate my differences because..."I Am" special.

And it is no accident that "I Am" special...I must realize that God has made me special for a specific purpose...He has chosen a job for me to do that no one else can do as well as I can...Out of the billions of applicants, only one is qualified...Only one has that unique right combination of what it takes...And "I Am" that one...

"I Am" special..."I Am" very special...AND SO IS EVERY OTHER HUMAN BEING.   (author unknown)

Communication—
The Key To Harmonious Relationships

I came into this world with a very specific purpose. I came to fulfill a mission. I came to Love Life and realize the Truth about me. I came to contribute to the salvation of this world.

"I Am" a part of God and the fullness of the Godhead dwells in me. In the Mind of God, no one, or no thing, is useless or meaningless. Everyone and everything is of critical importance to the balance and order of the Universe. Without me, God would not be complete. Without me, the Universe would lose its equilibrium.

All that is before me to do I do with Happy enthusiasm, for nothing is too insignificant. And never again will there be a sense of futility in my Life. "I Am" overflowing with Gratitude to the Father for the opportunity to be in physical form at this time. "I Am" so thankful to be right where I am, right now, serving all who come my way with Love, Joy, Understanding and Forgiveness.

Recognizing my true worth, I now go forth with uplifted vision. I see with the inner eye the Loving and Prospering activity of the Christ within. I see with my physical eyes lavish abundance everywhere. "I AM" Peaceful, Powerful and Poised, for I know who "I AM".

We communicate in a myriad of different ways, but our clearest message is always the example of our own behavior. For instance, when a child observes his parents doing something in a particular way, the child believes that is the way it should be done. If a child sees his parents continually responding with self-discipline, restraint, dignity, Harmony, and the ability to maintain order in their own Lives, then the child will come to accept that is the correct way to Live.

The key quality to effective communication is LOVE. Ultimately, Love is everything. When we Love something, it is of value to us, and when we value something, we spend time with it; we enjoy it; and we take care of it.

TIME is another very important factor in effective communication. When we devote time to our relationships, even when it is not demanded by glaring problems, we will perceive in them subtle needs for improvement.

We can easily make the necessary changes in ourselves and share with the other person our perception of the problem. Often, with gentle urging, administered with thoughtfulness and care, minor corrections and adjustments can be made that will make what seemed like a great problem melt into nothingness.

The *quality of time* we devote to our relationships, subsequently, indicates to the other person how much we value them. We can repeatedly profess our Love to another person verbally and mechanically, but if we fail to devote significant, high quality time to the relationship, our profession of Love will be perceived as hollow and empty. Again, our behavior is the greatest communicator.

When we truly LOVE people, we value them. When we spend quality TIME with them, we transmit the message that they are VALUABLE. The feeling of being VALUABLE is the foundation of our sense of self-worth and high self-esteem. The feeling of being valuable is also the cornerstone of self-discipline because, when we consider ourselves valuable, we will take care of ourselves in all of the necessary ways.

Self-Discipline Is Self-Caring. High Self-Esteem
Paves The Road To Fulfillment And Success

We can expand our communication skills by learning to quiet ourselves and asking our Higher-Self for guidance and Illumination regarding a particular relationship or situation. There are many things our Higher-Self will reveal to us when we take the time to ask and listen. We will learn things such as:

"I Am" not a victim of circumstance. "I Am" a creator of circumstance.

I have a purpose and reason for being.

The people I come in contact with in my Life are there for a reason. Whether the relationship is intimate or casual, each interaction is an opportunity for learning and growth.

No one knows what another person's learning experience is. Consequently, I do not always know what is best for another person.

I can only perceive a situation from my own frame of reference which may not accurately apply to the other person.

In other words—what is true for me *may not always be true for another*.

It's OK for me to share my perspective and opinion in a situation. It's also OK for the other person to perceive things differently from the way I do.

This doesn't necessarily mean that one of us is right and the other wrong. It merely means that we each have a different perspective according to our wisdom and experience.

It does not diminish my value or self-worth if another person disagrees with me.

The greatest gift I can give another person is the Freedom to experience the lessons Life is presenting according to his/her own Divine Plan.

I now realize that only my Higher Self can guide me unerringly to my highest potential, and I now know this is also true of every man, woman and child on Earth.

I believe the majority of our problems in communication result when we try to project our belief system onto a situation and then ASSUME the people involved are believing and experiencing the same things we are.

For instance, when I counsel couples, I first see each of them separately to hear their individual perception of what is occurring in the relationship. Usually, it's hard to believe they are involved in the same situation because they are each seeing things so differently. Each one is assuming the other person is seeing things just like they are, and therein lies the problem.

For example, she may say, "He doesn't Love me because he's not affectionate." In reality, what she means is, if she wasn't affectionate it would be because she didn't Love him. Instead of just projecting her feelings onto him, she needs to find out what *HE* means when he's not affectionate. When the subject comes up in a joint session, he is often shocked that she even felt he wasn't affectionate in the first place. From his perspective he may feel that he was being affectionate, and he might not understand at all what she means. It is clear that we need to stop playing the game of "mind reader," and we need to stop assuming our partners are "mind readers" too.

When we realize that each and every person has a very unique Life experience, we also realize that no two people see things quite the same way. By the time we're adults we have been through all kinds of experiences, both good and not so good. We have taken those experiences and molded them into our perception of what is real and true. Consequently, when two people are going through a situation or challenge, they are each seeing things very differently. What is more important however, is that they are each *SUPPOSED* to see things differently because they are each learning something different from the situation.

No two people are going through the exact same learning experience. Therefore, it is interference for us to try and force everyone to see things our way. We do that when we are feeling insecure or trying to validate ourselves by having others agree with us.

Again, the need to be "right" and have people approve of us will dissipate when we begin accepting our true God Reality. Then our methods of communication will be lifted into the Octaves of Harmony. Instead of saying "this is the way it is and you're wrong," we will be able to say "this is the way I feel when you behave in a particular way. This is what is going on for me in this relationship. What's going on for you? What are you feeling when you behave in that particular way?" We will then be able to learn a great deal about our relationships. We will also be able to let go of judgement, criticism, condemnation and fear.

Communication means to transmit information or feelings. We must evaluate our attitudes and see if we are really communicating or just trying to force our beliefs on others. A slight adjustment in awareness can turn each interaction into a truly fulfilling communion.

Center Of My Universe

Visualization preceeding the Affirmation:

The center of our Universe is the Sacred Flame of "I AM" in the Heart. Our Universe is every person, place, condition and thing in our Lives; conscious or unconscious, past or present, through obvious choice or through karmic liability. Within our Heart Flame we can Love our Universe Free of all lower energies and thus set ourselves Free, as well as assisting the forward progress of every other point in our Universe. This Affirmation is designed to open the flow for the Cosmic Force of Divine Love to pour through the Three-fold Flame in our Hearts. Then, instead of being victims to the circumstances in our world, we will be the masters of our Lives. Visualize yourself in the center of your Universe with every person, place, condition or thing in orbit around your Heart Flame, some close, some at a great distance. Visualize each one receiving a Ray of Force from the Love Flame in your Heart. In every case this Love is a greater Force than the energy of that person, place, condition or thing. Feel this activity of Loving Free every point in your Universe, from Its center, the Heart Flame of Love. Now, remaining in this state of consciousness, give this Affirmation slowly:

Affirmation:

"I AM" the Center of My Universe. (repeat 3 times and pause)

"I AM" a Force of Love to all of Its points. (repeat 3 times and pause)

"I AM" the Full Dominion of Love in Action through me. (repeat 3 times and pause)

"I AM" the Complete Master of Love over every vibration less than Love. (repeat 3 times and pause)

"I AM" Free…"I AM" Free…"I AM" Eternally Free. SO BE IT! Beloved "I AM"

Group Avatar

Visualization Of My True Being

I now look inside…in consciousness…AND I ABSOLUTELY KNOW, not just believe or even just accept, but absolutely KNOW…myself as a pulsating Being of Light. It is electronic Light rather than atomic Light. In the electronic vehicle the Light is free flowing, but in an atomic structure the Light is fixed in certain patterns. It is the electronic nature of God that must function through the atomic nature of man (the elemental structure), and it is the melding of these two that is *the next step*.

I see myself as a pulsating Being of Light, radiating through the flesh rather than the flesh structure attempting somehow to invoke this Being of Light and draw it through. "I AM" the God Presence. I simply feel myself as a free flowing sea of Light that blends so easily with the entire free flowing sea of Light that is the Universe.

Automatically, my consciousness is raised above the human for "I AM" not a human struggling to be a God—"I AM" a God Being resting in patience, knowing my time is very close when the physical structure can completely meld with the pressure of the Light of my own Being. Automatically, I feel my consciousness expanding like a beautiful balloon—it becomes larger and larger—and effortlessly takes on more of the perfection of the Universe.

I now acknowledge that "I AM" a firmly identified Being of Light working through the flesh. "I AM" now putting my attention upon my head centers—the Chakra upon my forehead, where the Twelve-fold Flame rests, the Chakra of the thousand petal Lotus at the top of my head and the

Source of Light at the base of my brain (the major ganglionic centers there). I feel these three Sources of Light now—not just coordinating Light that comes from my "I AM" Presence in consciousness, but rather as a Source of Light, three magnificent Suns radiating outward. This is the true Wisdom which is embodied in my highest Consciousness. I feel the pressure of Light now as it is literally training my brain structure to be a radiating center of this perfect Consciousness. And this Wisdom activity, combined with pure Divine Love flowing out constantly from my Heart Chakra, will give those around me an experience of Divinity—without words. I now make a firm agreement with myself to hold this identity of a Light Being as I affirm:

Affirmation Of My True Identity

"I AM" a Force of God moving upon this Planet.
"I AM" an upward rushing Force of vibration and consciousness which is my Heart Flame—the True Center of my Being.
"This Flame becomes my electronic Aura spiraling around me. Cosmic Energy flows through this Aura.
"I AM" a Being of Very Powerful Light.
"I AM" ONE with all Light, the Great Universal Consciousness.
"I AM" that "I AM".

Group Avatar

Code Of Conduct Of A Disciple Of The Holy Spirit

1.   Be ever conscious that you aspire to the full expression of God, and devote all your Being and service to that end, as expressed so ably in the First Commandment.

2.   Learn the lesson of harmlessness; neither by word nor thought or feeling inflict evil upon any part of Life. Know that action and physical violence are but the lesser part of the sin of harmful expression.

3.   Stir not another's sea of emotion, thoughtlessly or deliberately. Know that the storm in which you place

their spirit will sooner or later flow upon the banks of your own Lifestream. Rather, bring tranquility to Life, and be, as the Psalmist so ably puts it, "oil on troubled waters."

4.   Disassociate yourself from the personal delusion. Let self-justification never reveal that you Love the self more than the Harmony of the Universe. If you are right, there is no need to acclaim it; if you are wrong, pray for Forgiveness. Watching the self, you will find the rising tides of indignation among the more subtle shadows on the path of right, called "Self Righteousness."

5.   Walk gently through the Universe, knowing that the body is a Temple in which dwells the Holy Spirit that brings Peace and Illumination to Life everywhere. Keep your temple always in a respectful and cleanly manner as befitting the habitation of the Spirit of Truth. Respect and honor, in gentle dignity, all other Temples, knowing that oft times within a crude exterior burns a great Light.

6.   In the presence of Nature, absorb the beauties and gifts of Her Kingdom in gentle gratitude. Do not desecrate Her by vile thoughts or emotions, or by physical acts that despoil Her virgin beauty.

7.   Do not form nor offer opinions unless invited to do so, and then only after prayer and silent invocation for guidance.

8.   Speak when God chooses to say something through you. At other times remain peacefully silent.

9.   Make the ritual of your Living the observance of God's rules so unobtrusive that no one shall know that you aspire to Godliness, lest the force of their outer will be pitted against you or lest your service become impinged with pride.

10.   Let your Heart be a song of Gratitude, that the Most High has given unto your keeping the Spirit of Life, which through you chooses to widen the borders of His Kingdom.

11.   Be alert always to use your faculties and the gifts

loaned to you by the Father of all Life in a manner to extend His Kingdom.

12.   Claim nothing for yourself, neither powers nor principalities, any more than you claim the air you breathe or the Sun. Use them freely, knowing the God ownership of all.

13.   In speech and action be gentle, but with the dignity that always accompanies the Presence of the Living God that is within the Temple.

14.   Constantly place all the faculties of your Being, and all the inner unfoldment of your nature, at the Feet of the God Power, especially when endeavoring to manifest perfection through one in distress.

15.   Let your watchwords be Gentleness, Humility and Loving service, but do not allow the impression of Humility to be mistaken for lethargy. The servant of the Lord, like the Sun in the Heavens, is eternally vigilant and constantly outpouring the gifts which are in his particular keeping.

Holy AEolus

Loving Presence

Oh, Loving Presence, walk through me. Open the door of understanding so I may become increasingly aware of Perfection's radiance, and of abundant Universal Love for all people and all Life at all times.

As "I Am" growing in awareness, may my questing mind push through the denseness of materiality into the awakening and rising spiritual consciousness of my own Reality.

Let my sense of gratitude expand into a welcoming smile, a friendly greeting and an expanding Light. May I look upon all persons with the eyes of Love, knowing each as my friend, my brother or sister, and not as stranger. With this realization, the rising Christ of my Being will spread Its radiant Light to everyone I meet.

Oh, Loving Mind, thank You for the discovery that the consciousness of Divine Intelligence Lives within every one. May the Light of Truth Illumine my mind as I grow in greater awareness that "I Am" a Beloved Child of God.

As I place my hand in Yours to travel this Earth journey, guide me into doing the simple things that bring Happiness to others. Show me how to give wisely of myself and my talents in areas where they are truly needed and acceptable. Let me say with conviction, "I can" and "I will", as my thoughts dwell on the ascending spiral of right thinking, right feeling, and right action. And as "I can" and "I will" become a part of my consciousness, I open wide the gate of Divine Power within myself.

Thank You for the blessings that are mine. Thank You for the opportunities that come my way. May I ever praise and bless, give and receive, Love and be Loved, and rejoice in knowing that the Light of God is Eternally Victorious.

"I Am" a part of the Oness of all Life, and I rejoice in this Glorious Truth..."I AM"

Initiation Of Group Avatar

Surrounded in Harmony and Beauty, I gently close my eyes and immediately my whole Being is raised into a mystical Temple. All physical form disappears, and in its place is a Radiating Center of Light. I open my eyes and see again the Harmony and Beauty of my physical surroundings. I close my eyes again and re-enter the mystical Temple. I remain now with eyes closed, focused on the Radiating Center of Light, Sound and Color. Soon, before my eyes, there appears "a high Mountain of Divine Love." At the very top of this Mountain of Love is a magnificent Crystal Lake and around the Lake stand twelve Angels at different points, Angels from the Temples of the Twelve-fold Aspect of Deity around the Causal Body of the Father-Mother God. Suddenly, "The Word" is spoken by the Father God, and at His command, each Angel opens a floodgate, and "Twelve great Rivers of Life" begin rushing down the high Mountain of Divine Love. In each Lightbearer, the Holy Christ Self stands poised at the entrance of the Heart. As the Waters of Life rush down, they gain a tremendous momentum, and at the moment of contact with the Holy Christ Self, a beautiful Transformation takes place. The Holy Christ Self, becomes a Golden Disc and expands until It absorbs the four lower vehicles within It. Then words of Living Light flash before my consciousness:

"I AM" a Sun...my Love its Light...all else grows dim ...Earth fades from sight, and I know that "I AM" God the One, the Source, the Great, Great Central Sun.

I remain within this exquisite Peace, in the ever-expanding Golden Disc, until I gently reacquaint myself with the Harmony and Beauty of my physical surroundings and re-enter my lower vehicles. I open my eyes, and I accept the full force of this visualization remaining with me as I feel a magnificent Twelve-Pointed Crown of pure Light placed upon my head. I remain at Peace as a Cell in the Initiated Group Avatar.

Group Avatar

Available Tape Associated With This Chapter Is:
   D. DIVINE LOVE
See page *xxiv* for more information and order blanks.

CHAPTER 4

THE FOURTH ASPECT OF
DEITY IS PURITY

COLOR – WHITE
FOURTH RAY

**THE FOURTH UNIVERSAL LAW OF
VIBRATION–ALL THAT EXISTS
IS IN PERPETUAL MOTION
THE ASCENSION OF MATTER
INTO PURITY**

**THE ATTRIBUTES OF
THE FOURTH ASPECT ARE:**

**THE IMMACULATE CONCEPT
HOPE
RESTORATION
RESURRECTION
THE ASCENSION
THE HOLY BREATH
THE SACRED SUBSTANCE OF
THE MIND NATURE OF HUMANITY**

Purity Is The Heart Of Creation

Contained within the Fourth Aspect of Deity are extremely valuable qualities we can utilize in our return journey back to the Heart of God. As we understand more about these qualities, which are actually Sacred gifts from our Father-Mother God, we will realize how important it is for us to use them continually in our daily Life experiences. For instance, PURITY is a Living breathing pulsation at the core of every electron of energy evolving on Earth. Every particle of Life is comprised of electrons rotating around the central core of the atom. The atom is a miniature universe in itself and is the building block of ALL physical manifestation, including our physical, etheric, mental and emotional bodies.

The frequency of Purity at the core of every electron vibrates so rapidly that no discord can enter into it or contaminate its radiance.

If we could stop one electron of energy as it passes through the Universe, we would see that within the electron is contained the complete nature of God: all of God's Power, all of God's Majesty, all of God's Divinity. Every single electron contains within the central core of Purity, the totality of God's Perfection. Each electron is an intelligent Life force, and as it is projected forth from the Heart of God, it joyously and anxiously awaits the opportunity to serve Life and expand the borders of the Father's Kingdom. Each second, trillions and trillions of tiny electrons flow from the Heart of the Universal First Cause through our God Presence into the Immortal Three-fold Flame in our Hearts. We then send them forth into the world qualified with our thoughts, words, actions and feelings. We know the electrons themselves cannot be contaminated with our destructive behavior. The misqualification occurs, however, when we "clothe" the electrons in vibrations that are less than Harmonious. Limitation, illness, depression and various forms of darkness are the result of our placing a "cloak of shadow" around the electrons we send forth through our negative behavior patterns.

If we truly understand this process, we will realize that regardless of how bad our Life situation seems, or regardless of how bad our physical condition is, Purity and God's Perfection are *STILL alive in every electron*, and this pure God Light is waiting even NOW to be released from its "cloak of shadow" so it can manifest the perfection of God's original plan.

Remember, each electron is an intelligent form of Life that will respond to the command of the Three-fold Flame in our Hearts. Everything existing in our Lives is comprised of electrons, whether we're talking about a person, a place, a condition or a thing. The electrons that make up our Life experiences are reflecting our consciousness. They came from the Heart of God and answered the call to obey the magnetic pull of the Immortal Three-fold Flame within our Hearts. Once they entered the Flame, we had the free will to qualify them with any thoughts or feelings we chose.

Since these tiny Beings of Light (electrons) must obey the Divinity in our Hearts, we have the ability to speak directly to them and command through the Power of God "I AM" the continuous and permanent expansion of the Flame of Purity pulsating at their very core.

The Decree To The Precious Electrons

In the Name of the Almighty Presence of God "I AM", and through the full power of the Three-fold Flame pulsating in my Heart, I speak directly to the intelligence within every electron of Precious Life Energy now existing in my world. Blessed Ones, through the Power of God, I command that the Flame of Purity in the central core of your Being EXPAND, EXPAND, and EXPAND continuously and permanently.

I direct the Flame of Purity NOW to remove the effluvia (shadows) cloaking the electrons of my four lower bodies and every single electron existing in my environment.

Oh, Sacred Flame of Purity, Transmute into Light every rate of vibration which is discordant and all vibrations causing any form of limitation in my Life.

In God's Most Holy Name "I AM", I command that this be accomplished NOW even as I call, through the Most Powerful action of the Flame of Purity ever known on Earth. I Decree and experience this very moment, the Light of Purity expand-

ing in every electron until that which is limitation can no longer exist. As the vibratory rate of each electron is quickened, the cloak of darkness is cast aside, and the shadows created by my past misuse of God's Precious Gift of Life are instantly Transmuted into radiant Light.

I accept this done NOW with full Power, to be daily increased with my every call . . . So Be It! . . . "I AM"

Contemplate, for a moment, what you have just decreed. Can you fathom what a Blessing your Heartfelt call to the Flame of Purity is to the precious electrons serving you now in the physical appearance world? You have come to Earth to *Love Life Free,* and through your concentrated efforts–SO YOU SHALL!

Dispensation of Beloved Holy Spirit

In the Full Power and Authority of the Beloved Presence of God "I AM" and the Beloved Holy Spirit, we make this call to the Celestial Giver of ALL LIFE, that no longer may the electronic substance of the Universe be misqualified or imperfectly clothed.

We invoke a COSMIC DISPENSATION wherein the electrons will be INVULNERABLY CHARGED WITH PERFECTION'S FLAME IN ACTION, and passing through mankind's vehicles which are the open doors to Its expression in the physical world, the Electronic Light will remain within an invincible armor of Love, emitting Perfection, but allowing none of the discord of the lower vehicles to change the vibratory action, color or sound of its COMFORTING PRESENCE.

WE ACCEPT THIS CALL FULFILLED, AS GOD'S HOLY NAME, "I AM".

Group Avatar

The Miracle Of Resurrection

*"Keep your attention on The Sun of your Be-ing and, as It
expands, It will Illumine your outer consciousness,
bringing Wisdom through the Mind that was also revealed
through the Avatar, Christ Jesus."*

The Master

In the Kingdom of Heaven, where there is Eternal Life, ever increasing opulence of expression, and neither disintegration nor decay are known, the Power of the Resurrection Flame is not required. However, for the evolutions presently developing in the negativity on Earth, God, in His Infinite Mercy, has provided a Restorative Sacred Flame that, *if invoked and continually used,* will revivify every electron of our Beings with Its Lifegiving essence.

When Humanity abode within the Law of Harmony, neither disease, nor decay, nor disintegration was known upon the Planet or Its evolving Life. Then, mankind began experimenting with the Gift of Life and departed from the Harmonious qualification of God energy. At that moment in time, God perceived the shadow of misqualified thoughts and feelings taking form in the consciousness of Humanity. He knew the fruits of those seeds would be disease, disintegration and decay. He further knew that some means of Restoration would have to be provided to the children of Earth if they were ever to return to their original God Estate.

Our Father-Mother God, looking upon the children of Earth, knew the need of the hour. God perceived that a Sacred Force with the Power of Restoration was necessary for those desiring to return to their Divine Heritage. It was then decreed by our Father-Mother God that a Son would bring a Sacred Restoring Flame to Earth, by which Humanity could restore their minds, bodies and worlds to their rightful estate. God called this restorative power the Resurrection Flame.

"Before they have called, I have answered, and while they are yet speaking, I have heard."

God projected a Glorious Mother of Pearl Flame charged with the qualities of Resurrection into His aura. There, the Flame was fed by the Holy Breath of God until a Son, contemplating the nature of the Father, pierced through the blazing Light of God's aura, and perceived the Sacred Flame of Hope and Life. Before the Throne of our Father-Mother God, the Son asked that He might embody that Flame and bring it to Earth for the benefit of those who again chose to know Eternal Youth, Beauty and Life Everlasting. He was granted the honor, and through the Flame in His Heart, the quality and nature of the Resurrection Flame was anchored on Earth.

The Flame of Resurrection is the Hope of Redemption for the entire human race. It is the Essence by which the diseased, distorted and disintegrating substance generated by human thought and feeling, and imposed on the pure God energy, may be Purified, Transmuted and Restored to its natural God-Estate.

The action of the Resurrection Flame quickens the vibratory rate of the Light within the cells of the body. This enables the Inner Light to throw off the appearance of limitation and stand revealed in Its full Glory. The Resurrection Flame flows through the four lower bodies of everyone who invites It.

We all have the ability to draw the Resurrection Flame into our Hearts and project It, on the Holy Breath, through every fiber of our Beings. We can also project the Flame toward a given object, holding the beam of our attention as the conduit along which the Light flows into places of employment, hospitals, homes and human Hearts. We can direct the Flame into the psychic-astral plane, into all etheric records and memories of the past, dissolving and purifying the etheric records of every Lifestream, every nation, every continent and every injustice that has ever been perpetrated on any part of Life. The Flame can be directed into the accumulated manifestation of disease, poverty, despair, and into the tremendous accumulation of thoughtforms which fill the atmosphere, impinging themselves on the mental bodies of the people, thus blocking the God directives of the individual Higher Selves.

As we freely partake of the gifts and blessings of the Resurrection Flame, we have a wonderful opportunity to avail ourselves of Its Restorative Power by opening our four lower bodies to the Transmuting, Quickening, Raising Power provided to each of us by the Love of God.

As we reach into the Realms of Truth, we will be taught to use the Power of Resurrection to bring to Life the Divine Plan for ourselves, and also for those who are drawn into our sphere of influence. For optimum Power, we must invoke the Mother of Pearl Resurrection Flame through our entire Beings at least once in every twenty-four hour period. We must bathe in Its Radiance and restore every electron of our vehicles (physical, etheric, mental and emotional) to the Perfection we knew in the beginning, before even this world was. Feel the Resurrecting Power of Divinity stir into action, and allow It to flow through your Heart Flame into the world in which you presently abide. Thus, do we become Living Temples of Resurrection.

The Hand Of God

In the Name of the Father-Mother God "I AM", as Their True Son/Daughter, the Arisen Christ...

"I AM" the Flame of Resurrection in Action (3 times)

"I AM" the Sacred Fire Breath of God (3 times)

...charging through me, Loving Life Free.

As a Disciple of Holy Spirit, I have come to set right the vibratory action of all energy and substance in my world and in all the world. As a Disciple of Holy Spirit, "I AM" the Sacred HAND OF GOD, moving through this world, instantly re-establishing Divinity wherever this Sacred Fire is applied. I invite, invoke, focus, concentrate, manifest and sustain the Resurrection Flame. "I AM" a director of the Resurrection Flame, and "I AM" humble before Its Magnificent Presence, grateful to unleash Its Power of Love on the Earth...(pause)...

"I AM" the Hand of God, CHARGING the Electronic Substance, in, through and around all Life with the Resurrection Flame. (3 times)

In Oneness of Consciousness with the Holy Christ Self

of all involved, "I AM" the Cause of this Blessing of Holy Spirit; "I AM" the Bridge over which It flows; "I AM" Its final effects of Divinity re-established, the Divine Plan manifest in the world of form.

So be it, as the Holy Spirit in Action, "I AM".

Transformation By The Resurrection Flame

Oh, Magnificent Resurrection Flame, with all the gifts of our Father-Mother God, I invoke Your Radiant Presence to blaze through my every breath . . .

"I AM" THE RESURRECTION AND THE LIFE OF HOLY BREATH IN MY LUNGS (3 TIMES) and in the lungs of all Life.

"I AM" THE RESURRECTION AND THE LIFE OF HOLY BREATH THROUGH MY VOICE (3 TIMES) and through the voices of all Life.

"I AM" THE RESURRECTION AND THE LIFE OF HOLY BREATH CHARGING THROUGH MY CHAKRAS (3 TIMES) and the chakras of all Life.

"I AM" THE RESURRECTION AND THE LIFE OF HOLY BREATH PERMEATING MY FEELINGS (3 TIMES) and the feelings of all Life.

"I AM" THE RESURRECTION AND THE LIFE OF HOLY BREATH IN EVERY ONE OF MY CELLS (3 TIMES) and in every cell of all Life.

"I AM" THE RESURRECTION AND THE LIFE OF HOLY BREATH FILLING MY BEING (3 TIMES) and the entire Beings of all Life.

SO BE IT! AS LOVE IN ACTION, "I AM".

Group Avatar

Resurrecting The Divine Pattern Within

Each Spring an accelerated momentum of the Resurrection Flame begins to blaze in, through and around all Life on Earth. As it penetrates the Earth, it awakens the Elemental Kingdom. We can easily see evidence of this in the northern hemisphere as the trees and flowers burst forth with Life, and hibernating animals awaken from their winter sleep.

The beautiful birds return home, and men, women and children begin to express the buoyant Joy of Spring. This is a very Sacred time of year and provides for each of us an opportunity for expanded growth and service.

The Power of Resurrection pulsates within Life itself. It is renewal, survival and resuscitation. When we observe nature, we see this self-evident Truth as the influx of the Resurrection Flame brings the Divine Pattern of the flower contained within the seed to full manifestation. Each of us also has, pulsating in the "permanent seed atom" of our Hearts, the Divine Pattern of our own Lives. As we draw the currents of the Resurrection Flame through our four lower bodies, we begin to experience the Glory, Perfection, Beauty and mastery which is our Divine Heritage. IF we will ask our Higher Selves to project this Sacred Life-giving Essence through our Beings continually, we will activate the latent God Powers within our own souls.

As a wise gardener carefully prepares the Earth, and then opens his plantings to the Life-giving forces of nature, so our Higher Selves endeavor to always create the most beneficial atmosphere, and then await the flowing of spiritual currents which stimulate the awakening of our dormant Divine natures and potentials.

The Resurrection Flame reaches a crescendo on Easter or Resurrection Morn. Due to the number of people on the Planet turning their attention to the Resurrection of Beloved Jesus on that specific day, literally tons of this Sacred Light pour into the Planet. Consequently, if we will consciously draw the added influx of the Resurrection Flame through our Beings and channel It into the physical plane of Earth, we will not only benefit our own spiritual growth, but all Humanity as well. Remember, when we desire to expand the Divine Pattern within our own Being, we magnetize spiritual currents of energy which nourish and develop those slumbering spiritual centers within and arouse them to active expression through the outer consciousness.

Let's deliberately take advantage of the opportunity at hand each Easter season and continue to expand the Resurrection Flame throughout the year. Let's consciously tune into the Glory and Power of the Resurrection Flame and invoke this Sacred Essence through every fiber of our Beings and the Beings of all Life evolving on this Sweet Earth. Through the Power of this Holy Light, we will begin to truly experience the Heart Flame within, awakening from Its long sleep as It expands up toward God, invoking the Life-giving currents of the Resurrection, revitalizing the Divine Pattern that has lain dormant, bringing with It the miracle of a New Birth.

"I AM" the Resurrection and the Life of the Perfection of every particle of Life, now made manifest and sustained by Holy Grace! (3 times)

Resurrecting The Seed Of The Holy Christ Self In Your Heart

The Holy Christ Self is an intelligent Being of Light with a Pure and Perfect Consciousness. It is also the Silent Watcher and the Only Begotten Son of God—the Divine You—and if allowed Freedom of action in your individual world, It will act as the personalized Divine Director of all your material affairs.

When we have advanced on the Path, the outpicturing of the Christ Self through our physical body is what has been referred to as the Second Coming of the Christ, which must be an individual experience for everyone. Thus, we begin to understand why it is not enough to believe in One Christ, but each one must BECOME THE CHRIST within his/her own Being and environment now.

The Kingdom of God, Heaven, is within us. Our Loving attention must be continually held in our Hearts, focused on the Father within. Within our Hearts, God's Will is the only Will acting. Consequently, only His Perfect results are possible from this sacred place. The Reality is—*where our attention is, there we are, and what we put our attention on, we draw into our Lifes' experience.*

All feelings of unworthiness, low self-esteem, failure, fear, grief, sadness, loneliness, anger, desperation, depression, anxiety, etc., are nothing more than separation from God.

When we choose to turn away from the Holy Christ Self within our Hearts, we have withdrawn from our Divine Heritage and separated ourselves from God and all His Perfection.

Each day we must monitor our attention and observe whether or not we have chosen to be WITH God or WITHOUT God. God and all His Goodness are always WITH us. Where are we? By remaining within our Hearts, we will solve every limiting problem.

We must affirm continually:

"Not my will Oh Father-Mother God, but THINE be done in me!
I know it is done in me when 'I AM' ONE WITH THEE!"

Now, proceeding outward from our Heart Chakras, we feel the essence of our feeling world, our emotional bodies, the vehicles through which we are given the opportunity to feel the Presence of God as the Angels do. Let us now open all the doors and windows of our feeling worlds and ask the Great Cosmic Being, Archangel Gabriel, the Archangel serving on the Fourth Ray of Purity, to charge and amplify the substance of our feeling worlds with the joyous, buoyant, raising power of the Mother of Pearl Resurrection Flame.

We feel the Flame vibrating deep, deep into the substance of our feeling worlds–scintillating Light–going deep into the atomic structure that forms our feeling nature. Our feeling worlds become so uplifted by the Resurrection Flame they cannot register imperfection. We are connected with the Angelic Host, the Seraphim and the feeling nature of God, which becomes our spiritual Oneness with the Angels for all time.

Now, we put our attention on the Head Centers–upon our mental vehicles. The Twelve-fold Flame of the Aspects of Deity is alive and blazing upon our brows. Expanding around the entire circumference of our heads, we feel the full power of the Resurrection Flame penetrating deeply into our brain structures, into our etheric minds, into the structure of our mental vehicles. We feel the Light Rays from Beloved

Archangel Gabriel piercing into our brain structures, into our minds, into our thinking worlds. We feel Divine Order alive in every cell and electron of our brains, etheric minds and mental bodies. Now, we feel the full pressure of the Resurrection Flame blazing into our Head Centers—the centers at the base of our brains, our foreheads, the top of our heads—our etheric minds and our mental vehicles. We LET GO and let the Sacred Flame Transform all into a reflecting pool of the Divine Mind of God. (Silence)

We now take a deep breath and acknowledge to ourselves that we know we are electronic outposts of the substance of the Resurrection Flame, for it is the amplified substance of that Flame which Archangel Gabriel sends world-wide. Wherever He finds the fertile ground of a purified atomic structure, He creates His electronic anchorage point where electrons of that Flame can Live within the atomic structure of our Beings, radiating forth to all the Life we contact.

FEEL YOUR HOLY CHRIST SELF AWAKENING THROUGH THE POWER OF THIS SACRED LIGHT.

FEEL THE RESURRECTING POWER OF THIS MOTHER OF PEARL FLAME AS THE HOLY CHRIST SELF WITHIN YOUR HEART BEGINS TO EXPAND AND TAKE COMMAND OF YOUR FOUR LOWER BODIES.

Affirm with deep feeling:

"I AM" A CHILD OF GOD

"I AM" a Child of God on the return journey in consciousness to the House of my Father-Mother God. I do believe and accept my inevitable, instantaneous, miraculous and complete transformation into Christ Consciousness.

During this Cosmic moment in my Life "I AM" PURIFYING! PURIFYING! PURIFYING! my human consciousness with Sacred Fire through every thought, feeling, word, action and reaction in my Life.

"I AM" building a Life in Christ Consciousness. (3 times)
"I AM" my Holy Christ Self grown to full stature. (3 times)
I accept this for my Life and for all Life, as the Child of God which "I AM".

The Immaculate Concept

The Immaculate Concept is an often used but little understood term that has been expressed continually throughout the Christian dispensation. In this very sacred time of Planetary Transformation it is important for each of us to increase our level of awareness regarding this Divine Thoughtform.

The Immaculate Concept of any part of Life is the DIVINE PATTERN or the Divine Blueprint that is encoded within that part of Life as it comes forth from the very Heart of God. It is actually the Divine Pattern of Perfection, the highest potential that any particular part of Life has the capability of attaining.

There is truly a Glorious and Beautiful Divine Pattern for every expression of Life. When we put our attention on this *POTENTIAL* of Perfection instead of on the outer appearance of negativity in which a person may be temporarily clothed, we assist in bringing into outer manifestation the blessings of GOOD with which God endowed each person in the beginning.

At the inception of the Christian dispensation, Mother Mary was given the responsibility of holding the Immaculate Concept for Beloved Jesus, which she did from His conception until the Victory of His Ascension. By holding carefully to this Divine Concept, she greatly assisted Jesus in fulfilling His Divine Mission on Earth.

The Immaculate Concept means MAGNIFYING THE GOOD wherever our attention rests, thus minimizing the appearances of imperfection. This activity will help to bring more Light into our own realms of experience and to the Earth as a whole, rather than increasing the shadows.

If we will ask our Higher Selves and God to reveal to us the Immaculate Concept of every person, place, condition or thing we come in contact with, we will not only begin to experience the GOOD that is continually pulsating around us, but we will help all Life to succeed in reaching that potential of GOOD.

Mastery and completeness are within each electron of Life just as the oak tree is within the acorn. The smallest and most insignificant seed contains within itself, not only the pattern of its full flower, *BUT THE WAY AND MEANS OF EXTER-NALIZING THAT PATTERN.* We, as Human Beings, also contain within our Heart Centers, our Divine Pattern and Life itself endowed with self-sufficiency.

If we will but realize and accept it, the Light that flows in countless trillions and trillions of electrons into our worlds each minute contains the fullness of everything we desire– Healing, Prosperity, Love, Joy, Happiness, Illumination, Truth, Purity, Freedom and every other gift from God.

We must be Eternally vigilant with our thoughts, words, actions and feelings, knowing that whatever we focus our attention on, we amplify. Each moment we must ask ourselves, "What am I thinking and feeling now? Is this what I want to amplify in my Life?" If not, then ask yourself, "What do I want instead of this? What is the Immaculate Concept of this particular situation?" Then, we must focus our attention on the Divine Pattern instead of the appearance of negativity.

Remember, daily and hourly at every given moment– MAGNIFY THE GOOD!

"I AM" the Resurrection and the Life of the Immaculate Concept of the Planet Earth and all Life evolving hereon...NOW made manifest and sustained by Holy Grace!

To The Spirit Of The Immaculate Concept, Archangel Gabriel

As the Archangel Gabriel promised to come to Beloved Mother Mary and amplify the Divine Concept of the "I AM" Presence of the Master Jesus before His birth, so does Beloved Gabriel offer to come and direct His Cosmic Flame through the outer consciousness of every individual on Earth, stirring the remembrance of that one's own Divine Image and Likeness into active being.

Invoke the Presence of Beloved Gabriel. He will not fail you. Into the swirling confusion of thought and feeling, He will direct His constant Flame, and for a moment, the remembrance of the Perfection, the Glory, the Divinity of your own "I AM" Presence will stamp Itself upon your mind. Accept It in your feelings, and ask Beloved Gabriel to keep It sustained and help you, as He helped Beloved Mary, to nourish and develop that Divine Pattern through your outer self.

Archangel Gabriel. Come now into the atmosphere of Earth. Attend the consciousness of those gathered in the "upper chamber" seeking the true Way. Bring to their remembrance the full Glory they had with their Father-Mother God before even this world was. Sustain their enthusiasm until the Glory and Perfection of their "I AM" Presence is externalized in the fulfillment of their own Divine Plan, their individual Victory, for the encouragement and example to their brothers and sisters in the Family of Humanity.

Group Avatar

Note: The Flame of the Immaculate Concept is Crystalline White with a Madonna Blue Radiance.

The Goal Of Life Is The Ascension

The Ascension

From the Realms of God's Eternal Peace,
I feel the Power of Love's release;
And, in contemplation, now I see
My Beloved "I AM" Presence within me.
Its dazzling Light envelops all
As I, in adoration now do call;
As Loving arms enfold me 'round,
I dwell in ecstasy profound!

From within this pulsing Sacred Flame,
I hear revealed my Secret Name;
As I raise in consciousness, I stand
Ever holding o'er death the Victor's hand!
As I arise—Ascended—Free,
From deep within my Heart, the Light I see
Enfold all in its Power of Love—
The Sacred Tone from God above.

Now in Heaven's Realm, my voice I raise
In pouring forth Eternal praise

For the Love that strengthens and inspires,
And the Light Rays that are God's Sacred Fires.
"I AM" God's Love; His Power; His Might;
My one desire—all Life Free in the Light—
Returning now to God—the One—
The Source—the Great, Great Central Sun!

The Bridge To Freedom

The Ascension Flame is a frequency of the Fourth Ray essential to our ultimate Freedom in the Light. It is a gift from God that contains within Its very essence the Power to Ascend any condition in which we find ourselves, back into the Octaves of Perfection. It can Ascend limitation into Freedom; distress into Peace; poverty into Opulence; disease into Health; discord into Harmony. The Ascension Flame is one of the activities of Divine Alchemy which we have often misunderstood and failed to effectively utilize. If there are negative conditions in our Lives, if our souls are weighted down, if we are depressed, if we are existing in lack and limitation— then we must invoke the Ascension Flame into our Lives, and when we do, we will experience an Ascendency and Buoyancy of Light which will lift that negative condition and bring it into a natural state of Happiness and Harmony.

The Power of the Ascension Flame is a much needed quality on Earth today where there is so much pain and suffering. Humanity's etheric bodies are filled with the records and memories of the ravages of man's inhumanity to man. Our call to the Ascension Flame to blaze in, through and around the four lower bodies of all people will do much to help relieve the suffering. Even the elements that so selflessly serve us: the Earth, Air, Water and Fire, will greatly benefit from this Blessed Flame. The Ascension Flame can multiply substance and give physical nourishment to great numbers of people. It is tangible and practical in our Lives. All we have to do is "ask, and we shall receive" the benediction of this Transforming Gift. Through the invocation of the Ascension Flame, we can Ascend the substance of EVERYTHING, EVERYWHERE.

The Ascension Flame, like all Flames and Rays pouring into Earth from the Heart of God, is dual in nature. It is the descending, conscious stream of energy from our Father-Mother God, which is drawn and sustained upon the surface of the Earth by the self-conscious calls of Humanity, and it is also the Ascending energy of the mankind of Earth and all Life that is aspiring upward back to God.

Every Lifestream who has completed their Earthly sojourn and become God-Free has utilized the Ascension Flame to Ascend from the Realms of Earth into the Realms of Divinity. This Flame is constantly rising from the Earth as a Ladder of Light and Energy upon which any man, woman or child may Ascend when their mission on Earth is finished.

When we reach the point in our Earthly development where material things tend to lose their glamour, and we begin to reach out in the direction of Spiritual Enlighten-ment, we place our feet on the Pathway of Ascension. Our Ascension in the Light is the ultimate goal of our experience on Earth. At the moment of Ascension, we become One with our own Divinity, and therefore, ONE with our Father-Mother God. Our Ascension reflects our Mastery over all energy and substance, and we are Free to travel the full extent of the Cosmos. This is not, however, the end of our evolu-tion, but rather a new beginning. From this point, we com-mence a new period of development as a God Being.

Our conscious Ascension into the Realms of Divinity, upon completion of our Earth experience, is a natural step in the evolutionary process back to our Father-Mother God. The knowledge of this Truth had all but been forgotten by the masses on Earth after the "fall." Beloved Jesus came to bring to the outer consciousness of mankind the under-standing that the Ascension is the Ultimate Destiny for everyone, and His example was the Living proof for us to follow. Most people now consider the example of Jesus a unique expression of Mastery available only to Him and fail to remember His words: "These things I do, all men shall do, and greater things than these shall ye do."

The Ascension in the Light is essential for the full manifest expression of the Divine Plan for every Human Being, every Elemental (the Beings of the four elements) and every Angel now evolving on Earth. *The supreme and ultimate goal of every Lifestream is the Ascension into the Electronic Body of the "I AM" Presence*, where we then become forever FREE from discord, strife, and limitation of every kind. If we would only be willing to accept the possibility of our own personal Ascension instead of accepting disintegration, limitation, decay and death, we would experience the natural order of God's Divine Plan.

The Ascension is merely raising the purified energies of our Lifestream into the Perfection of our individualized "I AM" Presence. Our Father-Mother God has decreed that when ONLY FIFTY-ONE PERCENT of the *total* energy we have ever released in *any* existence, is qualified constructively, our Ascension is assured. FIFTY-ONE PERCENT! If only we could grasp the MERCY of that dispensation! It literally means, if we qualify just one percent more than half of our total Life energy constructively, God will Transmute the balance and assure our Ascension. That is a very small balance–ONE PERCENT over the midpoint of our Life Energy going back to the God Presence qualified with Perfection.

Now, that seems easy enough. We should all be Ascended and Free. However, THE AVERAGE PERSON USES ABOUT *THREE PERCENT* OF THEIR ENERGY CONSTRUCTIVELY. Twenty-five percent is used destructively through frustration, stress, anger, fear, pain, judgement, criticism, boredom, tension, exhaustion, depression, indifference, low self-esteem, failure, anxiety, disease, poverty and on and on. The Balance of SEVENTY-TWO PERCENT IS WASTED FORCE. Can we even begin to fathom that sacrilege? Seventy-two percent of our precious Gift of Life wasted! Seventy-two percent haphazardly spewn forth through oblivious thoughts and unconscious feelings. Everyday we receive TONS of Pure Life Energy–Pure primal Life flowing to us from God. That is the "down-flow." Everyday we return to God a trickle of positive energy qualified with good thoughts, efforts and intentions. That is the "up-flow." The Ascension is a scientific principle working with the Laws of physical matter (electrons). In order for matter to Ascend, the "up-flow" must balance the "down-flow," PLUS ONE PERCENT! In other words, FIFTY-ONE PERCENT.

During this very critical time of Planetary Transformation,

it is imperative that we remedy the present imbalance in our "up-flow." We need to be more cognizant of how we are using our precious Gift of Life from moment to moment.

If we will continually monitor our thoughts, we will observe whether or not our thoughtforms are Free of worry, distress and distortions. Are we focusing on the positive–MAGNIFYING ONLY THE GOOD? Are we releasing the accumulated misperceptions of the past? Are our thoughts holding the Divine Pattern and Plan of our own identity, as well as that of all Life? Are our thoughts only beneficial and constructive? If not, we must take command of our mental bodies, empty our minds of all destructive thoughts and replace them with the positive thoughts we wish to amplify. Then, we will experience with Joy, the purified thoughts flowing back to God, increasing the "up-flow" of our balanced Gift of Life.

Next, we must monitor our feelings to see if they are bogged down with depression and the negative feelings that arise from the acceptance of limitation, age and disease. We must observe whether or not our feelings are filled with displeasure and pain. Are our Emotional Bodies filled with Enthusiasm, Faith, Illumination, Understanding and Love for Humanity? Are they filled with Purity, Dedication and Consecration to our Father-Mother God? If they are not reflecting what we want, then we must again take command of them and Transmute every feeling less than Harmony back into Light.

Our Etheric Bodies are also an avenue for the misuse of our Gift of Life. Are they clear of all hidden resentments, rebellions, or injustices we perceive others have inflicted upon us? Are they Free of hurt and imperfect memories? Are they filled with memories of our Divinity and the Immaculate Concept of our Divine Plan? Are they Harmonious and Balanced at all times?

The final door for our Gift of Life, into the world of form, is our Physical Body. Again, our observation of this vehicle will reveal much to us. Are our Physical Bodies vibrant, alive, young and vital? Have they developed Dignity and Mastery? Are they charged with Power and Endurance?

The time is NOW! We are being called to greater service. We must practice, practice, practice–daily and hourly–the Purifying and Harmonizing of our four lower bodies so they will be in perfect balance, increasing and expanding constantly the "up-flow" of energy back to God for ourselves and the Planet Earth Herself.

Once we have determined, within ourselves, to consciously Ascend and abide within the Aura and Consciousness of our God Presence "I AM", we must disassociate ourselves from our four lower bodies, and recognize them as only the vehicles through which our God Self will express Itself in the physical plane. Our consciousness, centered within the "I AM" Presence, continually upholds and directs our four lower bodies, turning them ever upward as they occasionally plumet to old habits, tendencies and momentums. We must halt the downward fall of our vehicles, and kindly, but firmly, command to each body: "Come, we shall arise and enter the God Presence 'I AM'!"

When we find our Mental Body entertaining impure or imperfect thoughts, we must consciously command:

"MENTAL BODY, ARISE AND ENTER THE PRESENCE OF GOD 'I AM'!"

Negative, imperfect patterns of thinking cannot be sustained in the Presence of God "I AM".

When we find our feeling worlds generating and radiating disturbed, inharmonious feelings, we must consciously command:

"EMOTIONAL BODY, ARISE AND ENTER THE PRESENCE OF GOD 'I AM'!"

In the Presence of God "I AM", only Harmonious, Peaceful, Happy, Constructive feelings can abide.

When we find our Etheric Body conjuring up past memories of unhappiness, distress and pain, we must consciously command:

"ETHERIC BODY, ARISE AND ENTER THE PRESENCE OF GOD 'I AM'!"

Within the "I AM" Presence, the Glory of God alone is reflected.

When we find our Physical Bodies registering disease,

distress, passion, lust or discord of any kind, we must consciously command:

"PHYSICAL BODY, ARISE AND ENTER THE PRESENCE OF GOD 'I AM'!"

When in the Presence of God "I AM", flesh is Transfigured into Light.

Gradually, our vehicles will obey our command just as children respond to the wise parents who train the children entrusted to their care. Impersonally, but determinedly, the God Presence lifts the particular body which occasionally forgets its resolution and the fiat to ARISE and REMAIN in the Presence of God "I AM". Again and again, we must Lovingly and Patiently reiterate the command. Gradually, the Happiness, Peace, Power and Perfection of the "I AM" Presence will be so engrained into our Physical, Etheric, Mental and Emotional Bodies that none shall find any enticement for straying, even momentarily, into the inharmonies of the appearance world.

THIS IS THE PROCESS OF THE ASCENSION!

BELOVED JESUS SPEAKS OF HIS OWN ASCENSION

"My public Ascension was for the express purpose of showing mankind their ultimate Destiny. More and more, as the New Age comes into manifestation, shall I endeavor to impress upon the consciousness of every unascended Lifestream, the feeling of My full-gathered Cosmic Momentum of the Ascension in the Light as a possible achievement for every one of the human race. As I came under the same Law as all Lifestreams who choose the Planet Earth as a schoolroom, it was necessary that I keep the vibrations of My four lower vehicles Harmonious at all times. Throughout My Earth Life, I had to be consciously on guard so that I did not accept, through the avenues of the senses, the appalling human appearances with which I was surrounded. It took tremendous effort to not accept these appearances as real, but if I had allowed my consciousness to tie into the appearances of distress and imperfection around Me, the vibratory action of all My vehicles would have been lowered, and the resultant density of those vehicles would have shut off the flow of Spiritual Vitality required to achieve the public Ascension. You each choose, hourly and daily, the type of energy which you allow to enter into your minds, thoughts, feelings and actions. You are either Ascending or descending –according to that which you allow your attention to flow into. In your final hours, your Ascension will be determined by the vibratory action of your inner vehicles–as well as that of your flesh body. This I say–*your Ascension does not manifest as the result of a moment's Grace–but of entire embodiments of vigilance, self-control, self-mastery, aspiration, and service to God!*"

The Bridge to Freedom

JOHN THE BELOVED
SPEAKS OF THE ASCENSION OF JESUS

"I was one of those who witnessed the Ascension of Jesus. Beloved Jesus, His Mother Mary and I all knew beforehand of the coming of that magnificent Accomplishment. I was there when the Beloved Master arose early in the morning after making prayerful preparations for His Eternal Victory. Beloved Mary arose early as well, and in Her great kindness and wisdom, She gathered around Her the disciples and those other Lifestreams who were interested in the Ministry of Jesus.

"I watched the Shining Figure of Jesus as He began the ascent up the Hill of Bethany for the last time unascended. I watched to see the Sun shine on that fair head as He reached the peak of the Hill and then knelt there–with the Angels hovering all about Him. There He took His personal adieu from the Earth; from the beloved friends who had assisted him; and from all which had helped Him to enjoy Life as a young and vital man.

"I saw the Heavens open and the descent of the Divine Beings Who were to help Him in achieving the Eternal Victory of His Lifestream. I saw the Great Lord Maitreya (The Cosmic Christ) standing in the atmosphere and Jesus speaking to Him, the Great Maha Chohan (The Holy Spirit), Lord Michael, Beloved Saint Germain and many of The Heavenly Host; all of these were present in the atmosphere. The skies opened early that day–long before the noonday Sun had reached its zenith, and there was a period of suspension in space between the two Realms– the man Jesus taking His adieu from the world of form; and the Christ Jesus cognizing Divinity. This made a shining, strong and beautiful Bridge of Light between the human and the Divine.

"Then when We knew that He had finished with those necessary spiritual and personal preparations, Mary and the others began to move toward the base of the hill, from the peak of which the Ascension was to take place. Mary had kept this group together only by the energy of Her tremendous Love and the capacity which She had to weave the stories around the Life of Her Son–thus keeping them from taking from Him those few final moments of privacy.

"As the Beloved Mother and the rest of us ascended the Hill toward the Presence of the Master Jesus, one could almost see in the grass which had been trodden and by the marks upon the surface of the rocks upon the path, the many, many footprints made during the trips up Bethany's Hill which Mary had made during her times of prayer. This energy formed a part of the actual ascending current which Beloved Jesus was to use in this–His final Moment of Victory.

"We did not go too close to the Presence of that Magnificent One, for as His attention began to turn toward 'Home,' His body began to blaze with more and more Light. Through Him, His Holy Christ Self became more and more apparent, and that effulgent Light signifying to the others that something of unusual import was about to take place, also stirred within them the fear and uncertainty of the unknown.

"Thus, many who were present at that Cosmic Moment did not SEE the wonder when Heaven and Earth met for a moment; when a Son of God and of man triumphed over everything of this world–rising visible and tangible to the physical sight, into the Glory of His Father's Arms.

"And so it is–always, Beloved Ones. Cosmic Moments come and a few grasp them and their opportunities; then they go, and many who have been 'called' do not witness the magnificence of the Event!"

The Bridge to Freedom

THE BELOVED MASTER JESUS...

"Beloved Children of Life, beloved Children of the Father, beloved friends of many ages! You are those with whom I have shared so many pilgrimages, stood before so many shrines, worshipped at so many altars in the long course of evolution. You have been seeking the Kingdom of God, the right use of the energy of Life and the return of self-conscious mastery. Within the Heartbeat this mastery is part of the remembrance of the days before the shadows fell on Earth, when men and women walked in Freedom, Dignity and Mastery. The use of Life was Consecrated and Dedicated to widening the borders of that ever-expanding Kingdom of Heaven and the weaving into the pattern of form, the magnificent Perfection known at inner levels of consciousness.

"The restless, surging energy which propels the soul on the search for Truth is motivated by those memories of the Divine Mastery and Dignity, to which each individual consciousness was born and to which some day each consciousness must again return.

"I wish to convey to you, through the spoken word, a portion of My consciousness which throughout the ages you have sought. That consciousness overcame the shadows, limitations, chains and appearances of the world through confidence and trust in the Power of God!

"It is that confidence which comes through contemplation, through application and through the dedication of your vital energies until no longer do your feelings swear allegiance to the shadows; until no longer are the energies of your auras set into turbulent motion by those frightening appearances (in Truth, these appearances have no more Power than you give unto them); until each of you comes into the full maturity of your own Christ Consciousness. Such Christ Consciousness has overcome all sense of allegiance to the appearances that frighten, distress and disturb the mankind of Earth.

"*ONE SUCH MAN ANCHORED IN FEELING IN THE ALL-POWER OF GOD IS ENOUGH IN ANY AGE TO TRANSFORM THE ENERGIES OF THE MASSES.* It is to educate and develop within your feelings that surety, that conviction, that the Power of God invoked does act *without fail*, that We come again, again and again. In each such visitation We anchor a little more of the Fire substance of Our worlds through your feeling worlds, your mind consciousness, your etheric bodies and your flesh.

"After such a visitation, there is another portion of the energies of your various vehicles that is permanently God qualified and God consecrated and that can never again be qualified with the creation of the human octave.

"Wise is he who places his consciousness within and who places his bodies in the Living Presence of the Masters of Wisdom, and through contagion, absorbs into the energies of his Being that confidence and Faith in the Power of the Almighty!

"To you who cling so strongly to the belief of the ages, it seems a slow process, this Transmutation, this manifestation in works of that which your consciousness grasps mentally. Believe Me, however, the weaving of the chains and the drawing of the energies of limitation into your worlds has been an exceedingly slow process too. It has engaged the free will of your Life and the use of your faculties for millions and millions of years.

"Therefore, be not discouraged in your first endeavors to set the worlds of your consciousness in order, to drive from your individual Temples the many lurking fears and doubts, suspicions and uncertainties.

"If you could see with the inner sight the centuries upon centuries that your Lifestreams have spent in drawing those unpleasant visitors into your Temples, you would rejoice that you are finding Freedom and access to the Kingdom of Heaven as speedily as you are.

"Mankind so loosely accepts blessings. Even here below, the blessed Forces of the Elements that have served so ceaselessly through the ages have received in return scant thanks for Their constancy. Without Their service mankind could not have survived in the effluvia of their own thoughts and feelings.

"Still less has the Source of all Light, (the Father-Mother God) received the gratitude from those who use Life so freely, pressing it through the senses in the wanton use of free will, in the enjoyment of every passing pleasure. People have such Happiness in the use of Life, yet Loving Life itself so little that neither Reverence nor Gratitude has gone to the Source which has sustained that Life and that Individualized Consciousness for millions and millions of years on this Earth alone, not to speak of those aeons of time before incarnation on the Earth was a manifest fact.

"Mankind must come to an understanding today that the Source which supplies Life, which gives intelligence, which endows each separate consciousness with free will, has a purpose in such an investment! Mankind must come back to its Source and, bowing the knee before It, ask for revelation as to that purpose, then in humility, in Gratitude for opportunity, proceed to weave out of their own Lives the fulfillment of that purpose!

"Wherein is man's merit in doing the Will of God, the God from whence Life itself has come? Oh! the joy that should be within the Hearts of those who have even a mental concept of the Divine Plan! How willingly and joyously should the energies be Consecrated to the fulfillment of that plan, to the exclusion of all personal interest! To think that in the course of one short Earth Life, the iniquities of millions of years might be wiped out, should be a cause for tremendous Gratitude. How wonderful to know that in one Life of Gratitude in action there can be fulfilled the purpose for which individualization and sustenance of consciousness was ordained.

"Until mankind comes to this day, they shall not know Happiness; they shall not know Freedom. Those of you who have forsworn the world of pleasure; those of you who have returned to the feet of the Masters; those of you who have woven your energies through these years into the creation of these magnificent forcefields, are most fortunate among men and women, most fortunate that the vow which you took before the Source of all Light, is being fulfilled through your energies. At the close of this Earth Life, when you stand again in the Halls of Karma, you may say, 'I have fulfilled my purpose. I have fulfilled my vow. I have therefore returned with my sheaves of accomplishment in my hands.' You will hear the words of the Father, 'Well done, thou good, thou faithful servant.'

"Believe Me when I say, nothing matters on this Earth except that you make that record that you hold those sheaves within your conscious hands and that you have endured unto the end; that you have waited the summons of your Presence and passed yet in active service into the Realms of Light!...

"Your service is a voluntary one, Children of God. No one asked you to come, and no one asked Me. No one asked the great Saint Germain or My Holy Mother to come—only the Love of Life, the Love of God and the desire to see His Kingdom come prompted any Lifestream to bend the knee before the Karmic Board. Only such Love could take a vow to render a more than ordinary assistance; to bear a more than ordinary cross; to expiate karma not one's own and to abide in exile on a Planet groaning on its axis!

"Remember, Love prompted you to come and Love must bind you together while yet you here remain!

While that Love for God beats strong in your Heart, that Love fills your feelings for the Master and that Love passes through you for your fellow worker and your fellowman, you are secure! When that Love turns to bitterness, to resentment, to rebellion, to spiritual inertia, or spiritual depletion, then within the privacy of your own Hearts and rooms, call for the spiritual vitality, call for the spiritual assistance from above. Let it return to you that warmth, that Joy, that Enthusiasm which you knew before you took an Earth body, when you stood with Saint Germain in the Freedom of the inner levels and saw a Planet God Free. You then saw men and women in Freedom's robes; no sickness, no disease, no death known. More than once in the course of an Earth Life is it necessary for cosmic vitality and the infusion of spiritual energy to sustain you. No man is complete in himself. The great and mighty Archangel Michael, the Beloved Gabriel, the Beloved Raphael, all the members of the Archangels sustained My Mother, My Father and Myself. During that night in Gethsemane, the presence of the Archangels gave to me the courage to renew My vow! When I was all alone; when those who Loved Me best were sleeping; when the future held another sweet springtime, the birds sang sweetly and the early flowers were blooming, the salt spray from the sea was in My nostrils, and the Vital Fire of a body that never knew illness was invigorated by the pulsation of Resurrection, then I chose to give that Life!

"We see on—better than you know—We see the individual depletions and renewals! I but ask you to remember that as I received assistance, so may you! Wise are you that abide within it! Wise are you that expose your souls and spirits at every opportunity to the spiritual vitality that flows from the Archangels through the Earth...

"After the passing of My Father, one of the most difficult of My experiences was leaving My Beloved Mother and making that pilgrimage into the heart of Asia. There I met the Being Whom you know as the Divine Director. There I dwelt with Him, learning to measure My Own consciousness and learning to make My Own, the few short affirmations which He gave Me.

"One of the lessons which passed from His mighty consciousness to all of Us who gathered round Him, was that no prayer or mantrum, as He called them, no decree had efficacy unless the consciousness within itself, in feeling, both accepted and understood the Truth affirmed.

"We were taught there the Power of mental concentration upon the affirmation which was ours to use, and We were asked through the energies of Our Own force-field, Our Own auras, to draw forth the Truth of that affirmation until it was visible to the Master. We were not given another application until every fiber and cell of Our Beings confirmed Our affirmation, and We had made it Our Own in practical, manifest fact.

"Some remained for thirty or forty years working on the phrase 'I AM THAT I AM.' Some remained an entire embodiment upon 'I AM the Resurrection and the Life.' There was no favoritism. There was nothing that could forward our progress except the externalized Truth which was contained within the portion of the Law which the Master gave to us. He gave it to us sparingly, as though the Breath of Life contained within that aphorism could never be used again until the Kingdom was at hand!

"Mankind and the world does not realize the Reverence with which the great Masters and Teachers, the Sages and Saints, treat Life. Mankind that devours Truths, digests them little and makes them not their own, has much to learn about the disciplines that accompany the development of consciousness within the Retreats of the world.

"Many, many who applied to the Divine Director were not even given a single worded expression throughout that embodiment, for that great Being did not feel that their Light and consciousness warranted the investment of His energies and the corresponding responsiblity which would enter the world of the student, if he could not make the Truth fact!

"These aspirants sat within the aura of the Master throughout an entire embodiment, just content to touch the hem of His garment (aura). They were content to feel their own weak spiritual energies flowing upward on His constant upsurge of Adoration and Devotion to God. They were hoping that, perhaps within their own aura some day or hour, there might be kindled a magnetic spark which would draw even a flicker of interest from His eyes, a nod of His head or the benediction from His hand, and genuflecting to the ground when such recognition was accorded them without a spoken word.

"For Myself I joined those pilgrims with no announcement. I sat with the others in the nameless circle, and the Master, in deep contemplation and meditation, made no sign that He knew of My presence. I was not heralded as the Messiah, or singled out for favors. I was to rise or fall like any man or woman on My own Light. I would not have wished to have it otherwise! When mankind and students who strive for 'place' come to an understanding of this, their Hearts will know Peace.

"The moment the pupil is ready, the Master appears! The moment the pupil is ready for more knowledge, the knowledge is given. The moment the consciousness is ripe, the fruit is plucked. The moment the Earth is tilled, the new seed is sown. We, Who seem now so prolific in sowing of our seeds, do so because long after your world cycle is completed, and you stand in the God-Free Realm, there will be men and women who will base their Life upon this Law. As One Who took so eagerly that single phrase 'I Am the Resurrection and the Life', so grateful that I had been accorded the privilege and the honor of receiving from the lips of the Master some workable knowledge to make My Own, I say to you who are so blessed, receiving this instruction without limit, you would be wise to Reverence the gift and counsel given.

"Forty-eight hours after I had received the affirmation, 'I Am the Resurrection and the Life,' as you know, the fullness of My mission was revealed to Me, and I had accomplished the purpose of My visit. I shall ever be grateful to that Blessed One Who gave me the key. Remember, however, I prepared the soil for its sowing, and after it was given me, My Life had to nourish and develop the plant and the harvest. When I left, there was no farewell. The circle of hopeful ones did not even know one pilgrim was removed from their midst. The Master did not even open His eyes or gesture. All the way back across the hot sands of India, across the rough stones of the hills, I rejoiced over and over in the richness I had received from the Being, in that phrase alone–'I Am the Resurrection and the Life.' I built from it a ministry that stands today as a manifest example that it is not necessarily the amount of knowledge but the application of the knowledge given which brings results–proof of Mastery and Freedom to mankind!

"Take not these words and this instruction lightly! Take it home, into your consciousness and into your Heart. Weave into manifest form around you an aura so that your Teacher looking upon you will say 'this student is ready to be entrusted with more Truth, with greater Power, with a deeper Understanding of the Law!' "

The Ascended Masters Write The Book Of Life

SEAL THE EARTH IN THE ASCENSION FLAME

Beloved Mighty Victorious Presence of God "I AM" in me and in all Humanity, Beloved Legions of the Ascension Flame...

SEAL! SEAL! SEAL!

our dear Earth, Her atmosphere, all Her Governments and Her people in OCEANS of the MIGHTY ASCENSION FLAME!

Let Its Fiery ESSENCE penetrate and saturate them all,

lifting and raising all Life upon Earth out of everything human into all that is Divine!

Sustain that vibration forever!...making that Ascension Flame known and Loved by all belonging to Earth's evolutions. Let It return them all to the Father's House from whence they came, forever to remain in the Eternal Victory of God's Divine Plan Fulfilled!

IT IS DONE...for I have made this Call...AS GOD'S MOST HOLY NAME "I AM"!

ASCENDING INTO CHRIST CONSCIOUSNESS

Through the Sacred Fire of Divinity within our Hearts, we call to the Ascension Flame and the Presence of God "I AM"...

CHARGE! CHARGE! CHARGE!

Living Flames of Cosmic Christ Purity in, through and around our four lower vehicles, brains, feeling worlds and auras. Through the Pressure of Thy Light, EXPAND the Purity in every cell of our Beings, until all shadow of human appearance is no more.

Beloved Holy Christ Self, INTENSIFY the LIGHT of the Christ through our outer consciousness until THY INNER PRESENCE is realized.

SO BE IT...for "I AM" the Full Power of God acting here, NOW and FOREVER SUSTAINED.

Through the Christ "I AM" in me, I surrender now, in deep Humility, every thought, feeling, word and deed less than Christ Purity, and I step through the Golden Door of God Acceptance into the Heart of God, and claim my Divine Heritage! "I AM" FREE! "I AM" FREE! "I AM" ETERNALLY FREE!...GREAT UNIVERSAL "I AM".

THE COSMIC LIGHT OF JESUS, THE CHRIST

In the Full Power and Authority of the Beloved Presence of God "I AM"...

BELOVED ASCENDED MASTER JESUS, the CHRIST! BLAZE Your Heart Flame of COSMIC LIGHT into all LIFE on the Planet...and those to come.

Anchor within each embodied soul the COSMIC LIGHT required to draw out their constructive momentums, and enable them to respond positively to the increased LIGHT being released in this NEW GOLDEN AGE.

"I AM" THE RESURRECTION AND THE LIFE OF THE MOMENTUMS OF GOOD...in all Lifestreams on the Planet, now made MANIFEST and SUSTAINED by GRACE. (3 times)

We ACCEPT this Call FULFILLED...AS GOD'S HOLY NAME..."I AM"!

OVAL OF BLAZING WHITE LIGHT

In the Full Power and Authority of the Beloved Presence of God "I AM"...Beloved Legions of Light, I Love, Bless and Thank You for Your Great Service to me and all Humanity...

SEAL! SEAL! SEAL! me and all Humanity in Your Oval of Pure Blazing WHITE LIGHT which deflects those currents of energy which slow the vibratory action of my inner vehicles.

I DECREE the PURITY within every electron in my aura, feelings, mind, etheric and physical vehicles shall now EXPAND! EXPAND! EXPAND! and that which is limitation and shadow in my world SHALL BE NO MORE!

I ACCEPT this Call FULFILLED...
AS GOD'S MOST HOLY NAME..."I AM"!

Group Avatar

Available Tape Associated With This Chapter Is:
    E. PURITY
See page *xxiv* for more information and order blanks.

CHAPTER 5

THE FIFTH ASPECT OF DEITY IS TRUTH

COLOR – EMERALD GREEN FIFTH RAY

THE FIFTH UNIVERSAL LAW OF CYCLES
THE OUTBREATH AND
INBREATH OF EXISTENCE
DEDICATION AND
CONSECRATION OF LIFE

THE ATTRIBUTES OF
THE FIFTH ASPECT ARE:

ILLUMINED TRUTH
INNER VISION
CONSECRATION
CONCENTRATION
HEALING
DEDICATION
THE ALL-SEEING EYE OF GOD
THE EMPOWERMENT OF
ALL GOD QUALITIES ON EARTH

THE EMPOWERMENT OF ALL GOD QUALITIES ON EARTH THROUGH THE SUPREME INITIATION

If we will effectively utilize the Unified Qualities of the Fifth Aspect of Deity, we will realize the fulfillment of the fiat–"KNOW THE TRUTH AND THE TRUTH WILL SET YOU FREE!"

The gifts from God that pour into the physical plane of Earth on the Emerald Green Ray are Glorious beyond our greatest expectations. In this chapter, I am going to share with you a Sacred Initiation that, *if done according to the specific directions revealed herein*, will Transform your Life, lift you up into the Octaves of Perfection, Empower all of the Qualities of God within you and SET YOU FREE!!!, thus enabling you to be a Powerful vehicle through which the totality of God will Bless all Life on Earth.

We have become so immersed in the dense vibrations of our own self-created negativity that a great chasm has formed between our Higher Self and our four lower bodies, including our conscious mind and awareness. We have felt abandoned and isolated from the Realms of Truth. The Reality is, of course, that our God Presence ALWAYS RESPONDS TO OUR EVERY CALL, but if we are unable to reach up in vibration through the quagmire of our own mis-qualified energy effectively enough to perceive that response, then it is of no avail. It is necessary for us to raise our consciousness and our vibrations up sufficiently so the "STILL SMALL VOICE WITHIN" can be clearly heard.

Through the practice and use of the Initiation given in this chapter, we will be raised into the Realms of TRUTH. We will learn to perceive subtle Perfected energies at work in our Lives, and we will understand how to work with them efficiently. Through the rhythmic application of these techniques, we will recognize the intelligence within all Life. Our minds will be open and receptive to the Rays and Qualities of the Realms of Illumined Truth, and we will experience such exquisite vibrations that our entire Beings and environments will be flooded with Light.

As we reach up and reconnect with our God Presence, our

consciousness opens to the influx of pure Spiritual Energy. This Energy accelerates the growth of our awareness and Transforms our Lives powerfully and deeply, enabling our negativity to be Transmuted into Light.

During this Cosmic Moment in the Earth's evolution, we are receiving more assistance from on High than ever before, and dispensations are being granted that allow us to have access to Sacred Knowledge previously taught only to the High Initiates in Mystery Schools. We must accept this Sacred Knowledge with deep Humility and Reverence and use it ONLY as directed, knowing full well that if this Truth is used to perpetuate the ego or for self-agrandizement, the Law of the Circle will be instantaneous and just.

Before we begin this Initiation, we must be prepared to make changes in our Lives. The radiant Light of our God Presence will clearly expose the illusions and deceptions of our distorted belief systems. We must ask ourselves before beginning:

AM I READY TO OPEN MYSELF TO THE BLAZING REALMS OF ILLUMINED TRUTH?

AM I READY TO BECOME ONE WITH THE PRESENCE OF GOD PULSATING IN MY HEART?

AM I READY TO TRANSFORM MY LIFE AND MY PHYSICAL REALITY?

If the answer to all of these questions is YES, from the innermost part of our Beings, *then and only then*, may we proceed.

THE SUPREME INITIATION

All that exists in the Universe is the vibration of many spectrums of Living Light. Vibration is actually the Law of the Universe, and all Life breathes and expresses the essential nature of vibration through rhythm.

In order to attune ourselves with the vibration and rhythm of the Universe, it is essential that we master the technique of the Balanced Breath. Our ability to reach up in vibration into our God Presence is based upon the foundation of the Balanced Breath.

If we open our minds to the existence of Pranic Energy,

the Breath of the Holy Spirit, we will become aware of Its Presence. With every breath, we absorb this vital force of Life, and we depend on It to remain healthy and alive. Within our finer bodies there are specialized centers that serve as forcefields to magnetize and radiate forth this Holy Essence. These centers are seen as swirling vortexes of concentrated Light, and they are separate from the Chakra System. These centers vibrate at a higher frequency than our four lower bodies, and they are associated with the five Elements: Ether (Spirit), Air, Fire, Water and Earth.

Until the shift in vibration, which took place during Harmonic Convergence, these centers functioned only in the Fourth Dimension. In the physical plane they were considered dormant. With the acceleration in vibration of the Planet on August 17, 1987, we moved much closer to the Fourth Dimension, and not only were we brought into alignment with the Solar Spine of our "I AM" Presence and the Twelve-fold Aspect of Deity, but the five spheres of Elemental energy blazing in our God Presence began to awaken within our four lower bodies.

These five Elemental spheres continually magnetize highly Spiritualized Energy from the Octaves of Perfection, and NOW this energy is being released into the Elemental substance of our four lower bodies. Each center represents a force of Sacred Fire, the Breath of Holy Spirit, and with these centers activated through the Supreme Initiation, we will experience a Transformation in our physical, etheric, mental and emotional bodies at an atomic cellular level. The five Elemental spheres are receptive forcefields which receive energies from the Holy Spirit on the Holy Breath. This is a Feminine Energy Force that is being activated now as never before to accelerate the Feminine Ray Nature of Balance and Harmony through all Life.

The Supreme Initiation is a method whereby the Elemental centers will be deliberately awakened into full vibrant activity according to the Divine Plan of each individual. It is very important that this awakening process be done *slowly* and *thoroughly*.

In order to accomplish the Supreme Initiation we must continually manifest DIVINE TRUTH in our daily Lives.

Each of us must go within and earnestly endeavor to practice the Spiritual Truths we are now receiving consciously from the Fourth Dimensional Realms.

The Supreme Initiation is, of course, the initiation into the Reality of our true Being. This initiation cannot be accomplished through intellect. It will be attained ONLY through the perpetual practice of the Presence of God.

The veil has been lifted, and now through our open Hearts, our Invocation of the Light and our Reverence for all Life, we shall BECOME God Illumination on Earth–the Christ.

The Transformation taking place is occurring at an atomic cellular level. Consequently, through the five Elements comprising all manifest form, we shall pass through the steps of the Supreme Initiation into Christhood.

Through this Sacred Initiation, each of us will be Victorious over matter. Then, our bodies of Earthly expression will be Transformed into Light. We will then be "in the world, but not of it." We will be the Christ, grown to full stature, manifesting Celestial Lives of Beauty and Harmony in every single facet. Then, we will affirm with a KNOWING beyond the comprehension of our finite minds:

"I AM" a Sun/Son...My Love Its Light.
"I AM" a Force of God moving upon this Planet.
"I AM" ONE with all Light, the Great Universal
Consciousness.
"I AM" that "I AM".

STEP ONE OF THE SUPREME INITIATION
The Balanced Breath

Center
Yellow/Gold
WISDOM
Son-Daughter/The Christ

Left
Sapphire Blue
POWER
The Father

Right
Pink
DIVINE LOVE
The Mother/Holy Spirit

THE THREE-FOLD FLAME

The Three-fold Flame pulsating in every Human Heart re-flects the Three-fold Activity of God—the Holy Trinity. Through this Flame, Humanity expresses the Perfection of God in the world of form.

This exercise is designed to Unify the Three-fold Flame in our Hearts with the Three-fold Flame in the center of the Earth (third dimensional plane) and the Three-fold Flame in the center of the Great Central Sun (Fourth Dimensional Plane), thus creating a bridge over which this Planet will as-cend into the Octaves of Perfection.

To begin the exercise we sit comfortably with our spines as straight as possible and our bodies relaxed. We concen-trate on our breathing, gently counting in our minds the length of the IN breath and the length of the OUT breath. We then calmly adjust the inbreath and the outbreath to equal duration.

When we reach this calm, Balanced Breath, we begin to experience ourselves becoming aligned with the Harmony of the Universe. After a few minutes of Balanced Breathing, we begin to *feel* a force of subtle vitality growing and spread-ing through our bodies. This is Pranic Energy or the Breath of the Holy Spirit. This Holy Breath is the vital Life-sustain-ing essence that permeates and sustains all Life. We are not to force the conscious control of the breath, but just relax and practice this technique of Balanced Breathing until we per-ceive a definite sensation. As we do, we begin to accept and know that the breath is the most essential process of Life.

Only after we *FEEL* the vitality of the Holy Breath through the practice of Balanced Breathing are we ready to proceed to the next step.

After accomplishing the Balanced Breath, we focus our entire concentration on this symbol:

SACRED SYMBOL

After a minute or so we close our eyes and take this symbol within as we project it into our Hearts. With each breath we consciously affirm its presence there.

As we experience in our mind's eye this symbol anchored in our Hearts, we see it being Transformed into Living Light. The triangle becomes radiant Sapphire Blue Light. The symbol of the Three-fold Flame within the triangle becomes active and alive. We see a blazing plume of Pink Divine Love pulsating to the right, and a blazing plume of Sapphire Blue Power pulsating to the left. Rising from the center is the blazing plume of Sunshine Yellow Wisdom.

As the symbol grows, we FEEL a sensation of inner warmth in our Hearts. We FEEL the Power of this Sacred Symbol growing in intensity. As it becomes more and more Powerful, we project our Luminous Presence, a radiant forcefield of Light with a reflection of the Sacred Symbol blazing in the center, down into the Divine Momentum in the center of the Earth, the Sun of Even Pressure. In Consciousness, we anchor our Luminous Presence in the center of the Earth.

As the symbol pulsates in the center of the Earth, the Three-fold Flame of the Planet begins to rise up through the Earth and is magnetized into our Hearts by the Sacred Symbol anchored there. This creates a mighty shaft of Light from the center of the Earth into our Heart Flames.

We now project our Luminous Presence, containing a reflection of the Sacred Symbol, up into the Octaves of Perfection, higher and higher until we reach the center of the Great Central Sun. There again, we anchor our Sacred Symbol. As the symbol pulsates in the center of the Spiritual Sun, the Three-fold Flame of the Sun begins to descend down through the atmosphere, magnetized into our Hearts by the Sacred Symbol blazing there.

Once more, a mighty shaft of Light is created. These shafts of Light are unified in our Hearts, and a span of Light reaching from the Center of the Earth into the Heart of the Great Central Sun is permanently secured.

As we energize this span of Light, daily and hourly, on the Balanced Breath, the Bridge over which this Sweet Earth and all Her Life will ascend into the Octaves of Perfection (the Fourth Dimension) will be sustained.

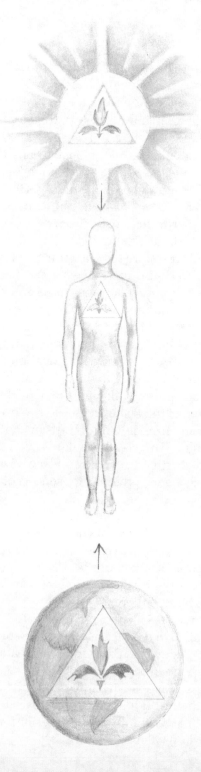

ON THE *INBREATH* THE SACRED FIRE FROM THE CENTER OF THE EARTH IS DRAWN UP INTO OUR HEARTS.
ON THE *OUTBREATH* THE SACRED FIRE FROM THE GREAT CENTRAL SUN IS MAGNETIZED DOWN INTO OUR HEARTS.

This is a very powerful exercise. As we daily practice this Balanced Breath, our perception will be elevated. We will witness changes occurring in our Lives. We will become vibrantly aware and experience the Glory of nature from a new perspective. We will be more Loving and Compassionate. Our sense of well-being and Happiness will be amplified greatly.

Through consistant practice, we will become a vehicle for God to work through to bring Illumination to our fellow Human Beings. Service is the key to growth. As we reach out to others, we will steadily rise to greater levels of awareness.

STEP TWO OF THE SUPREME INITIATION
The Ether/Spirit Sphere

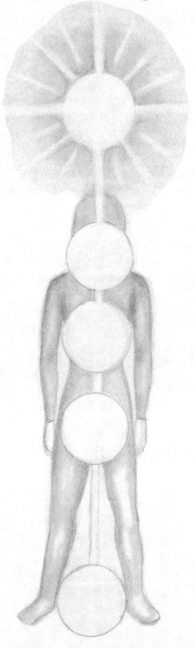

To begin Step Two of the Supreme Initiation, we sit comfortably in a chair with our arms and legs uncrossed, our hands resting in our laps with palms facing upward. We feel ourselves become relaxed, empty our minds of all thoughts and release all feelings of tension or stress–just letting go. We are enveloped now in a forcefield of Protection and Comfort. We are at Peace! We are Centered! We are One with all Life!

Once we have reached the relaxed state, we begin to observe our breath, noting silently the duration of each inbreath and each outbreath until we attain the Balanced Breath. In this Harmonious state we begin to feel the vital Life Force of the Holy Spirit flowing through our Beings. This Essence lifts us into a heightened state of awareness.

Now we concentrate our entire consciousness on the Three-fold Flame in our Hearts–the true center of our Beings. As this occurs, all of our senses are focused inward as each breath penetrates deeper and deeper into the Divinity within.

When we feel completely centered in our own Divinity, we move our focus of attention upward. It rises slowly until we reach a point twelve inches above our heads. There, we perceive a point of brilliant vibrating White Light. With the full Power of our Divinity we affirm into the center point of Light:

"I AM" THAT "I AM"

On each inbreath we affirm "I AM" that "I AM" into the Ether/Spirit Center above our heads, and on each outbreath, we visualize that center point of Light awakening into a blazing Sun. As it grows, it gathers intensity and momentum, becoming a rotating, pulsating vortex of Light.

As we continue to silently intone the affirmation into the Ether/Spirit Sphere, we feel the effects of the awakening Spiritual energy emanating into our consiousness, flooding our Beings with pure Life Vitality.

This experience is Powerful and intense. We are actually awakening to the center of pure spiritual intelligence within us. Every cell and atom of our bodies is affected and responds. From our new heightened awareness our view of reality begins to change. We release our attachments to the world of illusion, and we gradually perceive the Perfection of God's Will through the chaos.

During this period of awakening the Ether/Spirit Sphere, we will realize we are activating a part of our Beings that has been dormant. This process causes a flood of pure Light to enter our consciousness.

To completely activate this center, we must continue this exercise for a *MINIMUM OF FIFTEEN MINUTES EVERY DAY FOR SEVEN DAYS*. It is extremely important that we awaken the center fully and completely.

The Divine Plan for all creation is for the Perfection of the Immaculate Concept to reflect on the physical planes of matter. Through this process, physical matter Ascends into the Divine Blueprint.

THE LIGHT BODY–ETHER/SPIRIT

Through the above exercise, the Spiritual Light Body is activated, and if we will continually contemplate and apply the following guidelines, this step of the Supreme Initiation will be fulfilled.

GUIDELINES TO MY PERFECTION

1. "I Am" renewing my mind.
2. "I Am" lifting up my vision to see myself as God sees me–radiantly healthy and filled with Joy and Peace.
3. "I Am" whole, perfect and complete.
4. "I Am" meditating daily on my Divine Image.
5. I go about my business with an uplifted consciousness of health and well-being.
6. I Live the TRUTH of health.
7. "I Am" reprogramming my consciousness on a mental level. "I Am" also continuing my health work in the physical world of form.
8. My thoughts and actions are Harmonious and Balanced.
9. I eat and exercise properly and affirm perfect health, knowing the health of my body reflects my mind. It is the physical image of my mental atmosphere.

10. "I Am" aware of the total interrelationship of mind, body and Spirit in creating a state of well-being in myself.

11. My God Presence perceives only Perfection in me. It is the Will of God in individual expression.

12. "I Am" seeing my four lower bodies–physical, etheric, mental and emotional as my God Presence sees them–Perfect and raised into my LIGHT BODY. My Life is God's Life, and God's Life is Perfect.

STEP THREE OF THE SUPREME INITIATION
The Air Sphere

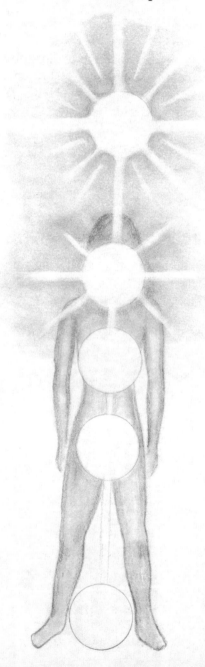

After completing seven consecutive days of activating the Ether/Spirit Sphere for a minimum of fifteen minutes each day, we are ready to proceed to the next step.

The Supreme Initiation is *always* done in ordered sequence, so Step Three begins by repeating Step One and Two for a few minutes. After silently intoning "I AM" that "I AM" into the Ether/Spirit Sphere for a few minutes, we visualize a shaft of pure, white, radiant Light flowing down from the Sphere above our heads to a point of blazing white Light in our throat centers. We feel the inrush of Light through this shaft activate the point of Light until it, too, begins to expand into a brilliant rotating Sun.

With the full gathered momentum of our Divinity, we silently intone into the Air Sphere awakening in our throats the affirmation:

"I AM" THE BREATH OF THE HOLY SPIRIT

On each inbreath, we intone the affirmation into the Air Sphere, and on each outbreath, we experience the sphere awakening into a blazing Sun.

This center must also be activated for at least fifteen minutes every day for seven consecutive days. During our sojourn within the Air Sphere, we will be lifted higher in consciousness, and our ability to express ourselves clearly will be enhanced. We will discover new ways to communicate, and we will be able to alleviate much of our past inappropriate verbiage. Our old belief systems that no longer apply to our present state of growth will also come into view, giving us the opportunity to release them and replace them with our new found insight.

THE ETHERIC BODY—AIR

Through the activation of the Air Sphere, our Etheric Bodies are lifted into our Light Bodies. If we contemplate and apply these guidelines, Step Three of the Supreme Initiation will be fulfilled.

THE PURIFICATION OF
MY RECORDS AND MEMORIES OF THE PAST.

1. "I Am" Purifying my subconscious mind—every ex-

perience of the past–Transmuting it–cause, core, effect, record and memory into Light.

2. My Etheric Body is Spiritually Pure. "I Am" Free of the world of illusion.

3. "I Am" reaching into the Octaves of Truth and breathing in the Holy Breath of God.

4. I invoke the Light of Clarity to shine on the records of the past and lift them into the Light of Understanding.

5. "I Am" developing the qualities of Divine Expression, Perception and Discernment.

6. "I Am" passing through the Truth of Discernment from the world of illusion into the Light of Reality.

7. "I Am" Balance.

8. "I Am" accepting my true God Reality.

9. "I Am" a focus of radiant, positive thoughts filled with Gentleness and Compassion.

10. My Life is a manifestation of my past thoughts. "I Am" changing my thoughts to be one with Divine Will. Therefore, "I Am" changing my Life.

STEP FOUR OF THE SUPREME INITIATION
The Fire Sphere

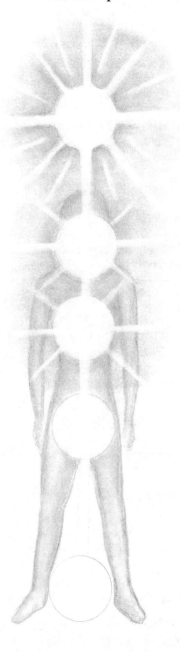

After completing seven consecutive days of activating the Air Sphere for a minimum of fifteen minutes each day, we are ready to proceed to the next step.

We begin by repeating Steps One, Two and Three for a few minutes. When the Spiritual Energy in the throat reaches its full intensity, we visualize another shaft of pure white Light flowing down until it reaches a point of Light pulsating at the base of our sternum in the center of our chests. As the Fire Sphere becomes activated, it begins to rotate and expand into a radiant Sun. With the full momentum of our Divinity, we silently intone into the Fire Sphere the affirmation:

"I AM" THE FIRE BREATH OF THE ALMIGHTY

On each inbreath, we silently intone the affirmation into the Fire Sphere, and on each outbreath, we visualize the sphere awakening into a blazing Sun.

As the sphere expands, we feel the warmth glowing and growing. The vibrations of Love touch our Hearts, and we feel more complete, centered and whole than ever before. The Divine Flame is a wonderous gift from our God Presence.

While activating the Fire Sphere, we become aware of the ways in which our vital energies are utilized daily. We begin to recognize ways in which we are allowing ourselves to be depleted. Through this observation, we will be able to make positive adjustments in the way we expend our Life energy. Positive growth requires effort and a will to change. Awareness always creates a responsibility to act on the knowledge gained.

THE MENTAL BODY–FIRE

Through the activation of the Fire Sphere, our Mental Bodies ascend into our Light Bodies. If we contemplate and apply these guidelines, Step Four of the Supreme Initiation will be fulfilled.

"I AM" ONE WITH THE DIVINE MIND OF GOD

1. Through the Initiation of Sacred Fire, I realize Love is the First Cause of all Life.

2. The Initiation of the Sacred Fire reveals my God Presence "I Am."

3. However brilliant the Mind, it must reflect the Love of God to be fulfilled.

4. The Sacred Fire Initiation brings warmth, Light and beauty to Life.

5. In the Fourth Dimension, Sacred Fire creates and gives Life.

6. The Sacred Fire Initiation opens a portal to Divinity.

7. Faith, Hope and Love are governing my thoughts. Faith is an inward knowing that all is working for my highest good. Hope is an ever-growing confidence in God's Wisdom. Love Illumines my Heart.

8. Through the Sacred Fire Initiation, I have the Power to Illuminate the world.

9. The Life and Love of God are my true Reality.

10. The Divine Mind of God floods my Being and enhances all my creative power.

11. Love Transforms Life, removing all that is unwanted, lifting each Lifestream into the Perfection of the God Presence "I Am."

STEP FIVE OF THE SUPREME INITIATION
The Water Sphere

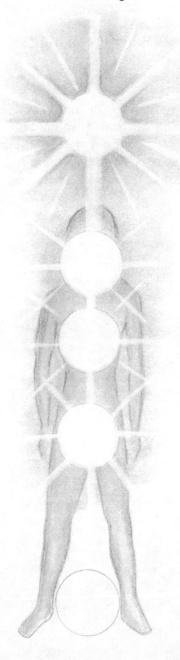

After completing seven consecutive days of activating the Fire Sphere for a minimum of fifteen minutes each day, we are ready to proceed to the next step.

We begin by repeating Steps One, Two, Three and Four for a few minutes. When the Fire Sphere has reached its optimum expansion, we visualize another shaft of pure white Light descending down until it reaches a point of Light vibrating at the base of our spinal column. As the shaft of Light penetrates into this seed point of Light, it begins to awaken the Water Sphere into a blazing Sun. With the full momentum of our Divinity, we silently intone into the Water Sphere the affirmation:

"I AM" THE HARMONY OF MY TRUE BEING.

On each inbreath, we silently intone the affirmation into the Water Sphere, and on each outbreath, we experience the Sphere expanding into a vibrant Sun.

The Water Sphere is associated with the emotional body, and it is often the most challenging center to awaken in the Supreme Initiation. Suppressed emotional energy rises to the surface to be Transmuted into Light during this step of the Initiation. The suppressed emotional patterns are a result of our distorted perceptions and programming from the past. These are the feelings and beliefs that have been keeping us struck in the past and blocked from moving forward into our highest potential.

THE EMOTIONAL BODY–WATER

Through the activation of the Water Sphere, our Emotional Bodies are raised into our Light Bodies. Through the contemplation and application of these guidelines, Step Five of the Supreme Initiation will be fulfilled.

THE HARMONY OF MY TRUE BEING IS
MY ULTIMATE PROTECTION

1. Be STILL and know that "I AM" God.
2. I have Transmuted all my emotions into Harmony by giving my God Presence dominion.
3. "I Am" gently leading my feelings and emotions into God's garden of Harmony and Balance.

4. "I Am" continually utilizing the God Qualities of Discernment and Discrimination.

5. I nurture my emotions with Humility and Simplicity.

6. "I Am" determined to Live Truth from my innermost Being.

7. My emotions are disciplined to be Tranquil and Patient.

8. "I Am" always calm enough to reflect the Vision and Voice of God.

9. "I Am" perpetually a manifest expression of Spiritual Truth.

10. I recognize my challenges and responsibilities as opportunities for growth, and I experience them with Joy.

11. I realize the Love, Wisdom and Power of God, therefore "I Am" experiencing a Spiritual Life filled with Light, Freedom and Divine Purpose.

12. "I Am" the Illumined consciousness of Tranquility and Peace.

13. I Anoint my Being with the knowledge of God, and "I Am" Serenity.

14. "I Am" cleansing and purifying my Emotional Body with the Violet Transmuting Flame of Love.

15. "I Am" focused on the Harmony and Balance of the Christ within.

16. I seek only God.

EXERCISE TO RESTORE BALANCE

As the Light of God pours through our Beings, It enters the electronic substance of our four lower bodies at a cellular level, thus pushing all of the frequencies of discord to the surface to be Transmuted at an accelerated pace. This often causes discomfort and some imbalance in our Lives. We must acknowledge that we are NEVER given anything we can't withstand, so it is important for us not to stop the process. There is, however, *an exercise that will alleviate the discomfort and help restore balance,* as the purification is taking place. Remember always, that once this process is truly complete, we will never again be prisoners of our painful past. We will be FREE to magnetize the incomprehensible Joy of the Fourth Dimension into our Lives. We will then experience the fulfillment of the invocation, "Thy Kingdom come, Thy will be done on Earth as it is in Heaven."

To begin the exercise, we sit comfortably and attain the Balanced Breath. Once we have experienced a definite sensation of heightened awareness, we visualize an intense Three-fold Flame blazing above our heads within the Ether/Spirit Sphere. As we breathe out, we send a stream of "The Fire Breath of The Almighty" in an arc from the Ether/Spirit Sphere around the front of our bodies into the Solar Plexus just above the navel. This is the spot in our bodies where our emotional energies are most intensely felt. As we breathe in the stream of Light, "The Fire Breath of The Almighty" radiates through our four lower bodies, absorbing every discordant frequency of vibration. The Flame then passes out our backs and arcs back up into the Three-fold Flame blazing in the Ether/Spirit Sphere where the discordant frequencies are instantly Transmuted into Light. Again on the outbreath, "The Fire Breath of The Almighty" arcs around our bodies into the Solar Plexus. On the inbreath, it passes out our backs having absorbed all discordant frequencies of vibration and carries them into the Three-fold Flame in the Ether/Spirit sphere for instant Transmutation.

This is a very simple, but extremely Powerful exercise, and we should continue to do it until the discomfort is dissipated and the balance restored.

I advise you again to follow the directions for the Supreme Initiation EXACTLY. It's important that we not become impatient and rush ahead. We have been waiting aeons of time for these Sacred Truths to be revealed to us. They have been held in abeyance because the Heavenly Host felt our consciousness was not raised sufficiently to enable us to use them correctly and safely. We are now being entrusted with these Sacred Truths. Let's prove that we are indeed trustworthy. Discipline is the key to Self-Mastery.

The Water Sphere must also be activated for fifteen minutes a day for seven consecutive days before proceeding to the next step of the Supreme Initiation, which is the activation of the Earth Sphere.

STEP SIX OF THE SUPREME INITIATION
The Earth Sphere

After repeating Steps One, Two, Three, Four and Five of the Supreme Initiation for a few minutes, we experience a cascading shaft of pure white Light pouring down from the Water Sphere to a point of Light situated between our feet. The Light begins to Illuminate the Earth Sphere as it becomes a brilliant rotating Sun.

Into the point of Light between our feet, we silently intone with our full Divinity, the affirmation:

"I AM" THE MASTER OF MY PHYSICAL REALITY

On the inbreath, we intone the affirmation; on the outbreath, we visualize the Earth Sphere expanding into a brilliant Sun.

As the Earth Sphere is activated, we become a Living, shining pillar of Light, a pure white radiant pathway of Light, linking all of our Elemental Spheres from head to foot.

The awakening of the Earth Sphere will be experienced by each of us as a tremendous relief, for we will now feel balanced in every respect. The major areas of our Lives that will arise during the activation of the Earth Sphere will be our physical, material realities. Our entire physical world will be surfacing for evaluation and adjustment. Physical possessions, attachments, care of our physical bodies and material needs will all be brought under scrutiny.

Through the Earth Initiation, we will learn how to effectively use the creative faculties of thought and feeling to project Divine Will onto physical energy (matter), thus creating Perfection on Earth.

THE PHYSICAL BODY–EARTH

Now, with the activation of the Earth Sphere, our physical bodies are raised into our Light Bodies. The fulfillment of Step Six of the Supreme Initiation will be accomplished through the contemplation and application of the following guidelines:

"I AM" THE PERFECTION OF GOD NOW MADE MANIFEST IN THE WORLD OF FORM

1. "I Am" aware that all energy originally came from God. Everything which seems like solid matter is, in reality, charged with Divine Energy and Light.

2. "I Am" Free from matter through the realization that all Life is One and responds instantly to the quality of Divine Love.

3. My physical body is healed and protected through my invocation of God's Will and Protection.

4. "I Am" going within to the Divine Flame in my Heart. Through this activity, the atomic structure of my physical body, at a cellular level, is refined and filled with Light. My body is etherealized. "I Am" residing in a body of Light while still in the physical world. *"I AM" IN THE WORLD, BUT NOT OF IT.*

5. The Divine Flame in my Heart calls forth the Love vibration within every electron of my Being, awakening each one to the voice of my God Presence "I Am."

6. Through the Earth Initiation, "I Am" lifted into the awareness that the purpose of my Earthly existence is to acknowledge and accept my Power of command over the five elements and all physical matter, thus becoming master of my physical reality.

7. I Invoke the Ray of God's Love into every electron of my Being and into every electron on Earth. My body and consciousness and that of all Humanity is NOW accepting the original Divine Plan of Perfection that has always been known in the Fourth Dimension.

8. Within every electron of the bodies of Humanity and the Elemental Kingdom, I FEEL the Cosmic Nature of Divine Love. Through this Divine Love, anything not of the Light is being Transmuted into God's Perfection.

9. "I AM" now seeing and feeling the original Crystal Clarity of every electron of precious Life energy evolving on Earth. Within this Crystal Clarity is held the Immaculate Concept of all physical matter.

10. Within the balance of the Masculine and Feminine Polarity of God an indisputable aura of Divine Love has formed on Earth, and the Christ within the Hearts of all Humanity is being called forth.

11. Humanity! Planet Earth! Awake! Step forth into the Fourth Dimension of Unconditional Love and *BE* the Perfection of your true God Reality on Earth.

STEP SEVEN OF THE SUPREME INITIATION
Directing the Light Force

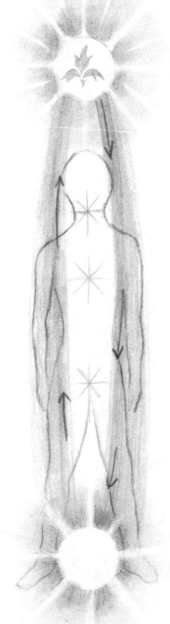

PINK
"AM"

BLUE
"I"

**BALANCING THE
MASCULINE AND FEMININE
POLARITIES OF GOD**

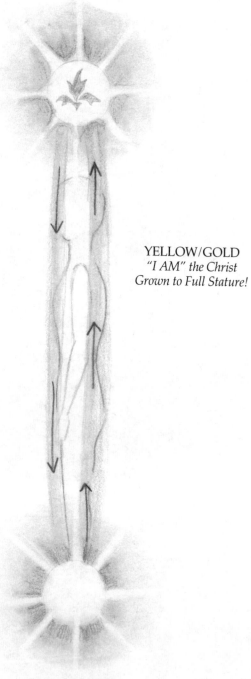

YELLOW/GOLD
"I AM" the Christ
Grown to Full Stature!

**BATHING THE
BODY IN PURE
CHRIST LIGHT**

To bring the activation of the Earth Sphere to fulfillment, the exercise must be done for a minimum of fifteen minutes each day for seven consecutive days.

Now that we have activated the five Elemental Spheres within our four lower bodies creating a tremendous pathway of radiant Light through our Beings from head to toe, we are ready to utilize this Powerful and Dynamic force to quicken the evolution of our consciousness and that of all Life on Earth. We are NOW an activated Light Body of God's Perfection, and through the conscious direction of this energy, we can assist in Healing the minds, bodies and emotions of all Life evolving on this Planet. The Supreme Initiation, therefore, enables us to elevate our Powers of service to our fellow Beings on Earth.

To begin attaining this greater Power, we must learn how to consciously direct this potent Light Force. To start the process, we stand and quickly pass through the six preceeding steps of the Supreme Initiation. After completing the Earth Sphere, we feel the Energy ascending from the Earth Sphere up the pathway of Light into the Ether/Spirit Sphere above our heads. Within the Ether/Spirit Sphere we see and feel the blazing Three-fold Flame of God. Pulsating to the right is the Pink Flame of Divine Love representing the Feminine Aspect of God—Holy Spirit/Divine Mother Principle. Pulsating to the left is the Blue Flame of God's Will representing the Masculine Aspect of God—the Father. Rising up from the center is the Yellow/Gold Flame representing the Son/Daughter Principle of God—the Christ/Wisdom. Now, as we breathe out, we feel the vibrant Blue Flame of God's Will flowing down from the Ether/Spirit Sphere above our heads, through the left side of our bodies down to the Earth Sphere between our feet. Then as we breathe in, we feel the crystalline Pink Flame of pure Divine Love rising up through the right side of our bodies from the Earth Sphere into the Pink Flame pulsating on the right side of the Ether/Spirit Sphere. On the outbreath, the Blue Flame of Divine Will flows through the left side of the body from the Ether/Spirit Sphere down to the Earth Sphere. On the inbreath, the Pink Flame of Divine Love ascends up the right side of the body from the Earth Sphere into the Ether/Spirit Sphere. This breath, designed to balance the Masculine and Feminine Polarities of God within us, is continued for at least five minutes.

Then, while still standing, we focus our attention on the Yellow/Gold Flame of the Christ/Wisdom in the Ether/Spirit Sphere. On the outbreath, we consciously direct the Golden Light of Christ from the Ether/Spirit Sphere down the front of our bodies to the Earth Sphere between our feet. On the inbreath, we magnetize the Golden Christ Light up the back of our bodies from the Earth Sphere to the Ether/Spirit Sphere above our heads. As we breathe out, the Christ Light descends, bathing the front of our bodies. As we breathe in, the Christ Light ascends, bathing the back of our bodies. This process is also continued for at least five minutes.

After doing Step Seven of the Supreme Initiation, "Directing the Light Force," for ten minutes a day for seven consecutive days, we are ready for the eighth and final step of the Supreme Initiation. Through this exercise, we will magnetize into our Beings and the atmosphere of Earth, the highest frequency of vibration this Earth has ever experienced. It is a frequency of the Twelve-fold Aspect of Deity from the Cosmic Holy Spirit in the Fifth Dimension. It is known as "The Fire Breath of The Almighty."

To begin this process we stand and pass quickly through Steps One through Seven of the Supreme Initiation. Then we witness, pouring into our Ether/Spirit Sphere from a focus of the Cosmic Holy Spirit in the Fifth Dimension, a spiralling Forcefield of Light blazing with the multi-colored Rays of the Twelve-fold Aspect of Diety. This spiralling shaft of Light is securely anchored in the Three-fold Flame within our Ether/Spirit Sphere. Now, as we breathe out, a cascading fountain of the Twelve-fold Aspect of Deity is projected from our Ether/Spirit Sphere in a profusion of glorious color in every direction in, through and around every electron of our bodies down to the Earth Sphere between our feet. On the inbreath, this Twelve-fold radiance of Light ascends up the center of our Beings through the Elemental spheres into the Ether/Spirit Sphere above our heads. Again, on the outbreath a fountain of cascading color radiates out from the Ether/Spirit Sphere through every electron of our Beings into

STEP EIGHT OF THE SUPREME INITIATION
Directing the Twelve-Fold Aspect of Deity
from the Fifth Dimension

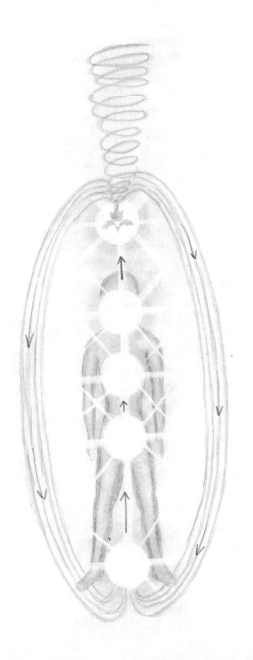

the Earth Sphere between our feet. Then, it is breathed up the center of our Beings into the Ether/Spirit Sphere again. This Sacred Activity should be repeated for at least five minutes every day.

It is through the consistent practice of this Supreme Initiation that our evolutionary growth will be greatly accelerated. With the perpetual discipline, we will create a vehicle through which our consciousness can Transcend the physical world of form and the wheel of Life and death forever.

It is the Pathway to the Ascension.

A PLANETARY HEALING

To expand our gift of the Supreme Initiation to bless this Sweet Earth and all Her Life, we need merely expand our consciousness of service. After we have individually completed the entire cycle–all eight steps of the Supreme Initiation–we are ready to expand this blessing to a global scale. This is very simply done through our conscious direction of the Light and our Heart's desire. As we stand preparing to begin Step One of the Supreme Initiation, we ask the Presence of God blazing in our Hearts to expand our Light Body to engulf the entire Planet Earth. We see ourselves standing within the Earth. Our spinal columns are in perfect alignment with the axis of this Blessed Star, and as we proceed through the Supreme Initiation, we ask God and the entire Company of Heaven to assist in this activity of Light. We ask that, as we activate the Elemental Centers within our own Beings, the activation will simultaneously occur within all Life evolving on Earth according to each Lifestream's Divine Plan. As we continue to awaken the centers within all Life day after day, we will clearly perceive the mass consciousness changing, and the Planetary Healing taking place through the process of Tranformation.

How very blessed we are to be able to assist at this critical time on Earth. How very honored we are to participate in the Victory of God!

THE HEALING OF PLANET EARTH IS AT HAND

Our Healing is NOW! It is in the air we breathe. It is in the Sun of the day and in the Moon of the night. It is in the rain and all nature. It is in our conscious thoughts and our Heartfelt knowing. Our Healing is at hand, and we accept it in deep Humility and Gratitude.

With every breath, we know our Healing is at hand. It is always present and ever available, abundant and plentiful. It is here, now, wherever "I Am." It is ours to silently accept. It brings Peace, Assurance and Blessings beyond measure. Its source is God, the Source that is Eternally Present. It is manifesting now and forever. It is within us every moment of time. We give Blessings and Gratitude for this Reality.

Through the All-Powerful Light of God...
"I Am" Healed and made whole.
"I Am" Eternal Peace.
"I Am" Heaven made manifest on Earth.
"I Am" that "I Am."

Available Tape Associated With This Chapter Is:
  F. TRUTH
See page *xxiv* for more information and order blanks.

CHAPTER 6

THE SIXTH ASPECT OF DEITY IS MINISTERING GRACE

COLOR – RUBY
SIXTH RAY

THE SIXTH UNIVERSAL LAW OF CAUSE AND EFFECT
THE LAW OF THE CIRCLE

THE ATTRIBUTES OF THE SIXTH ASPECT ARE:

SELFLESS SERVICE
HEALING
DEVOTIONAL WORSHIP
FOCUS OF LOVE
THE CHRIST-MAN WORKING THROUGH
PERSONALITY
THE DIVINE IMAGE EMBODIED IN FLESH

MINISTRATION IS
AN ACTIVITY OF GRACE

As we learn more about our purpose and reason for being, we begin to clearly see that our Spiritual growth and development is dependent upon our understanding and application of the Sixth Aspect of Deity–Ministering Grace. Selfless, giving service is the fastest, surest road to Spiritual development. It is not only the fastest, surest path but also the most fulfilling and rewarding.

Nowhere in the Universe do we have a better example of the benefits of Ministering Grace than in the Angelic Kingdom. If we will lift up in consciousness and observe these servants of God, we will learn lessons of selflessness that will enable us to Transform our Lives and carry this Planet Home, back to the Heart of God.

Whenever the Name of God is invoked, silently or audibly, the Angels of Ministration and Grace are there instantly with the fullness of God's Love, Blessings, Benediction, Healing, Faith and Power. The Blessings from God are given to us by the Angels according to our capacity to receive and accept them.

We Live, move and truly have our Being within the Living, breathing, intelligent body of the Universal God, and no matter how far we may have strayed in our behavior or thoughts, WE CAN NEVER LEAVE THE SAFETY OF GOD'S PRESENCE. All we need to do is *awaken to the reality* of our Presence within the safe, secure, Loving Heart of God, and we will be lifted in consciousness out of our self-created illusion of separation.

The Angels of Ministration and Grace are selfless servants of God, and it is Their great opportunity and Joy in the Divine Plan to minister to the people of Earth who have created painful experiences for themselves, and in their pain, sooner or later, invoke the Power of God to extricate them.

The Ministering Angels answer the prayers and calls of all Humanity. These Angels reach in graded order from the Heart of the Great Central Sun down to the depths of the most distorted frequencies of the psychic-astral plane. They are alerted the moment the Flame in our Hearts stirs, and the silent "God help me" arises within our consciousness. At that moment, according to our requirements, one or more Minstering Angels are sent into our auras to bring Grace and assistance.

Angels are the Messengers of God, and Their service to Humanity is not fully understood. There is a Cosmic Law which is inexorable and unchanging, which requires that THE CALL FOR HELP MUST COME FROM THE OCTAVE IN WHICH THE HELP IS NEEDED. This Law complies with our gift of Free Will. The Angelic Kingdom cannot intervene in our Lives unless we *ask* for It's assistance. Once the call for assistance has been made, however, on the return current of that very plea comes the Radiation, Presence and Power of the Angelic Host according to the requirement of the hour. The Angels abide in the atmosphere of Earth and are ever vigilant in Their watch for a flicker of Light which signifies an "SOS" from Humanity to the Heavenly Realms for assistance. The current need is evaluated; then the mission is directed to the Angels Who are trained sufficiently to hold within Their feeling worlds the particular quality of radiation which is needed to answer the prayer. That quality stimulates the Flame within the Heart of the person making the call, and as the Heart Flame is ignited with the necessary quality from the Angelic Host, the person is able to magnetize the answer to his/her prayer. Again, the answer comes according to our ACCEPTANCE.

It is by actual experience that the Angels grow and develop and learn the Joy that is within service. They are allowed to witness the change in our consciousness, as we are blessed with Their benediction. The Happiness and Joy that shines within the eyes of the Angels, when They see our Transformation, is beautiful to behold. They see our stooped forms straighten and our hopeless consciousness fill with Faith. They return to the Realms of Perfection charged with enthusiasm and a burning desire to return Earthward again and again until no Lifestream is left in either the Human Kingdom or the Elemental Kingdom which requires any assistance outside of the Flame of Divinity blazing in their own Hearts.

We can truly learn from the Angels. As we hold the Qualities and Virtues of God in our consciousness and breathe Them forth into the world with our every breath, we can understand the Joy and Enthusiasm the Angels experience as we convey Courage, Faith and Confidence to those we come in contact with our daily Lives. Then, with renewed vigor, we will want to return again and again to the Source of Perfection in our Hearts, magnetizing even greater God Light, increasing our capacity to radiate the Qualities of God to even larger spheres of influence.

If we will experiment with this daily, we will gradually become adept at maintaining a forcefield around ourselves that is perpetually charged with the Qualities and Virtues of God.

It is a Lovely, Powerful way to experiment with our Gift of Life. Each morning, we can think of a Quality of God that would benefit all of our friends, Loved ones and associates. It could be Love, Peace, Joy, Harmony, Kindness, Forgiveness, Compassion, Healing, Truth, Gods Will, Divine Purpose, Enthusiasm, Prosperity, Success, Victory, Freedom, Purity, Wisdom, Understanding, Clarity, Balance, Comfort, Grace and on ad infinitum. After choosing a Quality, we must focus the full power of our attention on that Virtue and fill our consciousness with It. Then, we invoke the Angels of Ministration that embody that particular Quality and ask Them to sustain It in our auras and feeling worlds throughout the day. We also ask that the Quality be intensified with every breath we take, thus expanding our forcefield of Perfection moment to moment.

As we practice this simple exercise each day, we will become more and more proficient at it, and soon we will be so anchored and efficient in our ability to maintain an aura of God Qualities that we will no longer be bombarded by the negativity emanating from the mass consciousness in our environment. When that occurs, we will truly be a Peace Commanding Presence, and our service will be a Healing benediction to all Life. At that point we will be *in the world but not of it.*

When we have learned to control our own auras and have them always qualified with God Light, we will be open portals through which the Light from the Octaves of Perfection and Truth can be projected in an instant to assist an entire city, a nation or a Planet.

THE FOURTH DIMENSION
IS ESTABLISHED ON EARTH

I would like to share with you now a message of Hope and extreme Joy. During these changing times, there is much confusion and often pain. It is easy for us to get caught up in the illusion of chaos and miss the Glory of this incredible moment on Earth. The Heavenly Realms are very aware of our struggle. Assistance and encouragement are pouring forth to reinforce us and give us strength. The following is such a message. Center yourself and ask your God Presence to envelop you in the Flame of Illumined Truth. Ask that, as you read these words, you experience the full magnitude and elation contained within each one.

May 22, 1988, Pentecost
MESSAGE AND RADIATION
OF THE BELOVED HOLY SPIRIT

"Beloved of this Earth, I come to you this day from the Fifth Dimension to bring to you the exclamation of Joy ringing through the Universe:

Victory is Ours! Victory is Ours! Victory is Ours!

"For aeons of time We in Heaven's Realms have awaited this moment of God Victorious Accomplishment. For aeons of time We have patiently waited as mankind groped in the darkness of his own self-created veil of maya and illusion for a flicker of Light, a spark of Truth. This Sacred Day, when millions of Lifestreams throughout the world celebrate the Baptism of Holy Spirit, I come to announce to you that the veil has been rend, and the cloak of darkness covering the electronic substance of Earth has been cast aside into the Violet Flame of Transmutation established on Earth by the Sons and Daughters of God.

"Since the inception of this unprecedented year of God

Light, 1988, the core of Purity within every electron of Precious Life energy evolving on Earth has been expanding. The expansion of Light has caused the negativity to surface at an accelerated pace, creating some extreme imbalances. As the Light increased, portals were opened in the sea of negativity surrounding the Planet. These portals have allowed the Light from the Fourth Dimensional Octaves of Perfection greater access into the third dimensional plane on Earth.

"As each Sacred month passed, the portals grew, forming greater openings through the psychic-astral plane of illusion into the atmosphere of Earth. Through the portals this month, the Solar Fire Breath of Holy Spirit has established the Fourth Dimension on Earth.

"With the influx of Holy Spirit that took place this day, this Blessed Planet and all Her Kingdoms have been lifted up in vibration out of the world of illusion into the Realm of Truth. The frequencies of the Fourth Dimension are now available to all Life on Earth, and as Humanity proceeds through this year, the new vibrations will be tangibly revealed.

"Now with the Fourth Dimension securely established on Earth, greater Octaves of Light shall be available to this Planet. The unified consciousness of the entire Company of Heaven is with Me today as I reveal to you the next step of your evolutionary journey back to the Heart of Our Father-Mother God. On this Holy Day, Humanity is being given the first opportunity to enter, in consciousness, a Sacred Temple in the Fifth Dimension. This is a Temple under My Direction, and it shall be known to you as The Temple of the Fire Breath of The Almighty. The opening of the doors to this Sacred Temple is giving you access to a higher octave of Holy Breath than you have ever experienced. The Flame blazing upon the altar of this Temple is a Radiant Kaleidoscope of the Twelve-fold Aspect of Deity. It sends spiraling circles of the Twelve-fold Flame in every direction, penetrating into all Dimensions. Until this day, the frequencies of this Flame were beyond your reach. Now, you may reach into the Fifth Dimension and experience a Realm of Bliss incomprehensible to your finite minds.

"All Life is evolving, and as you and your Planet step up in vibration, all dimensions above you move up in vibration as well. Consequently, the Body of God is ever expanding Its infinite sphere of Perfection. This day the Divine Mother Principle–the Feminine Aspect of God–Holy Spirit, has breathed this Planet and this entire System of Worlds closer to Her own Heart Flame. **The spiralling Twelve-fold Flame, the Fire Breath of The Almighty, is now entering the atmosphere of Earth, and as It is breathed into each person's Heart Flame on the** Holy Breath, the encoded pattern of each Lifestream's 'I AM' Presence is being released through the Solar Spine. These Divine patterns are reverberating now on Earth. *The 'I AM' Presence has returned.*

"Throughout the next several weeks, this momentum will build in intensity, strengthening the force of Divinity on Earth. Then, in August another influx of Holy Spirit will occur that will, through the co-operation of the Christ Presence on Earth, Group Avatar, adjust the axis of this Planet into Her rightful position in preparation for the establishment of the five additional Solar Rays of Light on Earth. The Rays will be projected into the Earth from the Electronic Belt around the Great Central Sun during the last five months of 1988. The five additional Rays of Light to be anchored on Earth have always been part of the Solar Spine of the 'I AM' Presence, but until the Earth Ascended into the Fourth Dimension, the frequencies of the Rays eight through twelve were beyond your perception.

"Now these Rays are going to be activated physically on Earth for the benefit of all Life evolving here. After the adjustment of the axis in August and the influx of Holy Spirit, the first of the remaining five Rays will be activated. This is the Eighth Ray, and it pulsates with the color Aquamarine. The God Quality most prominent on this frequency is Clarity. In September the Ninth Ray will be activated. This Ray is Magenta and expresses the Qualities of Divine Harmony and Balance. In October the Tenth Ray will engage, and the Earth will experience a Golden Frequency of Peace and Comfort beyond description. In November the Eleventh Ray will come into form on Earth, and Its Peach Radiance will bless all Life with the Qualities of Divine Purpose, Enthusiasm and Joy. Finally, in December the Twelfth Ray will be activated, and the Opal Essence of Transformation will bathe the Planet.

"When 1988 is brought to fruition, the Twelve-fold Aspect of Deity will be securely anchored on Earth through the Solar Spine of each person, and the Seven-fold Planetary Spine of each one will have completed Its ascent into the Solar Spine of the God Presence. Thus, the return of the 'I AM' Presence to Earth will be fulfilled.

"Blessed Ones, you have volunteered before the Throne of God to assist during this Cosmic Moment on Earth. Now, with the Fifth Dimension available to you for the first time, reach up in consciousness, and ask your God Presence to reveal to you your next octave of service. Your Divine momentum, your particular thread in the tapestry of Life, is needed now to assure the success of the Divine Plan on Earth. Reach up, and you will remember your promise to Love Life Free.

"Dear Ones, I envelop you now in the Sacred Fire Breath of The Almighty. 'I AM' One that is with you always. 'I AM' the Representative of the Cosmic Holy Spirit from the Sun beyond the Sun beyond the Sun."

Group Avatar

THE OPENING OF THE SEVENTH AND FINAL ANGELIC VORTEX

In the original Divine Plan, the Lifestreams drawn forth from the Heart of God, who were destined to inhabit the Earth, were divided into seven groups that were called root races. Each root race contained seven sub-races. In the original plan the First Root Race and the subsequent sub-races entered the Earth Plane and evolved through the 14,000 year cycle of the Seven Rays while developing the seven major centers along the spine, becoming completed Planetary Beings. Upon completion of this process, the evolving First Root Race Ascended into the Octaves of Light, and the Second Root Race embodied, beginning Its Earthly sojourn. After the Second Root Race and all of Its sub-races completed the evolutionary journey through the Seven Rays, they Ascended into the Octaves of Light, and the Third Root Race embodied.

To assist in Humanity's evolution, it was decreed by Cosmic Law that seven tremendous Angelic vortexes would be created. As each root race embodied, the original plan was for one of the Angelic vortexes to be activated, creating an open portal through which the Angelic Host serving the particular root race in embodiment would have access to the physical plane of Earth.

It was in the middle of the evolution of the Fourth Root Race that Humanity began experimenting and using our Gift of Life in ways that conflicted with the Will of God. As mentioned earlier in this book, that action resulted in the "fall of man" and caused the original Divine Plan to go awry. This glitch in the Divine Plan caused not only Humanity's evolution to be greatly delayed, but it also drastically affected the timing of the opening of the Angelic vortexes.

Since the time of the "fall", literally millions and millions of years have passed. The Fifth Root Race began coming to Earth prior to the Ascension of the Fourth Root Race. Subsequently, the Sixth Root Race began coming in, and now the Seventh Root Race is entering into the physical plane. The heaviness of this accumulated energy caused the Earth to groan under its weight, and it actually bent the axis of our Planet.

A major part of the Transformation taking place now is not only Transmuting the sea of negativity surrounding the Planet, but straightening the axis of Earth as well.

Several years ago, the Fourth Root Race finally completed its Earthly journey, but the Fifth, Sixth and Seventh Root Races are still evolving on Earth. A long time ago, the Fifth and Sixth Angelic Vortexes were opened after much delay. Recently, because of the urgency of the hour, a Cosmic Dispensation was granted, and Universal Law allowed the opening of the Seventh and final Angelic Vortex.

On June 11, 1988, through an event called Star*Link 88, a dimensional doorway was opened, and the Seventh Angelic Vortex was activated in the City of Angels at the Los Angeles Coliseum in California.

Several thousand Lifestreams gathered together during a six-hour event of unified consciousness in which a reactivation and initiation into multi-dimensional awareness occurred. This Blessed Planet and ALL Her Life were lifted up yet another octave in vibration, closer to the Heart of our Father-Mother God.

Through the activity of Star*Link 88, the Angelic Host, from frequencies beyond anything we have ever experienced, entered the atmosphere of Earth. These Mighty Seraphim from the Fifth Dimension assisted God in activating the pre-encoded memories that were implanted deep within Humanity's cellular patterns aeons ago. These patterns reflect our Divine Plan, our Purpose and Reason for Being. Humanity will now experience a great soaring and awakening, as we begin to remember our Divine Heritage.

A Cosmic Fiat was issued by the Godhead, and 1988 was decreed the year in which Humanity would step through the doorway into multi-dimensional awareness. This was accomplished as the frequencies of the third dimension were accelerated into the higher octaves of the Fourth Dimension.

During that sacred moment in time, Humanity was empowered with the increased Presence of the Angelic Host which is, even now, continually entering the Earth through the Seventh Angelic Vortex. The influx of Angels has formed an expanded bridge between Heaven and Earth–spirit and matter. Over this Sacred Bridge, the Rays of Light of the Twelve-fold Aspect of Deity from The Great Central Sun perpetually bathe the Earth.

The Light from these Ministering Angels is increasing daily and hourly. Moment to moment, the activated pre-encoded memories of our Purpose and Reason for Being, now reflecting at a physical cellular level within our four lower bodies, are reverberating through our creative centers of thought and feeling. As these currents of Wisdom and Illumination pass through our conscious minds, our God Presence sends a Ray of Light to help us tangibly grasp each Divine idea. Knowledge of our Divine Plan is now available to us as never before. We need only reach up and tap the Octaves of Illumined Truth.

VISUALIZATION FOR PERCEIVING YOUR DIVINE PLAN

Become quiet and relaxed.

Go within your Heart Center and experience a feeling of perfect Peace.

See yourself sitting on the Golden Throne in the "Secret Place of the Most High Living God."

Ask your God Presence to bring into focus before you the image of your purpose and reason for being.

Experience, deep within your Heart Flame, the innermost longing to fulfill this purpose.

Now, reach higher into the Octaves of Illumined Truth, and ask your Higher Self to reveal to you how you can begin to implement this purpose into your daily Life.

See the avenues of opportunity unfold before you.

Experience the feeling of elation as you begin to fulfill your Divine Plan.

Observe that as each opportunity presents itself, you joyously seize it, and feel a greater sense of accomplishment and self-worth than ever before.

You realize that in the simple act of fulfilling your purpose, your self-esteem is restored, and you feel whole and complete.

The emptiness that you have continually been trying to fill from the outside is now pulsating with the meaning and warmth of your Divine Plan.

You understand now, with greater awareness, that as you take advantage of each opportunity to fulfill your purpose, the Universe presents another one on the horizon.

Thus, your Divine Plan unfolds for you step by step.

INVOKING OUR DIVINE PLAN ON EARTH

Through the collective Wisdom Flame and God Illumination now embodied through Humanity, and in the Holy Name of God "I AM", we invoke now the Angelic Host from the Fifth Dimension, available through the Seventh Angelic Vortex, to guide, guard, direct and empower our Divine Plans on Earth. In our minds we hold a perfect thoughtform, the Immaculate Concept of our Purpose and Plans, and into this Planetary Force-field, we now CHARGE the God Qualities from the Heavenly Realms. Beloved Ones, RELEASE through this Thoughtform of the Unified Cup of Humanity, glorious Angelic Energies of Love, Wisdom and Power which we, as co-workers with the Angelic Host, do now INBREATHE AND ABSORB into Humanity and all Life, Victoriously Transforming all into the Golden Age of Spiritual Freedom.

In the Sacred Name of God "I AM", we now EXPAND AND PROJECT this glorious God Energy into Humanity and all Life, to further Freedom's Cause in all its magnificent ways, known and unknown, until every electron on Earth is completely saturated with the Love and Power of the Father-Mother God, and truly feels the Presence of God within itself. We decree that this release of Light, Love, Wisdom and Power, shall ACCELERATE all Life forward NOW toward its Divine Plan fulfilled.

"I AM" GRATEFUL for Wisdom's Flame now anchored in our collective God Presence. "I AM" GRATEFUL for the Sacred Essence of God which seeks Wisdom to establish Itself on Earth. "I AM" GRATEFUL to the Angelic Host and the entire Company of Heaven, our unseen Benefactors in the Realms of Light, assisting us to see our Divine Plan perfectly fulfilled.

I so decree this done Victoriously–as God's Most Holy Name... "I AM"!.

ACCEPTING THE POWER WITHIN– BECOMING THE DIVINE IMAGE EMBODIED IN FLESH

To change from a consciousness of low self-esteem and unworthiness to the acceptance of our true God Reality often seems like an impossible task, but in fact, it is just a SLIGHT ADJUSTMENT IN AWARENESS. Remember, the separation from our God Presence is self-inflicted. It is a result of years of distorted programming and erroneous beliefs.

Our God Presence is ALWAYS patiently awaiting our return to Truth. It is but a breath away, and our acceptance of this knowledge is all that is necessary for this part of our true Being to take command of our four lower bodies.

We are used to struggling and doing things the hard way. Consequently, it is difficult for us to believe that all we have to do is *ACCEPT,* truly accept, our own Divinity, and it shall be so. To our conscious minds that seems too simple, so we create a resistance, thus blocking our ability to realize and outpicture this Truth. It is time to let go of the resistance; time to stop putting up roadblocks of struggle and disbelief. It is now time to accept our true God Reality. It is time to change.

True change begins *within* and gradually manifests outward. It is a process that is always available and operates on all levels simultaneously . . . physical, etheric, mental and emotional.

There are several factors involved in the process of change. First, we need to center ourselves and go within to the Silence. This is accomplished through deep breathing, relaxation and meditation. When we reach the point of centeredness, we will more clearly perceive what beliefs and attitudes need to change in order for us to accept our own Divinity. Through Listening Grace, we will recognize our fears. Then, we will release limitations, old patterns and judgments. As we ask our God Presence for assistance, we will begin to Forgive ourselves for the separation we created. We will recognize the Truth of our Being and accept our highest good, our true God Reality.

ACCEPTING MY TRUE GOD REALITY

Begin this exercise by following the steps of "Getting in Touch with My Higher Self" listed in Chapter One (page 53). Then, gently bring your consciousness back to the moment of now and answer the following questions:

1. What is my present Life situation reflecting about my beliefs and attitudes, and the way I feel about myself and the choices I've made in the following areas?

   Relationships:
   Family/Home:
   Work/Career:
   Finances:
   Physical Health:
   Spiritual Growth:
   Service/Purpose:

2. What patterns and beliefs am I holding onto that are no longer relevant in my Life?

3. In what areas am I willing to let go of old patterns and beliefs?

4. What are my fears about letting go of my old programming and my old patterns and beliefs of the past?

5. What is going to be easy to let go of?

6. What is going to be difficult to let go of?

7. In what areas do I need to Forgive myself?

8. What do I consider my negative behavior patterns or character traits?

9. Am I willing to Forgive myself and let go of them?

10. What do I consider my positive behavior patterns and character traits?

11. Can I accept them and be Grateful?

12. What are four wonderful things about me right now that reflect my value as a person?

13. How do I accept and Love myself unconditionally right now?

14. What do I need to Love and Value myself more?

15. What is the most obvious change I need to make in my Life now in order to accept my own Divinity?

16. What do I need from myself to make this change possible?

Once our resistance and our blocks have been exposed to us through the preceeding exercise, they no longer have the same power to subconsciously manipulate us. When we look our fears in the face, they dissipate and loose their significance. Then, we can easily Transmute them through the Violet Flame of Forgiveness and proceed to the next step, which consists of establishing new patterns and beliefs that promote our highest good.

DECREE FOR TRANSMUTING THE PAST

*Through the Power of God pulsating in every Human Heart...
I invoke the full gathered momentum of the Violet Transmuting Flame of Forgiveness.*

Sacred Flame, come forth NOW from the very Heart of God and blaze in, through and around every electron of precious Life energy I have ever released which is less than God's Perfection.

Transmute NOW cause, core, effect, record and memory— every thought, word, action or feeling I have ever expressed which prevents me from KNOWING and ACCEPTING my true God Reality. I ask that this Violet Flame of Forgiveness continue to blaze through me, expanding moment to moment the maximum that Cosmic Law will allow, until "I AM" Free from every pattern or belief less than the reality of my God Presence.

"I AM" the Presence of God made manifest in the physical world of form, and I ACCEPT my Divine Reality NOW! SO BE IT! "I AM!"

This decree should be repeated daily with deep feeling until we experience the buoyant Joy of the Freedom it will bring. After reciting the decree for Transmuting the past, proceed to the next exercise.

SEVEN STEPS TO
CHANGE AND PERSONAL EMPOWERMENT

Begin by centering yourself in the present moment:

"I AM" here now!

"I AM" Happy and Balanced!

I Love myself and I enjoy what "I AM" doing!

"I AM" having fun!

STEP ONE

"I AM" LETTING GO OF ATTACHMENTS AND RE-
LEASING OLD PATTERNS AND BELIEFS.

1. I Love and accept myself as "I AM".
2. I release any belief or pattern that does not support
   my highest good.
3. I recognize the moment of my new beginning and my
   right and ability to change.
4. I move into change easily and joyously.

STEP TWO

"I AM" TRUSTWORTHY AND HONEST TO MYSELF

1. "I AM" experiencing the true integrity of myself.
2. "I AM" willing to know the Truth of who "I AM".
3. I trust the Truth, and the Truth sets me FREE!

STEP THREE

"I AM" WORTHY AND DESERVING OF CHANGE.

1. I Love and Forgive myself for any perceived transgression.
2. "I AM" a Child of God, and I deserve to be Loved
   and Forgiven.
3. "I AM" willing and able to restore every aspect of my
   Life.
4. "I AM" Healing myself physically, mentally, emotionally and spiritually.

STEP FOUR

"I AM" CHANGING THROUGH GRACE AND JOY.

1. Buoyant Joyous energy interpenetrates every aspect
   of my Life.
2. Laughter and relaxation are continually present

through my growth.

3. "I AM" willing to experience Joy and feel good about my changes.

STEP FIVE

I HAVE FAITH AND TRUST IN MY POWER TO CHANGE.

1. "I AM" in the Divine flow of my true God Reality.
2. "I AM" experiencing a patience, silence and inner calm through my changes.
3. "I AM" One with the Infinite Intelligence inside of me.
4. The Infinite Intelligence within me always makes correct choices.

STEP SIX

I LOVE MYSELF AND "I AM" GRATEFUL FOR MY GROWTH AND CHANGE.

1. I Love myself unconditionally right now.
2. I accept each opportunity with Gratitude and Love.
3. "I AM" Loveable, and all that is less than Love in me, I Love FREE!

STEP SEVEN

I ACCEPT RESPONSIBILITY FOR THE CHANGES IN MY LIFE, AND I ACCEPT THE POWER TO SUSTAIN THE CHANGES.

1. I support my Power within and know it is available as I accept my true God Self.
2. I choose to know now that "I AM" creating my own Reality moment by moment.
3. I choose to create only that which supports my highest good.
4. I choose to be my God Presence, *NOW!*

Our opportunity to fulfill who we really are is available to us now as never before in the history of time. This awareness is filtering into the consciousness of people throughout the world. The following article from the Quartus Report reflects that Truth and is an appropriate Thoughtform to close this chapter.

YOUR MISSION ON EARTH
by Michael Irving

BE WHO YOU ARE

Your mission on Earth at this time is to become who you really are. As YOU remember who you are you will awaken within others the remembrance of who they are. This effect will grow and grow and spread as a Fire of Realization across the once confused face of the Earth. At a specific Moment, soon to be reached, Humanity and the Earth will lift into a higher level of existence and John the Beloved's Vision of A New Heaven and a New Earth will become fulfilled. So Be It. This is our mission. Now is the time. Be who you are.

YOU ARE MYSTICAL–YOU ARE MAGICAL

You are a vast, unlimited, totally Free and open Being. You are a mystical, magical part of Creation expressing your unrestricted Power and Love through the beautiful physical form you have created on Earth. You have the Power and authority to create and be whatever you wish. Now is the time to bring your secret out into the world and express the miracle of who you are.

YOUR SECRET

You are a Starseed. You are a Starseed. You are a STARSEED. This means that encoded within your Being is the magical power and vastness of the Stars in the Heavens. If you are reading this, it is because you are a Being of Light who has come to Earth at this time to be in a physical form to assist Humanity through the rapidly approaching Time of Birth...when the Earth will rise in vibration and lift into a New Harmonic...into a higher sphere closer to the Heart of Creation.

NOW IS THE TIME

Now is the time for you to remember the Truth which has slept patiently as your Secret Within waiting for this Moment when the Truth will burst forth into your awareness as the greatest, most brilliant, most colorful Starburst ever to be experienced upon Earth. You are a Co-creator with God, and you have the Power and support to create Heaven on Earth. Now is the time.

WHO YOU ARE NOT

You are NOT the mass of confused mental energies buffeting around the Earth's surface which manifest now as adverse weather conditions and other disturbances. You are NOT the chaos surrounding Earth at this time. You are unlimited, creative energy. You are NOT the character that human society, tradition and culture have attempted to have you identify with. You are NOT a limited expression trapped within Creation as a restricted human personality. You ARE a totally vast and brilliant Being of Light. You are NOT your thoughts. You may identify yourself with the thoughts going on in your head–but you are NOT your thoughts. You are NOT the content of your physical/mental mind and brain. You ARE something far more purely intelligent...far more connected with the Power and Majesty of the vastness of Creation. You have the potential of being a God/Goddess on Earth.

THE PLAN

The Plan is OPERATION EARTH LIFT. This message is part of the briefing for Operation Earth Lift. Your mission is to come through physical birth into the confused energy field of Life on Earth. As you grow, you will realize more and more that you are different and separate from the confusion and sadness on Earth. You will become aware of a majestic, unlimited, tranquil, open and creative "Child" WITHIN the depths of your Being. In the present Earth years you will discover this New Child within yourself, and as you look into the eyes of this Child, you will see the Truth of yourself, and you will know your part in the plan.

YOUR PART IN THE PLAN

When the time comes–and the Time is here now for the Earth is to be lifted sooner than many realize–the Starseed within you will burst and full realizations will project into your awareness, giving you the knowledge of the Truth of Who You Are. This is your part in the Plan. Your mission on Earth at this time is to spontaneously switch from misidentification with human confusion and sadness and to instantaneously realize and correctly identify with the pure Spark of Light of unlimited Power and Beauty... the Source of who you are which, up until this time, has slept beneath the human character you erroneously identified with. Time is short. Your part in the Plan is to seek, to discover, to see and to become the Truth of who you are.

OPERATION EARTH LIFT

THE EARTH IS TO BE LIFTED. Higher Beings, Angels, Archangels, Masters, Saints, Intelligences from all parts of the Universe and Creation are focussing the Power and Love and Creative Will onto the Earth at this time. This Love-Will Energy is pouring into Earth from the Center within the Heart and Mind of Mother-Father God.

This Higher Energy manifests into the world of Humanity through your Heart and your Mind. This energy comes through you because at a deep level within your Being, you are AT ONE... you are in total communion with the highest levels of Creation... YOU are the Masters and the Angels... You are a Co-creator with God. The Plan manifests and becomes effective through your thoughts and your actions by your Living and Being the Truth of who you are.

"I AM" THE NEW CHILD

Surely it is now the time for the NEW CHILD to come forth from the shadows of my inner world into the Light of the Earthly world in order to fulfill the destiny which is encoded within the mystery of the deepest center of the Truth of my Being.

AS I LOOK WITHIN THE MYSTERY OF WHO "I AM", I gaze into the radiant eyes of my NEW CHILD, and I see a Flame which is as of the Sun, and in this glorious brilliance, my old self is burned away in a blissful, great purification to reveal, through an instantaneous burst of Light, a mystical, magical Being of incredible splendor and majesty…something I had long forgotten at the start of my search…something I had always secretly known and dared to hope I would one day be reunited with…THE TRUTH OF WHO I AM…"I AM" EVERYTHING THAT IS.

Available Tapes Associated With This Chapter Are:
    G. MINISTERING GRACE
    H. STAR*LINK 88
See page *xxiv* for more information and order blanks.

CHAPTER 7

THE SEVENTH ASPECT OF DEITY IS FREEDOM

COLOR – VIOLET
SEVENTH RAY

THE SEVENTH UNIVERSAL LAW OF
TRANSMUTATION

THE ATTRIBUTES OF
THE SEVENTH ASPECT ARE:

TRANSMUTATION
FORGIVENESS
MERCY
COMPASSION
RHYTHM
THE POWER OF INVOCATION

UTILIZING THE POWER OF TRANSMUTATION–THE VIOLET FLAME OF FORGIVENESS AND FREEDOM

Beloved Presence of God pulsating in my Heart . . .

Look into my Life and see what yet remains to be balanced by me to any person, place, condition or thing I may have wronged at any time, in any way, for any reason whatsoever. Reach Your Great Loving Hands of Light into all of the good energy I have released and draw forth TEN TIMES as much Perfection as I have ever done wrong. Fashion from that Substance of Perfection a Gift of Love, whatever is necessary to balance every debt I have created which still remains unpaid to any part of Life. Also, Beloved Presence of God–I ask You to FORGIVE every person, place, condition or thing which may have wronged me in any way, and balance all debts owed to me by Life everywhere.

I accept it done through the Power of God "I AM."

At this critical time in the evolution of the Planet, it is necessary for each of us to reach our highest potential. It is also crucial that we fulfill our purpose and reason for being. In order to accomplish this, we must learn how to Transmute the distorted thoughts, words, actions and feelings of our past that continually bombard us and create havoc in our daily Lives. This negative energy from our past returns, not to plague us or punish us, but rather, it returns to give us the opportunity to TRANSMUTE it back into its original perfection.

Scientifically, we know there is no destroying energy; therefore, we can't simply say "cancel, cancel" and erase the past. But, as I mentioned previously, this is a Cosmic Moment on Earth, and we are receiving more assistance and guidance from on High than ever before. We are moving into the Forcefield of Aquarius and into the embrace of the Seventh Ray of Spiritual Freedom. The radiance of this Forcefield contains within it the most powerful frequencies of Forgiveness and Transmutation this Earth has ever experienced. These frequencies are projected into the Earth through what is known as the *Violet Transmuting Flame of Forgiveness*. This Sacred Fire is a tool more powerful than our finite minds can conceive. If used effectively, it can Transmute every electron of precious Life energy we have ever misqualified at any time, in any existence, either known or unknown. By using this precious Gift effectively, we can move forward Illumined and FREE!

The Violet Transmuting Flame works as an atomic accelerator, raising the frequency of discordant energy into vibrations of Harmony.

The Violet Transmuting Flame Transmutes imperfect energy. When it is accompanied with the actual FEELING of Forgiveness for our own mistakes and those of others, It works wonders. When we call upon the Law of Forgiveness for all the mistakes we have ever made, and for THOSE OF ALL HUMANITY, It gives tremendous assistance, not only to us, but to Humanity as well.

The God Presence of every individual, even the most depraved, desires Perfection for that individual, and when we call to the God Presence of ALL mankind and ask for the Violet Fire of Forgiveness to blaze through them and FORGIVE their mistakes; it enables that God Presence to go into action when perhaps it has been aeons of time since It has been called upon, and thus given permission to assist that person.

Now, the Era of Freedom is at hand! We must seize the Opportunity while we may, making an earnest effort to undo all the mistakes we have ever made in thought, word and deed against ourselves and every part of Life, so that in times of crisis, we may have Peace and Protection in our worlds. We must do our best from now on to set up only those causes which bring Perfection as their effect. Every bit of Life ever entrusted to us must some time be purified and harmonized and returned to God qualified with Perfection as it was when it first came to us.

Strange things are taking place all over the Earth, and it is these imperfect, discordant, miscreations—created by Humanity and NOT BY GOD that are acting and trying to act everywhere. The use of the Violet Fire of Freedom's Love and calling upon the Law of Forgiveness are the most Powerful ways of preventing these negative things from acting in our world. When enough of Humanity use the Violet Flame of Forgiveness, we can prevent distressing things from happening all over the Earth.

The Violet Fire is a current of energy which has been qualified to seize imperfect energy and Transmute it so that it may be charged with Perfection once again. It is an activity of Love, Mercy and Compassion which can dissolve the Causes set up by Humanity whose Effects would be most distressing. Unless Humanity comes into this understanding and consciously USES this Violet Fire, we will have to meet up with our previous Causes that bring such suffering into our worlds. That is what is happening all over the world today.

Until a short time ago, the knowledge of this Sacred Fire was known and taught only in the Retreats of the Ascended Masters throughout the Realms of Light, but because of the short period of time in which certain things must be accomplished, It has been brought into the outer world where ANYONE can know of It, use It, and experience the Freedom which It brings.

The year 1954 was the beginning of the ERA OF FREEDOM for the Earth. It is a special time in the history of the Planet when Freedom is to take Its eternal dominion here. That means that the energy enfolding Humanity and in the atmosphere, which has been charged with impurity and discord, will be TRANSMUTED by this VIOLET FIRE, and when that is done, people will be FREE to again receive directions from their God Presence and the Ascended Host of Light, and thus every part of Life will have Freedom, not only Humanity, but the Elemental Kingdom, the four-footed creatures, and all that Lives will once again Live as God intended in the beginning–in Love, Peace, Harmony and Freedom–in Heaven on Earth.

When we call to our God Presence "I AM" and to the Great Beings Who serve on the Seventh Ray of Spiritual Freedom to blaze this Violet Fire through us, it will begin the removal of the miscreations in our emotional, mental, etheric and physical bodies, and we will experience a lightness and buoyancy in our feelings, a clearness in our minds, and a change in our physical bodies. We can now use this knowledge of the Sacred Fire—the VIOLET TRANSMUTING FLAME—and BE FREE!

The Sacred Fire of Forgiveness—the Violet Transmuting Flame—is made accessible to the sincere students outside the Ascended Masters' Retreats at this time to more quickly help the earnest and sincere to purify, redeem and sublimate the distress created by the misuse of the Gift of Life. As more and more individuals learn the efficacy of this Power of Sublimation, We shall have an expressed group of co-workers of Freedom who can, at will, Free themselves and others from the shadows which frighten, distress, and disturb them. Ponder well on the Power of Mercy to dissolve first the cause and core of the distress, and then to dissolve the effect before it can appear, act or manifest ever again.

The use of the Violet Fire of Mercy and Transmutation greatly assists earnest individuals to remove the CAUSES and CORES of discord in their own emotional, mental, etheric and physical bodies. Coupled with a conscious endeavor to sustain personal, family, national and world Peace, this brings VICTORY.

Patience, application, realization and invocation of the momentums of the Virtues which the Ascended Masters and Angels offer to mankind will assist all of us to rise to a point where we can receive the directions of our own God Presence, and eventually qualify to receive the directions of the Masters and Angels—through our personal edification. Individual development, if truly achieved, need not be proclaimed, but will be manifest in works!

The Violet Fire of Freedom's Love—The Law of Forgiveness is a part of the natural Law that governs this Planet Earth. As with all natural Laws, we are subject to them whether we believe in them or not. When we jump off a roof, it is irrelevant whether or not we believe in the Law of Gravity. We are going to fall to the ground just the same.

The beauty of the Law of Forgiveness is that we don't have to believe It; we don't have to understand how It works or accept It. ALL we have to do is ask for Its intervention in our Lives and USE It.

THE POWER OF INVOCATION

THE CALL FOR ASSISTANCE MUST COME FROM THE REALM WHERE THE ASSISTANCE IS NEEDED.

Each of us in the physical plane has the ability to invoke the Light of God that is Eternally Victorious into every one of our Life experiences.

The Violet Flame of Forgiveness is a specifically designed energy from the Heart of God that, *when invoked*, will pass through our four lower bodies and prevent those vehicles of expression from registering the chaos and conflict around them. It will also Transmute the discordant programming of the past.

If we would but invoke this gift of Light, we would be Free from tying into all of the negativity around us and Free from our negative belief systems. We would be Free to dwell in the continual guidance and Joy of our Higher Selves—our God Presences.

We must be persistent and invoke the Violet Light of Freedom rhythmically and continually. The result of this discipline will be our ability to remain detached from negativity. We will then begin to experience liberation and the ability to transmit endless Compassionate Love for others from that position of Peaceful detachment.

It is now time for us to rhythmically invoke the Violet Light of Freedom and wash from our vehicles all points of connection with negativity. We must detach ourselves from negative thoughts, feelings, memories or actions.

We are now capable of residing in the heightened detachment of Spiritual Freedom. We have the ability to channel Compassionate Love into our immediate environment and to the entire Planet as well.

We continually struggle with negative circumstances, but we must realize THAT ANY AND ALL OUTER CIRCUMSTANCES OR STIMULI THAT YET THROW US OFF OUR CENTER, ONLY DO SO BECAUSE THAT VIBRATION PASSES THROUGH OUR VEHICLES MORE RHYTHMICALLY AND WITH MORE POWER THAN

DOES THE VIOLET FIRE OF FORGIVENESS. In order to become detached from outer circumstances or stimuli, and therefore, not react to them or become impatient with them, we must rhythmically demand and command of our God Presence that the Violet Fire become a greater force in our consciousness than any outer situation, *no matter how distressing or repetitive it may be.* This is the Mastery we seek. This continual Loving demand of the Law of Life will eventually return our entire focus to the inner promptings of the God Presence and the directives of the Divine Plan we originally volunteered to serve.

We are at a point in our development when we can experience a New Age understanding of the exact Science of Energy and Vibration. We can now know precisely how to invoke, command and demand of Life "I AM" that our vehicles be charged with the actual flaming substance of the most powerful activity of Divine Love (the Violet Fire). And unerringly, each one of us can set the vibration of our own inner vehicles to a level that disallows the entrance of fear or any of its legions of imbalance. It requires Illumination as to the Law of Life and rhythmic application of the Violet Fire. Coupled with a firm determination, Self-Mastery is now available to all Humanity.

Prove to yourself the Power of the Violet Fire. Prove that It can overcome any force of imbalance currently manifesting in your Life. In private, repeat this affirmation constantly and rhythmically as an invocation . . .
"I AM" A FORCE OF VIOLET FIRE GREATER THAN ANY HUMAN EXPERIENCE.

Whether or not this activity of Violet Light registers on your five outer senses, you are still making a great deal of difference. Very quickly you will begin to perceive tangible proof in your Life experience that things are indeed improving.

Continue to rhythmically apply the Science of Invocation...focusing, concentrating, projecting and sustaining this Violet Light of Freedom until you attain full Mastery over all outer appearances.

The following exercises are specifically designed to enable each one of us to release the misconceptions of our past experiences, Transmute them through the Law of Forgiveness and reconnect with our Higher Selves.

RELEASING EXERCISES

The purpose of these exercises is to unlock and release, then TRANSMUTE, the destructive vibrations of our past thoughts, words, actions and feelings.

The negative energy that we have released during our Earthly sojourn pulsates in, through and around us. By unlocking, releasing and Transmuting these heavy discordant vibrations, we literally open the door to our Higher Self, thus creating a contact and communication that will guide us unerringly toward our highest potential.

As you begin, please sit comfortably in your chair with your arms and legs uncrossed and affirm with deep feeling:

"I AM" now enveloped in an invincible forcefield of protection. From this focus, "I AM" able to review my Life as an objective observer. I ask my Higher Self to push to the surface of my conscious mind every single experience, both known and unknown, that is in any way preventing me from attaining my highest good.

Blazing in, through and around my four lower bodies (physical, etheric, mental and emotional) is the full power of the Violet Transmuting Flame. This Light from the very Heart of God instantly Transmutes these negative thoughts, words, actions, feelings and memories back into their original perfection.

"I AM" at Perfect Peace.

As this information surfaces, I effortlessly let it go, without emotion, without pain and without fear.

I simply experience this negative energy being Transmuted back into Light and I Love it FREE!

Now follow with the Visualization for Problem Solving . . .

VISUALIZATION FOR PROBLEM SOLVING

Become quiet and relax. Gently close your eyes and go within to your Heart Center. Experience a feeling of perfect Peace. See yourself sitting on the Golden Throne in the "Secret Place of the Most High Living God."

Now ask yourself, "What are the negative concepts and beliefs about myself that are keeping me stuck in the past? What are the problems and concerns facing me now?"

As the beliefs and concerns begin to surface, see them appear before you but OUTSIDE of your forcefield of Peace.

Look at them, but feel the space between you and the concerns. As you visualize them before you, affirm with a great inner knowing:

"I AM" a FORCE OF VIOLET FIRE more powerful than any human creation. The Violet Transmuting Flame blazes through my Heart Flame into every person, place, condition and thing in my Life, conscious or unconscious, past or present, through obvious choice or through karmic liability.

The Violet Fire TRANSMUTES all energy less than God's Perfection back into Light.

A Ray of Force from the Violet Flame in my Heart is NOW projected to every point in my Universe. In every case, the Violet Flame is a greater Force than the energy of that person, place, condition or thing. I feel the Violet Fire Loving FREE every point in my Universe. The Violet Fire is Transmuting my experience into a Life of ABUNDANCE and FINANCIAL FREEDOM, STRENGTH and COURAGE, FULFILLMENT and SUCCESS, HEALTH and VITALITY, UNCONDITIONAL LOVE and REVERENCE FOR LIFE, HARMONY and ETERNAL PEACE, VICTORIOUS ACCOMPLISHMENT of my DIVINE PLAN, FORGIVENESS and FREEDOM, ILLUMINATION and TRUTH, GOD'S WILL and POWER, PURITY and TRANSFORMATION.

"I AM" FREE! "I AM" FREE! "I AM" ETERNALLY FREE!
IT IS DONE. SO BE IT. "I AM"!!!

Ask your Higher Self to reveal to you any other concerns, and again observe the concerns OUTSIDE of your space of Peace as they surface one by one. Each time affirm:

"I AM" A FORCE OF VIOLET FIRE GREATER THAN ANY HUMAN EXPERIENCE.

Maintain a space between you and the concerns. Now, for more indepth Purification and Transmutation, select one personal problem to focus on. See it OUTSIDE of yourself and stand back from it.

Ask your Higher Self to help you get a clear perspective on all of the different aspects of the problem. Feel yourself being raised into a space of Clarity.

What are you now sensing about the problem? What word, phrase or image would you use to describe how you are feeling about this problem from your new perspective?

Now ask your Higher Self to reveal to you, from this new point of awareness, what is the learning experience in this problem.

Take the time to allow the information to register in your conscious mind. If no Clarity comes immediately, feel yourself *reaching higher – now higher – now higher –* until you have reached the Realm of Illumined Truth. Experience each step along the way.

See the lesson and the solution unfold before you as you are gently and peacefully lifted out of the confusion of mass consciousness into the Octaves of Light.

Absorb the lesson. Anchor it securely in your conscious mind.

Often a problem or learning experience will have several "layers" for you to learn from. Accept each lesson as it is revealed to you and peeled away layer by layer.

Repeat this process of visualization again and again, if necessary, until you feel the problem is completely resolved. Feel the elation and sense of Freedom as the problem is dissolved in the Light of Illumined Truth and affirm once more with deep feeling:

"I AM" a FORCE OF VIOLET FIRE more powerful than any human creation. The Violet Transmuting Flame blazes

*through my Heart Flame into every person, place, condition
and thing in my Life, conscious or unconscious, past or present, through obvious choice or through karmic liability.*

*The Violet Fire TRANSMUTES all energy less than God's
Perfection back into Light.*

*A Ray of Force from the Violet Flame in my Heart is NOW pro-
jected to every point in my Universe. In every case, the Violet
Flame is a greater Force than the energy of that person, place,
condition or thing. I feel the Violet Fire Loving FREE every
point in my Universe. The Violet Fire is Transmuting my ex-
perience into a Life of ABUNDANCE and FINANCIAL
FREEDOM, STRENGTH and COURAGE, FULFILL-
MENT and SUCCESS, HEALTH and VITALITY, UN-
CONDITIONAL LOVE and REVERENCE FOR LIFE,
HARMONY and ETERNAL PEACE, VICTORIOUS
ACCOMPLISHMENT of my DIVINE PLAN, FORGIVE-
NESS and FREEDOM, ILLUMINATION and TRUTH,
GOD'S WILL and POWER, PURITY and TRANSFOR-
MATION.*

*"I AM" FREE! "I AM" FREE! "I AM" ETERNALLY
FREE!!!*

IT IS DONE. SO BE IT. "I AM"!!!

FORGIVENESS

Forgiveness is a word that vibrates with great warmth
and strength. It implies letting go . . . releasing. Forgiveness contains within it the Power to heal, soothe, reunite
and recreate.

Asking for Forgiveness and Forgiving others are processes
that involve our deepest compassion, empathy and wisdom.
Without Forgiveness there can be no lasting Love, no
change, no growth and no Freedom.

Forgiveness is a free will choice. To be Forgiven and to Forgive involve the same dynamics. If we want to be Forgiven,
then we must Forgive. If we are unable to Forgive others,
then we cannot expect others to Forgive us.

Forgiveness can never be realized in an atmosphere of accusation, condemnation, anger or fear. We will only begin to Forgive when we look upon the wrongdoers as ourselves.

All the people on this Planet are coping with Life in the best way they can, according to their wisdom and understanding. It is difficult for us to realize that, but for circumstances, we might have responded in the same way our so-called "wrongdoers" did. We divide our world into the good people and the bad people and see ourselves as being on the "good" side. Thus, we separate ourselves from the "bad" side.

In Truth, it is only by striving, through mercy, to understand our wrongdoers that Forgiveness and Compassion can begin. In the act of Forgiving and showing Compassion, we are very likely to discover new depths in ourselves and new possibilities for relating with people constructively in the future.

We will only understand and Forgive when we begin to perceive the people who have wronged us with Compassion—as feeling and vulnerable Beings like ourselves, capable of weakness, confused idealism, fear, panic, cowardice and frailty.

When we can connect sympathetically through understanding at a Heart and mind level with the other person, then we will have taken the first step necessary in piercing through our self-constructed walls of unforgiveness.

LOVE IS THE SINGLE
GREATEST SOURCE OF FORGIVENESS

In LOVE we are able to view the wrongdoer again as a worthy person. In LOVE we put the wrong in perspective and view the act apart from the person. We do not overreact. We strive, through empathetic behavior, to erase the boundaries between wrongdoer and wronged, even when we do not understand the behavior.

Through this process, we come together, renew our Faith, better understand and strengthen our present, and move forward in Trust again.

Forgiveness is a way of correcting our misunderstandings. It allows us to perceive the Love in others and the Love in ourselves. Forgiveness is a gift of Unconditional Love.

It is not, "I will Forgive you IF or WHEN," but rather, "I will Forgive you because I must, if I ever hope to Live fully and Happily again."

Forgiving and Transmuting does not mean that we condone the wrong. It simply means that THE ACTION IS PAST, AND FOR THE FUTURE'S SAKE, IT MUST BE RELEASED SO WE CAN RESUME LIVING AGAIN.

Unless we are able to Transmute the past, we'll never be Free of its Power to reawaken hurt, anger, hate and pain. We must learn from the pain and experiences of our Lives. Then, having become wiser, we must let them go, and move forward into tomorrow.

Why should we Forgive? We Forgive because the price we pay for not Forgiving is too great. To bear grudges, to harbor hate, to seek revenge, are all self-defeating and lead us nowhere. They neither satisfy or heal. They keep us from moving forward and starting again. They serve only to exhaust and deplete us. They keep us suspicious and hesitant to Trust again. They destroy our creativity and retard our growth.

There is no more personally rewarding moment than when we can truly Forgive and are Forgiven. At that instant, we become really Free, Free to move forward as fully functioning human beings. True Forgiveness is an act of the highest of human behaviors.

As a teacher once said, "Let go. Why do you cling to pain? There is nothing you can do about the wrongs of yesterday. It is not yours to judge. Why hold on to the very thing which keeps you from Hope and Love?"

As suggested in almost every Holy book–Judge not. Try to understand and have empathy, strengthened with Compassion. Then, Forgiving is easy. Remember, IT IS THE FORGIVER WHO IS FREED IN FORGIVING.

"Forgive us our trespasses as we Forgive those who trespass against us."

VISUALIZATION FOR TRANSMUTING THE PAST THROUGH THE VIOLET FLAME OF FORGIVENESS

Sit or lie down comfortably with your arms and legs uncrossed. Breathe in deeply, and as you exhale, completely relax and feel all of the tension just drop away. Gently close your eyes and visualize yourself in a beautiful relaxing place...lying in the warm Sun on a soothing beach or resting on the soft green grass in a peaceful meadow. Feel the warmth of the Sun as you feel safe and secure. With each breath you become more and more relaxed, more calm and serene.

As you are relaxing under the Sun, see yourself within a Forcefield of Peace and Protection. Then, see that a circle is beginning to form around you. You ask your Higher Self to bring into the circle every experience that is blocking your forward progress, every experience that is keeping you bound and stuck in the past. In the circle, you will find experiences of past hate and anger. There will be feelings of jealousy, fear, envy and doubt. You begin to realize that you are bound to these experiences, these people and these events from the past by ropes. You are not creating the ropes; you are merely recognizing that they are already there, created in the past through negative feelings and thoughts.

You begin to see experiences from the past that caused you pain, hurt and sadness. You see experiences that made you feel bad about yourself, experiences that made you feel worthless, not valuable, unimportant. You see experiences that robbed you of your dignity, your self-respect, your self-esteem.

All of these experiences, and the people involved in them, are bound to you by ropes. Any other experience that you have ever had that is preventing you from perceiving how very special you are, and preventing you from moving forward into a Life of Peace and Joy also begins forming in the circle. You recognize them, and you know them for what they are.

Now, to FREE yourself from the past, and to FREE yourself from these conditions, call forth again, through the Power of God anchored in your Heart, the VIOLET TRANSMUTING FLAME.

This Sacred Essence begins to pour into your Heart, and you project it forth from your Heart into the circle, filling the entire circle with the full gathered momentum of *Mercy, Compassion, Forgiveness, Transmutation* and *Freedom*. The Violet Flame blazes in, through and around every electron of energy within the circle. It becomes radiant and glows. It begins to Transmute and burn through the ropes.

Feel this crystalline Violet Flame FREEING you from all of this negative energy and FREEING those in the circle as well. Feel It blazing higher and higher as It burns through the ropes, dissolving all the negativity.

As the Healing takes place through the Law of Forgiveness, you begin to experience Liberation and Freedom. Now, you Forgive yourself and others for their negative behavior toward you, and yours toward them as you affirm:

LAW OF FORGIVENESS

With all the Power of the Beloved Presence of God "I AM", *and the Violet Ray of Eternal Love, Mercy, Compassion and* *Transmutation...*

I FORGIVE! I FORGIVE! I FORGIVE!

every person, place, condition or thing that may have wronged *me in any way, at any time, for any reason whatsoever, and I* *now LOVE FREE all debts owed to me by Life everywhere.*

I do now invoke the Law of Forgiveness for myself and all Humanity, for all misuse of God's Holy Energy since the beginning of time.

FORGIVE ME! FORGIVE ME! FORGIVE ME!

and as I am Forgiven, I send forth a gift of Love to balance all *debts to Life I have ever created which yet remain unpaid.*

"I AM" grateful for the Law of Forgiveness. "I AM" Loving *Life Free from the Wheel of Cause and Effect before it can act,* *manifest or longer be sustained.*

IT IS DONE! AS "I AM" GOD IN ACTION. SO BE IT!

See, feel and know the Violet Transmuting Flame is burning through the ropes. It is a beautiful feeling to know that whatever it was in the past that prevented you from recognizing your true God Reality is now leaving you once and for all. As you are released from the limitations, you radiate out into the circle, the pink essence of your Love. You also radiate pink Love out to everyone in your family, your friends and Loved ones, until your LOVE is literally flooding the Planet.

Love and acceptance flows through you to all Life. You are FREE, and they are FREE too. You then seal this activity of Light and affirm:

*I AM FREE! I AM FREE! I AM ETERNALLY FREE!
I ASK MY GOD PRESENCE TO SUSTAIN THIS
ACTIVITY THROUGH ME, INCREASING IT WITH
EVERY BREATH I TAKE.*

Feeling the buoyancy and Joy of this new found FREEDOM, gently return your attention to the room. Become aware of your physical body, breathe in deeply, and as you exhale, gently open your eyes.

"DECREE A THING AND IT SHALL BE SO"
THE POWER OF DECREEING

Within each spoken word is the Holy Breath, the Creative Power of God, that molds the Universal Light Substance into "forms" that correspond to the vibration of the words being spoken. Throughout ages of time, most of us have charged and surcharged our gift of speech with imperfection and discord. These distorted "forms" continue to pulsate in the atmosphere of Earth until they are Transmuted into vibrations of Harmony.

Decrees have been consciously presented to Humanity's intellect in order that we might use them as a balance for our misuse of the spoken word and for imperfect thought patterns created through the many centuries of embodiment. In order to shatter these distorted "forms", it is necessary to use energy vibrating at the same rate—but constructively qualified. In other words, a "form" created by wrong speech must be broken by a vibratory action of CORRECT SPEECH rather than by mental force.

A constructive decree is always an invocation to the

Godhead, or to the Ascended Host, or to one's own "I AM" Presence that becomes a "form" that God can fill with His Electronic Light Substance. This creates pulsating vibrations within the outer consciousness of a quality and activity that will bring a greater manifestation of the Divine Plan into expression.

When a decree is made in the Name of God "I AM", that decree Lives eternally, because it is ensouled by some God-Free Intelligence, Angel, Deva, Cherubim, Seraphim or Elemental, and those Beings use that decree and keep it in Living, pulsating "form" for the benefaction of the race. When a group of individuals with sincere intent and God-desire to help mankind gather together and give forth any type of constructive call, visualization or decree, there are always sent specific Angels and Devas Who are so Happy in that release of energy that They keep it sustained and constantly active.

When a decree is repeated three times, it signifies that the outer consciousness of our physical self, the consciousness of our Holy Christ Self (which Jesus termed the "Mediator between God and man") and the Omnipresent, Omnipotent, and Omniscient Consciousness of our God-Self (the "I AM" Presence) are all in one accord, agreeing upon the bringing forth of the same manifestation.

Another point in favor of the repetitive decree is the fact that, by hearing the decree voiced over and over again by ourselves or others in a group, we become more and more convinced of the Truth which we are voicing. That is why there is a tremendous efficacy in group decreeing. Also, in group work, we gain feelings of confidence by seeing and hearing others engaged in a common purpose.

The activity of decreeing for ourselves, Humanity and all Life in general is a tremendous privilege of God's Merciful Love. It enables God's promises to be fulfilled, for it is in accordance with His own Great Law. Gratitude for such an opportunity is the wide open door to more and more blessings in our daily Lives, and Life itself will bless and thank us for Loving it enough to decree it Free.

The following is a suggested format for a group meeting. As you become more familiar with the tools being presented here, your God Presence will guide you to wonderful ideas on how to expand and enhance your group work.

VIOLET FIRE CLASS

CANDLE LIGHTING::

Blessed Flame, come forth now to Bless all Life on Earth with your resplendent Presence.

Light Supreme, we acknowledge you in all Life, and we give Gratitude to the entire Company of Heaven as we invoke Them and the Great Angelic Host to Amplify the energy which we release in this class. May that Light expand and expand as It travels throughout the Universe, ever widening the borders of the Kingdom of our Father-Mother God in fulfillment of God's Holy Will..."I AM".

INVOCATION:

In the Name of the Beloved Victorious Presence of God–"I AM"–and the Beloved Holy Christ Selves within our Hearts and the Hearts of all Humanity, we dedicate this Class to the Violet Fire of Love, Mercy, Invocation, Transmutation, Forgiveness and Freedom for ourselves, all mankind and the Planet Earth. To that end, we call to You, Beloved Ascended Masters, Cosmic Beings, the Seven Mighty Elohim, and all Who are concerned with the Violet Fire and the Seventh Ray to our Earth to be with us in your Luminous Presence. Take up our humble efforts and amplify them without limit to bring instantaneous Perfection wherever the Blessed Violet Fire is called forth. We Love and Bless and thank you for the answer to this and our every Call to Light.

DECREES, AFFIRMATIONS AND VISUALIZATIONS:
(Select Several)

Dear Father-Mother God...

I invoke You to flood my Being and every single etheric record since the beginning of time with the JOYFUL experience of Forgiveness. In Forgiving, I let go of all the effects of misused energy impinging on my Life and the Lives of all Humanity. I let go of the ignorance, confusion and pain of this world. I have come to LOVE IT FREE, and so I shall!

This is now the HEART CENTER of my existence... the Joy of Forgiving Life as it enters my awareness ... setting it Free into a higher vibration with the gift of FORGIVENESS that you have given so freely into my keeping.

"I AM" a Chalice of the Violet Light of Forgiveness
flooding this Sweet Earth!

"I AM" THE JOY OF FORGIVENESS
"I AM" THE JOY OF FORGIVENESS
"I AM" THE JOY OF FORGIVENESS
SO BE IT! "I AM"

DECREES TO THE VIOLET FIRE
OF FREEDOM'S LOVE

IN THE NAME AND THE AUTHORITY OF THE POWER AND PRESENCE OF GOD "I AM"...BELOVED COSMIC BEINGS AND ASCENDED MASTERS CONCERNED WITH THE VIOLET FIRE AND THE SEVENTH RAY TO OUR EARTH...

* a) EXPAND! EXPAND! AND INTENSIFY DAILY THE MIGHTIEST ACTION OF VIOLET FIRE in, through and around every electron that makes up the atoms of our emotional, mental, etheric and physical vehicles, until they outpicture the God Perfection which Thou art! (Repeat three times from *.)

Hold it sustained and double it each hour. In God's Most Holy Name "I AM".

(use above pattern for the following...)

b) EXPAND! EXPAND! AND INTENSIFY DAILY THE MIGHTIEST ACTION OF THE VIOLET FIRE in, through and around all Nations, Races and Creeds in every Country of the World, and in, through and around their homes, places of occupation and general environment until the Perfection of the Divine Plan does manifest for all Life.

c) EXPAND! EXPAND AND INTENSIFY DAILY THE MIGHTIEST ACTION OF THE VIOLET FIRE in, through and around the CAUSE and CORE of the CREATIVE CENTERS of all doubt and fear in the Earth, on the Earth, and in its atmosphere.

BELOVED PRESENCE OF GOD "I AM"...BLAZE, BLAZE, BLAZE AND EXPAND, EXPAND, EXPAND THE VIOLET FIRE OF PURIFICATION AND TRANS-MUTATION IN, THROUGH AND AROUND THE LANDED SURFACE, THE WATERS AND THE PEO-PLE OF _____*_____ AND INTENSIFY AND ESTAB-LISH A MIGHTY FOCUS OF THE VIOLET FIRE IN THE ETHERIC REALM OVER THEM.

* 1. The United States, including Puerto Rico...
* 2. Canada, Central and South America and Cuba...
* 3. India, China, Korea, Japan and Viet Nam...
* 4. Egypt and the Continent of Africa...
* 5. England, Scotland and Ireland...
* 6. The Soviet Union, Germany, Greece, Turkey and the Continent of Europe
* 7. Malaysia, Indonesia and the Continent of Asia...
* 8. Australia, New Zealand and the Islands of the Pacific...
* 9. The Planet Earth...

SO BE IT!!! IN GOD'S MOST HOLY NAME "I AM"!!!

***LEGIONS OF THE VIOLET FIRE...BLAZE, BLAZE, BLAZE THE VIOLET FIRE OF FREEDOM'S LOVE AND TRANSMUTATION AS OF A THOUSAND SUNS IN, THROUGH AND AROUND...

a) All the Forces of the Elements, the Elemental Kingdom, the Kingdom of Nature, birds and four-footed creatures and every Living thing, until the Perfection of their Divine Plan does manifest.

(Repeat three times from ***)
We so decree it! As God's Most Holy Name "I AM".

(use above pattern for the following...)

b) All substance and food used for human consumption which does not raise the vibratory action of the vehicles, until Divine Perfection does manifest in our worlds.

c) All space activities throughout the World until every Nation unites in co-operative service that God's Will may be manifest.

d) All Humanity, so that each Lifestream may individually acknowledge and accept the IMMACULATE CONCEPT for all Life.

e) All religious teachings so that Divine Love, Truth and Universal Brother/Sisterhood will quickly manifest.

f) All incoming children, the young Generation, their Parents and Guardians, until the Youth are raised up to carry out the Directives of their God Presence.

g) All youth centers and activities; all schools, colleges and universities; all leaders, teachers, instructors, and professors in every line of endeavor, until the Flame of God Illumination is manifest and is eternally sustained.

h) All places of incarceration; all employed there; every judge, jury, and Court of Law until Divine Justice is manifest.

i) All doctors, nurses, healers, hospitals and institutions of healing everywhere, so that Divine Healing may manifest.

j) All in our Governments at the local, state, and national levels, and through all Governments on the Earth, until the Plan for Divine Government and Eternal Peace does manifest and is eternally sustained.

k) Every part of Life on the Planet Earth, until God's Divine Plan does manifest for all.

l) All thoughts, words and deeds which do not bless,

until every radiation is a benediction upon all Life.

m) Every part of my physical, etheric, mental and emotional bodies, and those of all Humanity, and hold it sustained until all human creation there, its cause and core, is dissolved and Transmuted into Purity and Perfection.

Beloved Silent Watcher over every city, town and village on the Planet Earth. . .reach out Your great Loving Arms and raise up a limitless number of individuals in every center who will awaken to the reality of the faithful use of the VIOLET TRANSMUTING FLAME OF COSMIC CHRIST MERCY AND COMPASSION. See that each such individual completely understands the full import of the opportunity now offered them to Free themselves and their fellow Humanity from all human distresses. We decree that their conscious acceptance and use of this Mighty Power from the Heart of God will cause to be established within and over every one of these centers, great purifying Foci of the VIOLET FIRE, through which the inner bodies of all in their vicinities may pass at least once each day and more often if desired.

This we ask in God's Most Holy Name "I AM".

THE VICTORIOUS VIOLET FIRE OF FREEDOM'S LOVE now . . .
Heals our bodies . . .
Harmonizes and stabilizes our feelings . . .
Illumines our consciousness and sets us FREE . . .
raising us into full mastery over all human appearances, desires and feelings, now and forever sustained. (3 times)

In the Name, Love, Wisdom, Power and Authority of the Beloved Mighty Victorious Presence of God "I AM" in us, we speak directly to the Heart of the FREEDOM FLAME... Enfold us in Your Purifying, Forgiving, Healing Substance that causes the consciousness and feeling of FREEDOM to flow forth from us constantly to all the Life we contact. Let this Purifying Essence saturate the atmosphere around us everywhere we move so that Its miracle-working Presence will give daily, tangible proof of Your Reality to all. Send Legions of Your ANGELS OF THE VIOLET FIRE to INTENSIFY and GUARD this FLAME OF FREEDOM around us in order that we may use our Life and our Light to Their fullest in our service to all Life and the CAUSE OF FREEDOM throughout the Earth.

This we ask in God's Most Holy Name–"I AM".

O Beloved Victorious VIOLET FIRE OF FREEDOM'S LOVE–WE LOVE YOU! We do NOW most earnestly and sincerely call You into dynamic action in, through and around our Beings and worlds, knowing that YOUR HEALING PRESENCE will always bring us Happiness and release from all not of the Light. Enfold us with Your Heavenly Presence, Substance, and Power of Light, and TRANSMUTE all imperfection into perfect Divine Order through Divine Love, and keep it eternally sustained. In Your great Wisdom, release to and through us now ALL THE POWER OF YOUR AC-TION that You feel we are capable of using, and we thank You for Your Presence in the Universe and Your Service of setting all Life Free everywhere.

Beloved Presence of God–"I AM"–in us and in all mankind... all Great Beings, Powers and Legions of Light ...In the Name and by the Power of Almighty God, we call for the Light of Cosmic Forgiveness, the Light of the

VIOLET FIRE OF FREEDOM'S LOVE, the Great Cosmic Light, and the Light of Cosmic Victory to flow out from Cosmic Sources to penetrate the atmosphere of Earth and TRANSMUTE, TRANSMUTE, TRANSMUTE all that is not of the Light—Cause, Effect, Record and Memory, before it can act, manifest, or longer be sustained. Replace it by the Cosmic Three-fold Flame, and the full Power of the Cosmic Flames of Freedom and Illumination until Earth's Victory is assured and the Permanent Golden Age becomes a reality.

We so decree It in God's Most Holy Name "I AM".

Group Avatar

TRANSMUTING MIS-QUALIFIED ENERGY TO MORE QUICKLY AWAKEN THE CHRIST-SELF

Electronic Substance is the emanation of an Intelligent Flame giving off a radiation of Light.

In the physical appearance world, the substance thrown off from the bodies of the people has been called the psychic or astral substance, because Its Pure Primal Essence has been qualified with impurity and imperfection.

Calls for Purification, the use of The Violet Transmuting Flame and the drawing forth of the Sacred Fire through the lower atmosphere of Earth are the greatest Services that can be rendered to Humanity in changing the quality of energy in which we constantly move.

When these calls are made by sincere individuals to the Sacred Fire and the Forces of the Four Elements to clean and Purify the atmosphere, the resulting Purification will enable the people to more quickly awaken to the Christ Self, and more readily respond to the impressions and directions of the Higher Intelligences from the Realms of Illumined Truth that are so eager to assist Humanity out of our self-inflicted chaos.

When you call to your God Presence "I AM", your Holy Christ Self and all the Legions of Light who serve on the Seventh Ray, to blaze the Violet Fire of Forgiveness and

Transmutation through you, It will begin to remove the miscreation in your physical, etheric, mental and emotional bodies, and you will experience a lightness and buoyancy in your feelings, a clarity in your mind, and a change in your physical body.

CLEANSING EXERCISE

Stand in your room and call the Violet Transmuting Flame into action in, through and around you for at least nine feet in every direction. Raise your hands and ask your Higher Self, your God Presence, to qualify your hands with the Purifying Power of the Violet Transmuting Flame. Visualize your hands blazing with Violet Light–pulsating as Amethyst Suns.

Then, starting at your head, pass your hands down over your body to the feet, taking in as much of the body surface as you can reach with your hands. Envision that your hands are mighty magnets, pulling every electron of negativity out of your body.

Now, with the left hand, sweep down over the right shoulder, arm and hand, and with the right hand, give the left shoulder, arm and hand the same treatment.

Repeat this activity in its entirety four times, once for each of the four lower vehicles (physical, etheric, mental and emotional). Periodically shake your hands from the wrist to cast off the heavy, discordant energy that is being removed from your bodies and visualize the negative energy being Transmuted in the surrounding Violet Fire.

If not just yet, eventually, you will be able to see with the inner sight what takes place during this exercise. In the first part of the exercise, it is as though a close fitting garment of dark substance is being removed from the body with the hands. The second time you go over the body, the "garment" removed is of a grey substance. The third time, it is of a lighter grey color, and the fourth time, even lighter. Day after day, as you proceed with the exercise, this astral substance becomes lighter and lighter in color and texture until it is entirely removed from the body.

This is real substance–with actual color, vibration and feeling, created through the misuse of energy throughout our Earthly sojourn.

On completion of the exercise, visualize the Violet Transmuting Flame expanding through your Heart Flame, flooding the entire Planet and affirm:

Beloved Presence of God in me...EXPAND! EXPAND! AND INTENSIFY DAILY THE MIGHTIEST ACTION OF VIOLET FIRE in, through and around every electron that makes up the atoms of my emotional, mental, etheric and physical vehicles, until they outpicture the God Perfection which Thou art! (Repeat three times)

In the Name of the Almighty Presence of God "I AM" and the Creative Fire pulsating in every human Heart...Beloved Presence of God "I AM" in me and that of all mankind...

SATURATE MY FEELING WORLD WITH THE VIOLET TRANSMUTING FLAME (three times)

SATURATE MY MENTAL WORLD WITH THE VIOLET TRANSMUTING FLAME (three times)

SATURATE MY ETHERIC WORLD WITH THE VIOLET TRANSMUTING FLAME (three times)

SATURATE MY PHYSICAL WORLD WITH THE VIOLET TRANSMUTING FLAME (three times)

In God's Most Holy Name "I AM".

BENEDICTION:

Sealed in the Violet Transmuting Flame, Beloved Presence of God "I AM" in us and in all Humanity, Great Host of Ascended Masters and Cosmic Beings, the Angelic Host and Elemental Kingdom Who have served us this day, we thank You for your outpouring of Light and Love. We thank You for Healing, Supply, Wisdom, Protection, Perfection and Your Blessings of every kind. Hold them sustained in, through and around us, and pour them through us for the blessing and raising of all Life on our Planet Earth.

May the BENEDICTION and BLESSING OF THE MOST HIGH LIVING GOD and the PEACE which does surpass the understanding of the human mind be with you, each one. May the God of Mercy protect and guide you on your Spiritual Path toward Enlightenment and Freedom.

Angels of Ministration and Ceremonial, we Love, thank, and Bless You for Your wondrous service to us this day. Take up our humble efforts and amplify them with Your Mighty Love. Take them North, South, East and West, and cover our dear Planet Earth with Love and Light, with Peace, Illumination, Healing, Freedom, Victory, and the Will of God made manifest through every electron belonging to this Planet and Her evolutions in any way. THIS SHALL BE, for We have spoken in God's Most Holy Name "I AM".

CANDLE EXTINGUISHING:

Blessed Flame, Expression of the Light Essence of the Supreme Source "I AM", we thank you for your obedient service to the Children of Earth. Clothed in the Gratitude from our Hearts, return Thou now to the Heart Center of Creation, to be again called forth at the Invocation of Humanity to expand the Borders of the Kingdom of our Father-Mother God.

We realize the Oneness of all Life, and in humility, we bow before the Light of the Cosmos, as we all serve as Pulsations of Light in the Body of the Supreme Source "I AM".

The decrees used here were taken from the Group Avatar Book of Invocation with permission of Group Avatar. If you would like to order this very beneficial book please write to:

Group Avatar
PO Box 41505
Tucson, AZ 85717

THE SEVEN STEPS TO PRECIPITATION: THE SCIENCE OF SUCCEEDING IN YOUR PURPOSE

Now is the moment in time when we must learn to accept our Divine Birthright. Our Birthright includes the Law of Precipitation–the Science of Creation–and if we utilize this science as it was originally intended, we will no longer haphazardly create misery and suffering in our Lives. By applying the scientific principles of precipitation, we will become and REMAIN Masters of our Earthly experience.

The Seven Aspects of Deity we have covered in the book thus far reflect the Third Dimensional Realm, the physical plane of Earth. These Seven Rays contain within Them the Seven Steps to Precipitation, which give us Mastery over this physical plane.

Precipitation is actually the science of succeeding in our purpose. It is the way and means by which we bring our goals into physical manifestation. It is the Law of Creation for our Universe. It is our path to Freedom.

The only way for us to *permanently* raise ourselves out of the various kinds of limitation we have created and foolishly accepted as normal in our Lives, is for us to Transmute the previous causes of our distress through the Power of the Violet Transmuting Flame. Then, we must set into action *NEW* causes, which will create *NEW* effects in the physical world. Change in our Lives will not be *permanent* unless we learn the Seven Steps of Precipitation, and apply them through our own conscious efforts. However, once we learn the skills and prove to ourselves the accuracy of this science, we will be more than willing to continue the process and sustain our newfound Freedom.

FOLLOW THESE STEPS CAREFULLY, AND PROVE TO YOURSELF THAT YOU ARE TRULY THE MASTER OF YOUR OWN FATE.

Often when we talk of being Masters of our own Lives or Creators of our own Reality, people feel that somehow we are trying to usurp God's Power or negate God's authority as THE Creator or the Universal Source of all Life. Quite the contrary. When we accept our Divine Heritage as Sons and daughters of God, we realize "ALL THAT THE FATHER HAS IS OURS." Through this Illumination, we exalt and

Glorify our Beloved Father-Mother God.

We have been given the gift of Free Will, so that each of us will learn, through our own self-conscious efforts, to use our Gift of Life to expand the Borders of The Kingdom of our Father-Mother God, creating Harmony and Balance on Earth.

As we learn to become Masters of the physical plane, which is our purpose and reason for being on Earth in the first place, we evolve into co-creators with God, reaching our highest potential and fulfilling our true God Reality. Then, we can affirm with true KNOWING:

"I AM" THE DIVINE IMAGE OF GOD, MANIFESTING PERFECTION IN MY BEING AND WORLD, AND FOR THE CHILDREN OF GOD, EVERYONE, EVERY-WHERE, IN GOD'S SUPREME NAME, FOREVER!

WHEREVER "I AM", MY VERY PRESENCE IN THE UNIVERSE IS A CONSTANT OUTPOURING AND RE-LEASE OF GOD LIFE AND LIGHT, GOD TRUTH AND GOD FREEDOM TO ALL I CONTACT EVERY DAY IN EVERY WAY!

I would like to issue a word of caution at this point. There is no mocking the natural Law of Cause and Effect. If this process is ever used for selfish or impure motives, our man-ifestation will not be permanent, and we will suffer much through the misuse of this creative process.

However, if we use the Science of Precipitation for the highest good of all concerned and for the enrichment and Illumination, not only of ourselves, but all Humanity as well, we will be Blessed beyond measure. Our supply of money and every good thing will constantly increase as we use the knowledge and wisdom we have gained. This will give us complete FREEDOM and independence. We will no longer be trapped in miserable situations, struggling to supply the needs of our physical existence. Instead, we will be daily and hourly creating Lives that are fulfilling and rewarding in every way. We will be co-creators with God, spiritual Partners with the entire Company of Heaven, manifesting greater Glory on Earth for ourselves, and all the evolutions of this sweet Planet.

This knowledge is being given to Humanity at this critical time on Earth by the Ascended Beings of Light and Love Who have set Themselves Eternally Free from all human limitation by the correct application of these Laws. The Beings of Light are graciously offering us this Wisdom, so we, too, can enjoy our Eternal Freedom. If we will joyously accept the Blessing of these Sacred Laws and utilize them as though they were meant for each of us alone, we will experience the ultimate mastery of our physical reality. Then, we will be inspired to use this knowledge for the benefit of our fellow Human Beings and all Life on Earth.

As you read these words, ask your God Presence to fill every fiber of your Being with the Gratitude, Reverence and Humility worthy of this gift of knowledge.

THE SEVEN STEPS TO PRECIPITATION:
Step One: Under the Direction of the Elohim of the First
Ray of God's Will
Color – Sapphire Blue
DECISION – THE WILL TO DO

Everything that has ever been accomplished on the Earth-plane or on the plane of Heaven has been accomplished by men and women of decision who have voluntarily chosen to combine the energies of their Lives with the WILL TO DO. Without the WILL TO DO, which is the first step in the Science of Precipitation, there is no permanence of accomplishment. It is what we WILL that we manifest! What we WILL, we draw to ourselves, for the WILL is the magnetic power of God in our Hearts which does invoke and bring to us that which we desire.

If we state calmly, with the dignity and mastery of our own Hearts: *"I WILL TO BE GOD FREE"*, we will feel ourselves being empowered by the strength of our God Presence. We will lift our chins, straighten our spines, and proceed along Life's path, refusing dissolution, poverty, limitation and all the chains that bind us to misery of any kind.

The First Step of Precipitation is DECISION, and the WILL

to create whatever it is we desire in our Lives. We must always ask, of course, that our desire be in alignment with God's Will, and the highest good for all concerned.

Step Two: Under the Direction of the Elohim of the Second
Ray of Enlightenment and Perception
Color – Sunshine Yellow
PERCEPTION – WISDOM – CONCENTRATED POWER
OF ATTENTION

Contained within the radiance of the Second Ray is the Concentrated Power of our attention. Without the focus of our attention, our mind could not conceive or know anything.

The Power of our attention is the open door to our minds and our entire consciousness.

Our mental bodies receive, through our attention and through all the activities of the senses, everything our attention connects with–good or otherwise–and then we draw back into our mental bodies, the pictures or forms that register in our mind. If our attention is on negativity of any kind, whether we see it, hear it, feel it, or experience it through any of our sense consciousness, that discord enters our mental bodies and adds to the accumulation there. Our mental bodies are cluttered with the cobwebs and distorted human concepts of the past. There is much stored there that is in the process of disintegration; some of the conglomeration is even petrified. It's time for us to LET GO of the distortion of the past. We must now deliberately control our attention and focus it only on the things we want to maintain and sustain in our Lives. Through the Power of the Violet Transmuting Flame, we can sweep away the clutter and the cobwebs of the past. Then, through the Power of the Sunshine Yellow Ray of Enlightenment, we can begin to focus our attention on what we really want to manifest.

Our mental bodies were originally created to be magnetic fields, which, through the Power of our attention, could draw into themselves Divine ideas from the Mind of God, thus enabling us to create Perfection on Earth. Through practice, we will again reach up into the Mind of God and PER-CEIVE clearly the Divine Plan for Earth. Then, through the correct application of the Seven Steps to Precipitation, we will manifest that Divine Plan permanently.

The Second Step of Precipitation is PERCEPTION–THE CONCENTRATED POWER OF OUR ATTENTION.

After making the DECISION and developing the WILL TO DO, we must PERCEIVE clearly what we want to create in our Lives and focus the full Power of our ATTENTION on that goal.

Step Three: Under the Direction of the Elohim of the Third Ray of Divine Love
Color: Pink
DIVINE LOVE

Divine Love has caused to come into being every electron or particle of Life belonging to this Planet. The positive quality of Divine Love is the magnetic, cohesive Power which drew into being the precious Earth upon which we stand, the physical bodies in which we presently function, and every other manifestation which appears here. Every form which we enjoy is a part of Life, held together by the Flame of Love. If Divine Love, which is COHESION, were to cease to be, all in the Universe would return to the unformed and become again part of primal Life.

Without Love, nothing is permanently accomplished. Without Love, the clearest vision remains but a cloudy vapor.

LOVE IS CONSTANCY UNDER THE MOST TRYING OF CIRCUMSTANCES, AND ACTION AT THE MOMENT WHEN IT IS REQUIRED MOST.

Whenever we want to expand the activities of DIVINE LOVE, whose qualities are Adoration, Magnetization and Gratitude to Life, we need only ASK, AND WE SHALL RECEIVE.

The Third Step of Precipitation is DIVINE LOVE. After we have PERCEIVED clearly our desired goal, we must invoke into our thoughtform, the cohesive Power of DIVINE LOVE which draws the unformed into form. This is the Power which draws primal Life into the patterns or ideas held in our minds and sustains them in the physical plane in tangible manifest form. The more sincere feelings of LOVE we put into our goals, the more beautiful they will be, and the more quickly they will manifest. This is true whether our goal is something we wish to create for personal use or whether we are creating something for the benefit of all Humanity. The more LOVE we put into our service, the greater our manifestations will be, the higher their qualities will be, and the more plentiful their blessings to the world of form.

Step Four: Under the Direction of the Elohim of the Fourth
Ray of Purity
Color – White
PURITY – THE IMMACULATE CONCEPT

Held within the Mind of God is the Immaculate Concept for each and every particle of Life. The Immaculate Concept is the blueprint or pattern of Perfection that we will one day fulfill. It is the true potential of our God Presence and the purpose of our Lives.

This Divine Pattern contains within it all the qualities and virtues of God, which include Prosperity, Joy, Vibrant Health, Peace, Love, Happiness, Harmony, Truth, Freedom and on and on ad infinitum.

We must ask God and our Higher Selves to reveal to us the Immaculate Concept of our Divine Plans and our desired creations. Then, we must hold our attention continually on these perfect patterns, energizing them with LOVE until they are physically manifest.

The action of this Law is mechanical. *It is absolutely and positively a science of vibration.* The speed with which electrons revolve around the central core of each atom in our minds (mental bodies) is determined by the thoughts we entertain. When those thoughts are on Perfection and on the expansion of God's good in the Universe, the vibratory action of the electrons in our mental bodies accelerates and deflects away from us the mass thoughtforms of destruction which float in the atmosphere of Earth. Then, we are Free to hold steady the *pure* pictures of our goals, not distorting them by any opinions or desires of our lower selves. At that point, we are pure, clear crystals through which the Immaculate Concept of our desired goals are magnetized from our God Presences and projected into matrixes to be filled with Light substance and formed into matter.

We must continually invoke our God Presences to sustain the original Divine Designs, so that, even unconsciously, we won't impose upon our goals any change that may not be for the highest good of all concerned. In as much humility and selflessness as possible, we must hold to the PURITY of the Divine Ideas (Patterns) which we received from our God Presences, always reaching up higher and higher in consciousness to assure that PURITY will be eternally sustained.

The Fourth Step of Precipitation is PURITY–THE IMMACULATE CONCEPT. After we have invoked the cohesive Power of DIVINE LOVE into our thoughtforms, we need to magnetize the IMMACULATE CONCEPT/DIVINE PATTERNS from the Mind of God through our Higher Selves into our thoughtforms, thus creating matrixes around which our Divine Patterns will be formed. Within every electron which is released from the Heart of God is the Power to create and sustain the Kingdom of Heaven on Earth for ourselves, our families, our Loved ones and all entrusted to our sphere of influence. Right within the brazier of our own Hearts, we contain the most powerful activity of an "Atomic Accelerator" ever imagined–our Spark of Divinity–the Victorious Immortal Three-fold Flame. By holding to the PURITY of God *within*, the Immaculate Concept of our own Divinity will flash through our minds and fill our feelings with Happiness and Ecstasy, as our Etheric Bodies are charged with God's Patterns of Perfection. Then, we will be the clear, open portals through which our Divine Plans and goals will flow into the world of form.

Step Five: Under the Direction of the Elohim of the Fifth
Ray of Truth and Concentration
Color – Emerald Green
CONCENTRATION – CONSECRATION – TRUTH

Without Concentration there is only mediocrity. To bring our manifestations into Reality, we must persevere through the Power of Concentration–CONCENTRATION OF ENERGY TO FOLLOW THROUGH TO VICTORY.

CONCENTRATION involves holding the pattern and channeling energy into it until it is completed in every detail. The mind must be held in focus on the goal and not allowed to fly off on various tangents or schemes until the Divine Pattern is wholly completed. Through the Power of CONCENTRATION, our goal is fed and nourished.

It is far better for us to do one thing well than to do a hundred things halfheartedly. We've all heard the phrase "Jack of all trades and master of none." It is imperative that we not allow fear and doubt or ridicule from others to make us believe we cannot succeed. When ideas are flashed in our minds, and we focus on them and form the mental pictures, we have taken the first action necessary in deliberately drawing forth the Reality of those ideas. Then, if we will hold on to the ideas and apply the Seven Steps of Precipitation, they will become tangibly manifest in the physical world. For instance, if we want financial Freedom, we must *HOLD TO THAT IDEA*, and see that substance visible in our hands and use now. If we want Eternal Youth and Health in our minds and bodies; if we want Freedom from limitation of any kind; if we want fulfilling, Loving relationships; if we want careers, both financially and creatively rewarding; if we want the Joy and Happiness that comes when we are actively fulfilling our Divine Plans–then we must develop clear, definite pictures in our minds of *exactly* what we want, and STAY WITH THAT *ONE* IDEA until we have brought it forth into physical manifestation. If we Love Life and ourselves enough to stay with one idea; if we are consistent and humble enough to let God do His Will through us; if we will only CONCENTRATE upon one thing at a time, then it is impossible to fail. THE LIGHT OF GOD IS *ALWAYS VICTORIOUS!*

WHAT THE MIND CAN CONCEIVE,
THE PERSON CAN ACHIEVE!

The Fifth Step of Precipitation is CONCENTRATION. After we have magnetized the IMMACULATE CONCEPT from the Mind of God into our Pattern, we must CONSE-CRATE and CONCENTRATE our Life energies to fulfilling our goal. CONCENTRATION and CONSECRATION are almost one and the same, because, whatever we are going to do that amounts to anything, requires the CONSECRA-TION of our Life energy. It is the CONSECRATION of all of our energies to fulfilling our goals that will give us mastery over this world of form. Through the correct use of our Gift of Life, which is electronic Light substance, we must de-velop the CONCENTRATION of purpose and CONSE-CRATION of our energy to follow through to the VICTORY of ACCOMPLISHMENT.

Step Six: Under the Direction of the Elohim of the Seventh Ray of Invocation, Rhythm and Freedom
Color: Violet

INVOCATION – RHYTHM – FREEDOM

Note: In the Seven Steps of Precipitation, the Sixth Ray of Peace and Ministration, and the Seventh Ray of Invo-cation, Rhythm and Freedom are inverted. The reason for this is that the RHYTHM of building and creating, the part of the service of the Seventh Ray, is necessary to allow the coalescence of Universal Light into form. The Sixth Ray, expressing Ministration and the Radia-tion of PEACE, is necessary for the final steps of sol-idifying the perfect design.

In the beginning of our individualization, God created each of us as a Divine Self-conscious Intelligence–"I AM"–a White Fire Being from the Universal First Cause. We had the capacity to draw forth from Life every God gift we might ever require in order to manifest Perfection. In the great scheme of things, God answers the Heart call of every individual, and when that Heart call, deeply and sincerely from within itself, desires to release Life which has become trapped in humanly created negativity, that portion of Life is given FREEDOM from all manner of suffering and limitation of every description. It can then express its true self. Within that Life is the fullness of God.

Life, which is Light Essence quiescent, contains within Itself all the Power of the Universal First Cause. This same Life (Light) flows from the Heart of God into our Beings, animating our worlds. Within that Light is EVERYTHING we require to exist in perfect Harmony and Joy on Earth.

Whenever we sincerely desire FREEDOM, and in constant RHYTHM, choose to INVOKE and COMMAND IT into our Lives, we shall receive assistance from on high until we experience that FREEDOM physically manifest.

If we will observe Nature, we will easily recognize the absolute RHYTHM by which all creation takes place; the rising and setting of the Sun; the ebb and flow of the tides; the recurrent seasons; the inbreath and outbreath—all in absolute, perfect RHYTHM. RHYTHM is a key factor in Precipitation and must always be applied faithfully. The RHYTHM OF INVOCATION is a science of the Seventh Ray and a very necessary part of our process of creation. Perfection is drawn forth by the Power of Invocation, and the INVOCATION must be done RHYTHMICALLY. Once we establish a RHYTHM in INVOKING our specific manifestation, which simply means INVOKING our goals every day at approximately the same time for the same duration, we must *stay within our pattern* until the energy required flows into our goal and brings it into form. RHYTHM provides nourishment for the form. In our own Precipitation, the RHYTHM which we establish will determine the symmetry, beauty, accuracy, efficiency and general Perfection of our manifest design.

The Sixth Step of Precipitation is the RHYTHM of INVOCATION. This is the constant nourishing of our desired goal which is formed from Life energy. We must nourish our goal until it is not only manifest, but symmetrically perfect as well. Remember that constancy of RHYTHM gives symmetry to the form being created. RHYTHM and constancy of application are absolutely essential to bring about the manifestation of our desired design.

After we have CONSECRATED our Life energies to fulfill our goal and projected the full Power of our CONCENTRA-TION into the process, we must RHYTHMICALLY IN-VOKE our plan into form. This is necessary in order for the Light of God to consistently flow into our creation. This constant flow of perfect Light, called forth from the Heart of God, makes it possible for our goal to be kept Free from the contamination of the outer world.

If we will observe a certain RHYTHM and INVOKE the Light of God into our goal at the same hour everyday, we will draw much greater concentration of Power, and we will accomplish our goal much more quickly. When we spasmodically try to fit our application into our spare time, we dissipate our efforts and delay our success.

Our RHYTHM of INVOCATION may be in the form of decrees, visualizations, meditations, prayers, silent mental thoughts or any other reverent application to God.

If the Seven Steps of Precipitation are carefully applied, nothing but our own "giving up"–abandoning our project before it is completed–can possibly prevent our eventual precipitation. We must not stop the RHYTHM of INVOCA-TION before our manifestation appears. "Keep on Keeping on!" Then, when our precipitation stands completed before us, we will know that it did not come to us by happenstance, and that it is not just a gift of Faith. We will know that it is a precipitation direct from the Universal, and we will understand, as never before, what it means to be co-creators with God.

Step Seven: Under the Direction of the Elohim of the Sixth
Ray of Peace and Ministration
Color: Ruby
PEACE – MINISTRATION

This final step completes the Seven Steps of Precipitation. These Seven Steps are the unalterable process of all God-Creation–finite and infinite. Through this Sacred process, each and every one of us CAN, and one day MUST, draw forth, direct from the Universal, the gifts of Light's Perfection which are the Will of God for us to enjoy and to give to all Humanity.

We must now KNOW and ACCEPT that *the ability to precipitate is a natural attribute and Power of our "I AM" Presence.* Our "I AM" Presence originally became conscious of Itself as a Living, breathing Being when It was first directed out of the Universal First Cause. When the Presence found Itself to be an Individualization of God Consciousness, It chose to draw to Itself the substance of Primal Light (Life) and qualified it with the God Ideas of Its own personal consciousness. This qualified Light was then sent forth by the God Presence to create and expand the Beauty, Glory and Ecstasy of Creation.

Since the very nature of God Light is to expand Perfection, the "I AM" Presence determined within Itself to leave for a time the Heart Center of Its Creator and explore the Seven Spheres of Learning which surround the Godhead–the Sun from whence It came, eventually descending into the Earthly plane of form. Then, Its co-creation with God became physically manifest.

The Seventh Step of Precipitation is PEACE. After we have fed and nourished the forms we wish to precipitate through the power of RHYTHMIC INVOCATION, the manifestations must then be held within the feeling of undisturbed PEACE. Otherwise, they will disintegrate and return to the Universal from whence they were originally drawn. We must not allow discord of any kind from ourselves or others to destroy them. It is necessary for us to seal our precipitated forms in the Ruby Flame of PEACE and hold them inviolate against the disintegrating forces of human thought and feeling.

Through Divine PEACE, our goals can be sustained and expanded as gifts which will Live for Eternity. Where Harmony, PEACE and Tranquility abide, that which we have drawn forth cannot either be taken away from us or disintegrate. PEACE and the Harmony of our feelings seals our entire creation in Divine Protection.

Summary of the Seven Steps of Precipitation

These seven steps are absolutely mathematical in their precision.

Step One: DECISION – THE WILL TO DO
Step Two: PERCEPTION–WISDOM–
             CONCENTRATED POWER OF
             ATTENTION
Step Three: DIVINE LOVE
Step Four: PURITY–THE IMMACULATE
             CONCEPT
Step Five: CONCENTRATION–CONSECRATION–
             TRUTH
Step Six: RHYTHM OF INVOCATION –
             FREEDOM
Step Seven: PEACE – MINISTERING GRACE

This information on the steps to precipitation is derived from the discourses given to Humanity by the Seven Mighty Elohim. For the complete text see: "The Seven Mighty Elohim Speak on The Seven Steps to Precipitation" available through:

The Ascended Master Teaching Foundation
PO Box 466
Mt. Shasta, CA 96067

Available Tapes Associated With This Chapter Are:
I. TRANSMUTING THE PAST THROUGH
   THE POWER OF FORGIVENESS
J. FREEDOM
See page *xxiv* for more information and order blanks.

CHAPTER 8

THE EIGHTH ASPECT OF DEITY IS CLARITY

COLOR – AQUAMARINE
THE EIGHTH RAY

THE EIGHTH UNIVERSAL LAW
OF POLARITIES

THE ATTRIBUTES OF CLARITY ARE:

VIVIFICATION
DIVINE PERCEPTION
DISCERNMENT
LUCIDITY
**THE QUALITIES OF A SPIRITUALLY
FREE BEING**
DIGNITY
COURTESY
ROYAL CHARM

THE REBIRTH OF OUR PLANETARY IDENTITY INTO OUR GOD IDENTITY

1988 was proclaimed the year of the return of the "I AM" Presence to Earth. It was the year of Initiation. Humanity was Initiated at inner levels into a new identity, as we each became one in vibration with the Solar Spine of our "I AM" Presence. All Life on the Planet was Initiated into the Order of a new Cosmic Day, and this Blessed Earth was Initiated into a new vibration for Planetary orbit. All of the Sacred Forces in the Universe came to assist in these Divine Initiations. They formed a Bridge over which Humanity passed at both inner and outer levels into a consciousness, Celestial and Divine.

Now, it is time for the Initiation of our true "Rebirth". We are "born again" when we conquer "self" and Ascend into the Presence of God "I AM". Our "Rebirth" occurs when we once again Unite in consciousness with the Universal flow of God's Will, God's Wisdom and God's Divine Love in action. It occurs when we merge our Spiritual Beings with the actual Flaming Substance of God "I AM".

The Initiations that will bring us to the moment of "Rebirth" are transpiring now. Under the influence of the Feminine Ray of Holy Spirit now anchored on Earth, the Initiations taking place are both Planetary and Solar. Every Being who has graduated from the Earth plane has passed through these Initiations. Every one of us must some day pass through the Seven Planetary and Twelve Solar Initiations on the return journey back to our Father-Mother God.

The Seven Planetary Initiations were accomplished by Jesus, Who exampled for us perfect Christ development under the Sixth Ray Dispensation. He sought out the Wisdom of the Ages during His eighteen missing years, and after He found the Truth of the Planetary Laws and applied them to His Life, He passed quickly through each Initiation. Once He passed through the Seven Planetary Initiations into Christhood, He united with the flow of the Universal "I AM" Presence. With this personal Victory, He accomplished His complete Avatarship for the entire 2000 year cycle of the Sixth Ray Christian Dispensation in just THREE SHORT YEARS.

We are now being given the opportunity to do likewise. When the "I AM" Presence returns to Earth THROUGH THE CHRIST, neither time, nor space, nor circumstances can block Its flow of Perfection to Earth. Humanity is now experiencing this flow of Perfection, and we are being lifted up into Christ Consciousness. We are destined to become millions and millions of magnificent Christ Beings whose brilliant Light Illumines and Transforms the Planet IN A FEW SHORT YEARS. But, as it was for Beloved Jesus, our inner preparation is the keynote in order for this Divine Plan to be brought to fruition according to schedule.

Enough of the Lightworkers on Earth are approaching the completion of their Planetary Initiations that Solar Initiations can now begin taking place. The Twelve Solar Initiations are held within the Twelve Electronic Belts around the Sun. They have always been considered Sacred Mysteries in the past, but now it is necessary for the Solar Energies of Perfection to enter the physical plane in order for this Earth to Ascend into the Realms of Light. Humanity has awakened, and there is no returning to the sleep of the dense veil of illusion and maya.

Now is the time for us to approach our Adeptship. The Lightworkers on Earth represent the Hope of the world. It is through us that the Solar Energies will enter the Planet and be practically applied to our everyday Lives. We are the portals, "the open doors which no one can shut." We volunteered, prior to coming to Earth, to be the instruments of God. That is why we have been allowed entrance into the physical plane during this Cosmic Moment.

Each of us should evaluate the nature of our development and contemplate our potential for Cosmic Service. This is the time foretold long ago, "when Humanity shall dance with the Light of the Sun." This is the time when our four lower bodies will dance with the Twelve Solar Rays of our God Presence "I AM". As this transpires, we will more readily identify ourselves with our God Presence as "I AM" Beings, rather than as human beings struggling to become Free. When we are in the flow of our "I AM" Presences, even our human egos, with all of their treachery, cannot block God's First Cause of Perfection.

With the return of the "I AM" Presence to Earth, our planetary spines, with their seven chakric centers, are ascending in vibration into the frequency of our Solar Spines with twelve chakric centers. The Solar Spine is the spinal column of our God Presence "I AM". This great rod of Light continually reflects and magnifies the Rays of the Twelve Electronic Belts that pulsate as the Causal Body around the Sun, representing the Twelve Aspects of Deity. As we Live within the Light Bodies of our God Presences, we will do the same thing on Earth, reflecting continually the Twelve Aspects of God as we accomplish our Solar Initiations. We can Live within this greater body of Light as easily as we Live in our flesh bodies, drawing the Light of the Sun into Planetary Life. As Humanity recognizes and accepts this acceleration of consciousness, Planetary Transformation will occur, and the full Light of God will enter the realms of Earth where it is needed most. Then, this Cosmic Moment on Earth will be fulfilled with God's Victorious accomplishment.

VISUALIZATION TO EXPERIENCE THE SEVEN CHAKRA CENTERS BEING REBORN INTO THE TWELVE CHAKRA CENTERS

In this exercise, we will experience our physical spine being brought into alignment with the spiritual spine of our "I AM" Presence.

Begin by standing straight with your feet a few inches apart. Now, feel the flow of Sacred Fire Ascending from the Root Chakra at the base of the spine up the spinal column into your Crown Chakra at the top of your head and back down to the Root Chakra again. This Sacred Fire is a spiraling forcefield of your Father-Mother God, a Blue Flame reflecting the Masculine Polarity of God and a Pink Flame reflecting the Feminine Polarity of God, spiraling up and down your spine in a great dance of radiant Light. Breathe slowly and rhythmically. Clear your mind of all thoughts and concentrate on this Sacred activity of Spiritual evolution.

(Pause)

The Masculine and Feminine Flames now spiral in perfect Balance and Harmony, performing their dance of Light as the Universal Life Force courses through your four planetary bodies (physical, etheric, mental and emotional). FEEL the Seven Planetary Chakras, each reflecting the completion of its purpose. Feel each planetary chakra in perfect balance, reflecting its Masculine/Feminine Aspects in absolute Harmony.

Root Chakra – Red
Central Chakra – Orange
Solar Plexus Chakra – Yellow
Heart Chakra – Green
Throat Chakra – Blue
Third Eye Chakra – Indigo
Crown Chakra – Violet

When the Sacred Fires of your Father-Mother God are in perfect balance within your four lower vehicles, you begin to experience a moment of rapid absorption into the greater vibration of your "I AM" Presence. Instantaneously, but very gently, you feel the great rod of Solar Fire blazing with Twelve Chakras along your spine. These Twelve Chakras are like blazing Suns, and reflect the Perfection of each of the Twelve Aspects of Deity.

At the base of the Solar Spine is the White Aspect of Purity. Next, the Opal Aspect of Transformation. Then:

the Violet Aspect of Freedom,
the Ruby Aspect of Ministering Grace,
the Peach Aspect of Divine Purpose,
the Gold Aspect of Peace,
the Pink Aspect of Divine Love,
the Magenta Aspect of Harmony,
the Blue Aspect of God's Will,
the Aquamarine Aspect of Clarity,
the Green Aspect of Truth,
the Yellow Aspect of Enlightenment.

The lesser Planetary spine is absorbed into the greater Solar Spine; the Planetary identity becomes the heightened Identity of a God Being. This greater identity is an Electronic Pattern of free flowing Light rather than the atomic pattern of fixed proportions of atoms and molecules you have accepted as being your physical identity on the material plane. It is this Electronic pattern of your Divine Identity that literally dances with the Light of the Sun. Like a Celestial Gem, Its aura captures a spectacular aureole of Solar Radiance, Cosmic Colors and Divine Qualities. It is this Electronic Pattern of Celestial Light that is your permanent identity. It is this Electronic Pattern that assimilates the totality of God's Perfection and continually radiates those Divine Blessings forth to all Life.

As you accept and know your Divine Identity, affirm with deep feeling:

"I AM" the Eternal Flame of Life...a White Fire Being from the Heart of the Almighty.

I dwell within my Twelve-fold Ray from out of the Great Central Sun...crowned with the Twelve Diamond Rays of Attainment.

I abide upon my Sacred Lotus Throne of Light...letting my Love flow out to all Creation.

"I AM" a Sun in the Infinite Palace of Light...my world the Altar of Infinite Space...my Radiance...the Peace of the Great Solar Quiet.

"I AM" the undying Flame of Life everywhere, the Great Eternal Joy, Glory, Perfection of Existence.

"I AM"..."I AM"..."I AM"...Twelve times Twelve "I AM".

I wear pure golden sandals with ribbons of Light, a Crown made of Sun Rays, a Cloak of God Might. I carry a Scepter, my focus of Power. I pour forth Pure Christ Light each moment...each hour.

Group Avatar

even-Fold Planetary Spine

Twelve-Fold Solar Spine

Planetary	Solar
VIOLET	**YELLOW** Enlightenment, Wisdom, Understanding, Illumination
INDIGO	**GREEN** Truth, Consecration, Dedication, Concentration, Inner Vision
	AQUAMARINE Clarity
BLUE	**BLUE** God's Will, Illumined Faith, Power, Protection
	MAGENTA Harmony and Balance
GREEN	**PINK** Divine Love
	GOLD Eternal Peace
	PEACH Divine Purpose, Enthusiasm, Joy
YELLOW	**RUBY** Healing, Devotional Worship, Ministering Grace
ORANGE	**VIOLET** Forgiveness, Mercy, Compassion, Transmutation, Freedom
	OPAL Transformation
RED	**WHITE** Purity, Restoration, Resurrection, Ascension, Hope

THROUGH THE RAY OF CLARITY, THE TRAPS OF THE WORLD OF ILLUSION ARE REVEALED

During this critical time of Planetary Transformation, there is much confusion and chaos surfacing in people's Lives. The term "New Age" is popping up everywhere, and every conceivable form of psychic-astral entrapment is being placed before the seekers of Truth, creating stumbling blocks that lead us astray. Our belief systems reflect the gamut of extremes from people who believe everything is Light and Love–"there is no such thing as evil," to those who believe that everything existing on Earth is evil–"the work of the devil." We are truly in the latter days, and the Bible warns us continually of the deception that will manifest during these times. We are told that we must have discernment. This is the time of the "false prophets" when Jesus told us we would hear, "Lo, I am here, and lo, I am there", *but* "By their works alone shall they be known."

With the Aquamarine Ray of Clarity now Illuminating the darkness, we can more readily recognize deception. As we are raised up into the Realms of Truth, we begin to perceive and KNOW the Reality of what is occurring on Earth at this time. I would like to share with you now the Inspired Truth pouring into the physical plane on the frequencies of the Ray of Clarity. As you prepare to read these words, ask your Higher Self, the radiant Presence of God anchored in your Heart, to envelope you in an invincible forcefield of God's Will and Protection. Ask that you be filled with the essence of Truth and Divine Perception, so every trace of interference will be cast aside, and you will acknowledge the Truth that will set you Free from the entrapment of the world of illusion.

I know it is uncomfortable to read some of these things, but if we understand the logistics of what is occurring on Earth now, we can easily lift ourselves above the chaos and progress unencumbered into the Lives of Joy awaiting us in the frequencies of Light.

If there were no such thing as evil, God would not have commanded Humanity to not partake of the tree of knowledge of good and evil, as demonstrated in the allegory of Adam and Eve. God knew that our environment would reflect our consciousness. If we did not know of evil, we would not have that knowledge in our consciousness, and therefore, it would never be reflected in our environment. Unfortunately, we did partake of that tree, and as described in Chapters One and Two, Humanity, at a certain point in our evolution, began experimenting with our Gift of Life in ways that were contrary to God's Will.

It is true that evil was never part of the Divine Plan for Earth. Actually, it was never part of the Divine Plan for any of God's creation, but God gave us the gift of Free Will, and through the abuse of that gift, WE, *the Children of God, created evil.*

Never, since the beginning of Creation, has a single electron of Light come forth from the Heart of God that is less than Perfection. This is true of all of God's Creations, every particle of Life in all the Universe.

The original Divine Plan was that we, as Children of God, would enter the physical plane of existence and use our creative faculties of thought and feeling to manifest Perfection in the world of form, thus becoming co-creators with our Father-Mother God, as we evolved back into the Octaves of Perfection.

When we began to use our Free Will to create thoughts and feelings that were not in alignment with God's Will, the negative energy released in such activities began to accumulate in the atmosphere of Earth. Negative thoughtforms and discordant feelings began to form a veil around the Planet, and as Humanity misqualified more and more energy through the abuse of Free Will, the veil became thicker and thicker. *All energy is intelligent Life,* and as this negativity became denser and denser, it began to form a mind of its own. It began to perceive itself as a lifeform separate from God, and even began to see itself as being independently sustained and powerful. In actuality, this accumulation of negativity had separated from God. Since it was humanly created through our Free Will choice, God would in no way interfere with its development. God, however, would not release one electron of energy to sustain this human miscreation. Therefore, the only way this realm of chaos could survive was by Living parasitically off of Humanity's negativity.

Each time we sent forth negative thoughts or feelings, we fed this veil of illusion now known as the psychic-astral realm. Throughout time, this realm of chaos grew. Every inhumane thing Humanity did to another part of Life added to this cloud of darkness around the Planet. This psychic-astral plane is seething with the etheric records and memories of the atrocities Humanity has perpetrated on our fellow Human Beings throughout time, as well as our abuse of every other part of Life. This HUMANLY CREATED psychic-astral realm is the dimension referred to in the world religions as "hell".

Many of the world religions teach that, if we are "bad", we will go to "hell" when we leave this physical plane. On some levels that concept may be perceived as true. When we leave the physical plane through so-called "death", we are magnetized into the frequency of energy that is compatible with our level of consciousness or spiritual development. We can observe the behavior patterns of some people in the physical plane and determine very destructive levels of consciousness. When these people "die", they don't sit on a white cloud and play a harp for eternity. They are drawn to their like vibration. Consequently, these destructive souls end up in the psychic-astral plane and are trapped there until, *through their own Free Will choice,* they decide to move into the Light and into the higher schools of learning in the Heavenly Realms where they are prepared to again enter the schoolroom of Earth. Because some of these souls refuse to move into the Light, they often remain in this dimension known as "hell" for what seems an eternity.

With this greater level of insight, we can see that the very dense, dark frequencies of the psychic-astral plane contain not only the records and memories of Humanity's negative thoughts, feelings, words and actions accumulated over time, but this realm also contains trapped souls that have fallen far from Grace. These discarnate souls, many of them trapped in this "hell" for hundreds of years, have become so destructive that frequently they are perceived as demonic or satanic entities in both appearance and consciousness.

In the Biblical teachings of the latter days, we were told that there would be a time when "Satan would be loosed on the Earth." This is occurring not as God's punishment, but simply as a sequential step in the process of Planetary Transformation. It is VERY IMPORTANT that we clearly understand what is occurring on Earth during this time of change, not to instill fear or concern, but rather to give us the incentive to Protect ourselves and lift ourselves up out of the chaos. It is imperative that we KNOW the psychic-astral realm has ABSOLUTELY NO POWER OVER THE LIGHT! The greatest influence this dimension has over us is for us to believe it doesn't exist. Then, we don't Protect ourselves, and we carelessly open ourselves up to the forces of imbalance, which are struggling to survive by feeding off of our negativity. We do not have to do battle with this realm. *We need merely invoke the Light and lift ourselves above it.*

The reason for the increased confusion and interference from the psychic-astral realm at this time is because of the awakening taking place within the Hearts of all Humanity. The Divine Fiat has been issued, and this Blessed Planet is being called Home to Her Divine Heritage of Heaven on Earth. The discord and the negativity of the psychic-astral realm cannot move forward into the Octaves of Perfection. The intelligent Life in this dimension of chaos is aware that it is in the process of being Transmuted. This dimension is vibrating at such a frequency of pandemonium that it cannot perceive it is being given the opportunity to move into the Light at an accelerated pace. Instead, it thinks it is being destroyed and is desperately fighting for its Life. It is striving with every fiber of its being to prevent Humanity from recognizing our own Divinity. It is ever-vigilant, waiting for opportunities to deceive and confuse the seekers of Truth. This force of imbalance is well aware that, once we tap the Power of God within our Hearts, we will not be feeding the psychic-astral plane any longer with our destructive behavior patterns, thoughts and feelings.

Remember, God will not give one electron of energy to sustain this humanly created realm of chaos. The only way it survives is through our negative energy. When we stop misqualifying our Gift of Life and become one with our God Presence "I AM", this realm will be dissipated and Transmuted forever. In the meantime, it is diabolically working to prevent us from attaining our eternal Victory in the Light.

Whatever we put our attention and energy into, we draw into our Lives, so we must not dwell on the forces of imbalance or the psychic-astral realm, but we must be informed and aware of the deceit and traps they create to snare us.

The increased Light of God is entering the physical substance of Earth at an atomic cellular level. Any frequencies of vibration that are discordant are being pushed to the surface to be quickly Transmuted into Harmony. This purification is causing extreme imbalances all over the Earth, particularly in the psychic-astral realm. Because of this fact, we are experiencing what the Bible referred to as "Satan being loosed on the Earth."

The intelligences within the psychic-astral plane, which I will refer to as the "forces of imbalance", are using their cunning powers of deception in ways that would boggle our finite minds. BUT, IF OUR MOTIVES ARE ALWAYS THAT WE ARE STRIVING TO BE THE GREATEST FORCE OF GOD LIGHT POSSIBLE, IN DEEP HUMILITY, WITH NO SENSE OF SELF-AGRANDIZEMENT, OUR GOD PRESENCE WILL GIVE US THE NECESSARY DISCERNMENT NOT TO BE LED ASTRAY, **IF WE ASK!!!**

At the present time many, many people are being deceived by the forces of imbalance, and are being led away from their Divine Plans. We must realize that the forces of imbalance whisper "sweet nothings" in our ears and tell us whatever we need to hear to feed our egos. They do not say, "I'm the sinister force, and I've come to ruin your Life." They say, "I'm God. Follow me." This treachery is occurring now as never before. Daily and hourly, sincere Lightworkers are being tricked into being used as pawns for the forces of imbalance. This is definitely a time when we MUST NOT CONFUSE SINCERITY WITH TRUTH. Many of the people who have been ensnared are now obliviously leading other people astray themselves.

Humanity is currently being bombarded with every conceivable form of gimmick or psychic trick. Unfortunately, most of these traps are being called "New Age." Consequently, *the Truth of the New Age* is getting lost in the illusion of the "New Age," and many people are rejecting the Reality of what is occurring on Earth at this time because of all the fraud. I want to state clearly, *that is exactly what the forces of imbalance are trying to accomplish.* This intelligence does not have to take us over or possess us. It only needs to confuse and deceive us to the point that we stop growing and fulfilling our Divine Plans, which is certainly what happens when we refuse to accept the Truth. When we reject ALL of the information associated with the New Age because of the confusion, we, in essence, "throw the baby out with the bath water" and play right into the hands of the forces of imbalance.

Interestingly, this force has no Power over us whatsoever other than what we give it. The way we most frequently get involved with this realm of deception is by naively giving our Power away to other people, and by willingly giving this force dominion over us by listening to its lies and buying into its charades.

At the present time, there are myriad ways in which we are being trapped and deceived: psychics, trance channelers, conscious channelers, mediums, spiritualists, hypnotists, past life regressors, life readings, aura readers, astrologers, seances, fortune tellers, palmistry, numerology, graphology, craniology, tea leaf readers, tarot card readers, UFO's, space brothers, extra terrestrials, walk-ins, holistic healers, all kinds of body work and therapies, crystal healers, various "New Age" machines for energy balancing, chakra balancing, psychic phenomenon, ESP, psychokinesis, dowsing, mind control, mind links, astral projection/out of body travel, psychic fairs and seminars, New Age teachers, "living masters," gurus, mantras, mandalas, crystals, ouija boards, pendulums, y-ching, runes and on and on ad infinitum.

Occasionally, some of these things can be utilized as a valid and important part of our growth and development. But often, they can be absolute deception. The problem, of course, is how do we determine if a particular person or technique is an asset or a hindrance to our growth as we strive to become one with our God Presence "I AM".

I used to believe that if a person was not working with the Light it would be obvious. I thought I would be able to easily spot them and avoid their services. Unfortunately, that is not always the case. Because of the cunningness of the forces of imbalance, many sincere people are being tricked into thinking they are reaching the Octaves of Truth, when in actuality, they are being used as pawns of the psychic-astral plane. The forces of imbalance always give us enough Truth to make us think we've reached the Realms of Light, but then they throw in their plan of deception to trap us in darkness. I have experienced dedicated, Loving, sincere people who were genuinely trying to help others according to their wisdom and understanding, but who were, unbeknownst to themselves, being totally manipulated by the forces of imbalance. I will emphatically stress again, THIS IS A TIME WHEN WE MUST NOT CONFUSE SINCERITY WITH TRUTH!!!

It is also a time when we must not deny the opportunity and knowledge being provided to Humanity by the Realms of Truth to assist us during the most intensified activity of Transformation ever manifested in the Earth's evolution. It is a time when we must invoke the Light of Discernment and SEPARATE THE WHEAT FROM THE CHAFF.

The key factor in all of this is Understanding. With the Ray of Clarity Illuminating the darkness, we can easily see how we have been deceived in the past and how to avoid it in the future. Now that we understand there is a veil or forcefield of negative energy surrounding the Planet, it becomes obvious that we must pass through that forcefield in order to reach the Realms of Light. When people go through a near-death experience, and Live to tell about it, they consistently describe "passing through a dark tunnel into the Light." The dark tunnel is the passage through the psychic-astral plane. What is occurring now, unfortunately, is that many people don't accept or understand the Reality of this veil of negativity.

There is a tremendous awakening taking place, and people are becoming more sensitive. They are becoming more clairvoyant, more intuitive, more perceptive. All of this is a perfectly natural part of our growth. It is not supernatural or mystical. It is purely human development–evolution. All of the great Avatars of the past ages developed their extra-sensory perception and came to show us the human potential. Beloved Jesus, with all His gifts and powers said, "These things I do you shall do, and even greater things than these shall you do." As these extrasensory abilities begin to develop in people, they get excited and overanxious. They begin to open up their receiving circuits without caution, and accept whatever they receive. These wave lengths go out as signals into the psychic-astral plane. Discarnate entities trapped in this realm are then magnetized to the unaware person. These entities can say they are anybody. They will tell us they are one of our Loved ones who have died, or they will say they are our "guides," Ascended Masters, or even Jesus. They will whisper "sweet nothings" appealing to our egos, telling us how special or powerful we are. Sometimes, they will even tell us they want to use our bodies to help Humanity. They then ask us to allow them to possess us for a period of time, such as in trance channeling. Initially, the words we hear will always be sweet and Loving. These masters of deception know exactly what to say to convince us they are who they claim to be.

To the neophite just awakening, this seems like a miracle. The more in awe they are, the more they carelessly open up and the more entrapped they become. Before long, the innocent seeker has offered to be an open door for the deceptive force and a pawn to lead Humanity astray.

At the present time there are innumerable trance channels. These are people who willingly allow an entity to take over their bodies. For a time the person leaves their body, and the entity steps in to give a message to Humanity. During the time the entity has control of the channel's body, it is siphoning the Vital Life Force of the body in order to have the strength to animate the vehicle and use the vocal chords. This leaves the channel exhausted and drained. Many trance channels drink alcohol, smoke or take stimulants to keep going.

The messages from trance channels vary from trite ramblings to what appears to be valid information, but remember, we are dealing with the realm of deception. Even if the information appears to be Truth, sooner or later, the "zingers" that will lead us astray will infiltrate the message.

We must Understand, this realm is fighting for what it perceives to be its Life, and it *does not* want us to become Illumined and FREE, for then we will not feed it with negativity. One of the guidelines that will help with our discernment is knowing that when we reach through the psychic-astral realms into the Octaves of Illumined Truth, the Beings of Light abiding there to do God's Will communicate with us *consciously and telepathically*. Ethical Beings DO NOT POSSESS BODIES. No Being of Light would *ever* drain another person's Vital Life Force by taking over his body. If a person is in a trance—meaning out of his body—and an entity has taken over, THE ENTITY IS FROM THE PSYCHIC-ASTRAL PLANE. This is true *regardless* of how sincere the trance channel is, *regardless* of who the entity claims to be or *regardless* of how pure the message appears.

In addition to the entities that brazenly take over another person's body, there are those that control people and manipulate them from a distance. The forces of imbalance can lead us astray by giving false information to the people we seek out to inquire about our Lives. They have the ability to interfere with astrologers, psychics, life readers, hypnotists, past life regressors and all other forms of guidance that reach beyond the physical third dimensional plane.

This realm of deception can also contaminate legitimate tools and healing techniques by working through the person using the particular technique. The energy pouring through the hands, machines, crystals, cards, pendulums, mandalas or whatever the healers are using, IS ONLY AS CLEAR AND PURE AS THE HEALERS THEMSELVES.

Another way this realm of deception leads us astray is by drawing our attention to destructive thoughtforms. What we think about and what we put our Power and attention into, we draw into our Lives. The forces of imbalance are very aware of this Natural Law, and they are feverishly striving to focus our attention on negativity and chaos. All we have to do is observe the incredibly destructive thoughtforms that are being created through the movie industry and the music industry. They are projections straight out of the psychic-astral plane.

The entities working through trance channels are likewise focusing attention on gloom and doom, earthquakes and catastrophies. Even some of the Christian religions are continually empowering the devil through their constant attention, as well as their focus on a possible global holocaust and nuclear war.

Our environment is a reflection of Humanity's consciousness. If the forces of imbalance can manipulate Humanity into focusing on all the chaos, we can indeed bring all the destructive predictions into manifestation. If however, we choose to focus our attention on the Light of God, we can Transform this Planet into Heaven on Earth which is the invocation and prediction of the Lord's Prayer.

This information is coming forth now, not to condemn or judge anyone, but rather to protect and assist the seekers of Truth. It is extremely rare that anyone is deliberately and consciously allowing themselves to be used as a pawn of the negative force.

However, the reality is that anytime we are using extrasensory abilities, dealing with knowledge or energy fields beyond the normal five senses, there is the possibility of tapping into the psychic-astral realm by mistake, IF WE DON'T TAKE THE NECESSARY PRECAUTIONS.

With greater knowledge and Clarity on how we are being deceived, we can take the necessary steps to protect ourselves and lift ourselves up into the Realms of Truth where we belong. Then, we will truly be the effective teachers and healers we are striving to be.

The good news is that the psychic-astral realm of deception has absolutely no Power over the Light. It also has no ability whatsoever to possess us or interfere with our Lives unless we give it the Power to do so, which as I have explained, is usually done innocently through over-enthusiasm and lack of awareness.

If we will take the time to consistently establish an invincible Forcefield of Protection around ourselves and be patient enough to wait until we have raised up in consciousness and vibration through the psychic-astral plane into the Realms of Illumined Truth *before* we allow ourselves to open up, the forces of imbalance won't be able to touch us or whisper "sweet nothings" in our ears to lead us astray.

The ultimate goal of the awakening taking place is for each of us to become so in tune with our God Presence "I AM" that we are able to easily reach into the Realms of Illumined Truth for guidance without having to depend on *any* outside source. Only our God Presence knows exactly what our Divine Plan is, and He/She is constantly prodding and prompting us forward to fulfill that plan. Only our God Presence will lead us UNERRINGLY to our highest potential. This should be a Communion we strive for daily in our meditations.

As we invoke the Light of Discernment, we will clearly see that, if the motive of *anyone* at this critical time on Earth, is to teach us anything other than how to go within and tap the force of our own Divinity for guidance and Illumination, they are *not* serving our highest good.

All of the tools, all of the gifts, all of the techniques, are only being given to us at this time to accelerate the process of *re-unification with our God Presence.*

In Chapter One the exercise "Getting In Touch With Our Higher Selves (page 53) is specifically designed to protect us and lift us up past the confusion of the psychic-astral plane, so we can safely commune with our God Presence and the Beings of Light in the Realms of Illumined Truth. I recommend you use this process each and every time you meditate to secure your safe passage through the psychic-astral plane into the Octaves of Light.

In addition to this exercise for meditation, we must *always* envelop ourselves in a Forcefield of Protection first thing in the morning and feel it secured around us throughout the entire day, as we go about our business. Then as we retire at night, we must again reinforce our Protection so it will be sustained throughout the night. The discipline of Protecting ourselves in Forcefields of Light should be as automatic as breathing. Once we truly establish the habit, we'll feel naked without our Mantle of Light.

MANTLE OF LIGHT DECREE
Beloved Presence of God "I AM" in me, I gratefully

acknowledge in my mind and accept in my feelings the Living Reality of your Mantle of Electronic Light Substance enfolding me in a blazing aura of ever-expanding Protection.

From within my Heart I feel the pulsation of the Flame of Divinity, the Presence of The Christ, radiating through my consciousness . . . through which flows at all times the virtues, qualities, and blessings from God to me and through me to all Life everywhere.

I also acknowledge and accept the mighty armor of Light and invincible momentum of Faith so Lovingly offered to me by Archangel Michael and my own Angel of Protection, and with Loving conviction, I decree:

The Light of God is Eternally Victorious (3 times)

I Live this day in God Light (3 times)

God is in control wherever "I AM" (3 times)

THE HARMONY OF MY TRUE BEING

IS MY ULTIMATE PROTECTION

I do now invoke the added assistance of God's magnificent First Ray. I see a sword of Blue Flame extending from my Crown Chakra, down my spinal column and out through the bottoms of my feet. It radiates out through my four lower bodies cutting FREE, cutting FREE, cutting FREE anything that is not of the Light.

"I AM" now forming around my four lower bodies a ring of blazing White Light. This is a "ring pass not of Flame" which prevents anything that is not of the Light from penetrating into the space around me.

Being projected into my forcefield now are bolts of Violet Lightning from the Heart of God which instantly Transmute every trace of inharmony, every negative thought, word, feeling or action back into God's Perfection.

"I AM" now placing Blazing Sapphire Blue Crosses in front of me, in back of me, on either side, above and below me, establishing the invincible guard of God's First Ray of Protection.

Finally, my entire forcefield is encapsulated in a frequency of Pure Light from the Fifth Dimension. It is a mirror-like substance that makes me invisible and invulnerable to all not of the Light. It is called The Mirror, Blue Substance of Invisibility. When any negativity peers into my Forcefield, it is merely reflected back onto itself for Transmutation into the Light.

Beloved Presence of God "I AM" . . . keep this ACTIVITY OF LIGHT sustained around me and my world, so that only the WILL OF GOD may manifest in ALL my activities, in ALL places and at ALL times.

I make this call... As *God's* Most Holy Name "I *AM*"

As we daily invoke this Forcefield of Protection, it will build in momentum. Gradually, we will know and feel its tangible, physical Reality, and as we become familiar with all of its aspects, we will be able to secure them in a flash with a single thought. Through this activity, our eternal VICTORY IN THE LIGHT will be assured.

> Available Tape Associated With This Chapter Is:
>   K. CLARITY
> See page *xxiv* for more information and order blanks.

CHAPTER 9

THE NINTH ASPECT OF DEITY IS HARMONY

COLOR – MAGENTA NINTH RAY

THE NINTH UNIVERSAL LAW OF HARMONY

THE ATTRIBUTES OF HARMONY ARE:

BALANCE
SOLIDITY
ASSURANCE
CONFIDENCE IN BEING IN THE WORLD
BUT NOT OF IT
FOCUS ON THE EARTH ELEMENT
PHYSICAL SUBSTANCE
THE SACRED SUBSTANCE OF
THE BODY NATURE OF HUMANITY

HARMONY AND BALANCE
THE PATH TO OUR ETERNAL FREEDOM

Beloved Presence of God "I AM"...Oh Beloved Immortal Victorious Three-fold Flame of Life...EXPAND within us, and in the fullness of Your Divine Powers, raise us into Your Mighty Perfection. Blaze forth visible to the sight of all Life, and enfold all within Your dazzling Presence of Harmony and Balance. May all Humanity hear and obey Your Mighty Command for Perfection to manifest NOW upon the Earth. Reveal Your Eternal Law of Life...the Mighty TRUTH and REALITY of Your Own Being. Set all Life FREE, and hold Your Dominion within us and all Humanity forever. The Beloved Immortal Victorious Three-fold Flame of Almighty God is within each Holy Temple. Let all the Life on Earth adore Its Mighty Power and be at Peace...in humble, willing, adoring, Illumined Obedience to this...our ONE SUPREME SOURCE OF LIFE!

Through the HARMONY of my True Being, I perceive and externalize, every minute, PERFECT HEALTH in every cell, organ and electron of my four lower bodies.

Through the HARMONY of my True Being, I receive and externalize, every minute, GOD SUPPLY in limitless abundance filling my every need.

Through the HARMONY of my True Being, I create and externalize, every minute, an AURA OF PERFECT PEACE, HARMONY AND BALANCE which acts as a natural conductor of God's Will to all Life wherever "I AM."

Through the HARMONY of my True Being, I perceive and externalize, every minute, the WILL OF THE FATHER in Understanding, Illumination and Freedom.

Group Avatar

Within the Immortal Victorious Three-fold Flame of God blazing in our Hearts, pulsates the Kingdom of Harmony. By the complete surrender of our outer consciousness, our human personality or ego, to the Immortal Three-fold Flame of Divinity within, we allow the Kingdom of Harmony the full God authority to act through us. Through this radiance of Harmony, we will clearly hear the guidance of the "still, small voice within," and we will allow it to produce and sustain for us our Eternal Freedom. The God authority of this Sacred Flame of Harmony will produce Peace in our feelings, our minds and our etheric records, as well as our physical bodies.

As we daily practice the surrender of the outer personality to the Flame of God in our Hearts, we find that the Kingdom of Harmony within begins to externalize, and our Lives and environments are Transformed. Perfection and Beauty manifest all around us, and we finally realize what the term "Heaven on Earth" really means.

Often, people believe, in order for energy to be Harmoniously qualified, it must be spent in devotion, prayer, ceremonial services and solemn invocations directly concerned with spiritual aspirations. The Truth is that anything we do constructively and Lovingly is a natural Harmonious expression of our gift of God's Life, whether it be helping a friend, performing some needed chore with Enthusiasm, fulfilling our jobs with Joy or interacting with friends and Loved ones Peacefully. Any activity we participate in, if done in an attitude of Love and Joy, will raise us into the vibration of the Kingdom of Harmony within. Daily and hourly, we receive many opportunities to deal with our Life experiences Harmoniously. Each time we choose Harmony over discord, we are raised into an Octave of Peace which is our rightful estate in the Kingdom of Heaven within.

Many times we separate the activities of our daily Lives from our so-called "spiritual work." We often feel that working, cleaning, preparing meals, taking care of children, repairing the car and shopping are all distractions that prevent us from being as spiritual and Harmonious as we would like to be. Actually, our daily activities are the greatest opportunities we have to develop our spiritual skills. Our God Presence "I AM" is always directing us to the exact situations necessary to enable us to practice the skills or disciplines we need to learn most. In order to learn our lessons and Transmute the energy we've misqualified in the past, our actions need not be spiritually qualified, as long as they are constructively and Harmoniously qualified.

This opens the door for a great deal of thought and contemplation. Just think, all of us have responsibilities and moral and monetary obligations. Isn't it wonderful to know our spiritual unfoldment is not delayed by reason of our daily obligations, but rather we can use *any* state of circumstances to accelerate our spiritual unfoldment?

The Law is that Energy MUST BE HARMONIOUSLY RELEASED, not necessarily spiritually released, to insure our Eternal FREEDOM! This literally means that, no matter what we have to do during the day, if we will do it Harmoniously and constructively with Joy, it will enhance our spiritual growth.

Every single opportunity provided to us during the day is being presented to us by our God Presence to give us the chance to develop the skills we need to become the masters of our Lives. Just think of it–EVERY SINGLE OPPORTUNITY. This means there is no such thing as interference or distractions from our growth. Those things that we have always considered a nuisance, a bore, a problem or a hindrance to our spiritual advancement are, in fact, the very experiences we need to perpetuate our growth.

Isn't that a wonderful thought? We can now enter into each and every day with a feeling of enthusiasm and expectation, knowing that no matter what happens, it is the perfect opportunity we need to practice the Law of Harmony and develop the skills we need to attain our Eternal Freedom. What a Blessing!

Harmoniously qualified energy is invulnerable. We must consistently draw it forth from the Flame of Divinity in our Hearts, and utilize it with every thought, word, action or feeling we express. Harmony is an assurance against chaos. It is our responsibility to maintain a Harmonious flow of our own God Energy regardless of what external disturbances might manifest in our Lives. We usually guard our worldly possessions with great care, but we allow the most precious possession of all–our Harmony–to be shattered on the slightest pretext of an unkind word, a challenging situation, fear, anger and a multitude of other instances.

When we consciously and constantly maintain Harmony, there will be no set of circumstances or experiences of seeming importance that will have the power to throw us off center or cloud our awareness of the omnipresent, omnipotent and omniscient Presence of God within our Hearts. In our cloak of Harmony and Balance we will be fearless, undaunted, protected and a source of blessing to all.

All of the qualities and aspects of God pouring into the Planet to benefit the evolving consciousness of Humanity and all Life are embodied in the essence of Harmony and Balance. Whether it is the Harmony that radiates through Divine Purpose and Ordered Service, or the Harmony which comes from Wisdom and Understanding, the Harmony within Divine Love and Beauty, or the Harmony which encompasses the Scientific Balance of Life, the Harmony of Devotional Worship, Forgiveness and Freedom, or the Harmony of our ultimate Ascension in the Light, every single facet of God pulsates within a forcefield of the uninterrupted frequency of Divine Harmony.

As we grow and aspire to Godliness so we may be of greater service to this Blessed Planet, we must take concerted, conscious effort to monitor the Life Force flowing through us moment to moment. In order to constructively and Harmoniously use ALL of the energy of our Lifestream, we need to *stop* the conscious churning of thought processes such as impatience, irritation, thoughtless words, and frustration. These activities requalify God's Pure Life Energy with discord and chaos. As long as we are undisciplined in this area, our God Presence will not increase our Gift of Life, and we will be limited in our ability to serve Humanity. If we are still capable of having an emotional outburst and contaminating that precious Gift of Life with negative frequencies of vibration, our God Self will withhold it from us as an act of Mercy and Justice until we learn to dispense the small allotment of Energy we now receive from God constructively. Needless to say, negativity interferes with our effectiveness and our ability to be the Powerful Force of good on Earth that we have the potential of being.

When we become Balanced and Harmonious, and the

energy released through our bodies is NEVER qualified discordantly, there will be no such thing as the deterioration we presently associate with old age or disease. When we release our vehicles at the close of that phase of our Earthly experience through the process we now call death, we will be in as perfect a condition as when our Holy Christ Self first magnetized the unformed primal Life substance into physical form before the "fall of man". If we focus our attention on the vibratory actions we allow to pass through our bodies, and qualify those actions *only* with Harmony and Balance, we will experience a state of perpetual Beauty and vibrant Health. With the knowledge now pouring into the Earth from the Realms of Illumined Truth, we have the opportunity to create bodies, through the correct application of the Law of Harmony, more glorious than we could ever imagine. Not only do we have the opportunity to do so, we have the *responsibility* to do so. The Holy Christ Self of each one of us is as beautiful as the most perfect Celestial Being we could possibly conceive. If we will consecrate and dedicate our precious Life Energy to the Law of Harmony, our Holy Christ Selves will duplicate that beauty and perfection through our physical bodies.

If we choose to put forth the necessary effort to discipline ourselves through self-control, we will be marvelous examples before the world, and we will prove the Kingdom of Harmony within far more powerfully than our verbal declarations ever could.

It's time to take inventory of our behavior patterns to see what improvements we can make, individually and collectively. What changes do we need to make in order to externalize absolute, unconditional Harmony? What changes will insure our inexhaustible strength, energy and perfect health? What changes will accelerate our infinite supply of all good and the abundance of God? What will activate the amplification of every facet of Perfection?

This is the assignment being given to us by the Octaves of Truth. We are being asked to become the permanent manifestation of Harmony, Beauty and Perfection on Earth NOW. Through the orbits of our own individual worlds, our homes and spheres of influence, we must be the examples of Truth.

Within our very physical forms is the Presence of the Almighty Living God, the Presence that enables us to say "I AM". We must return to that fundamental Truth within ourselves. The Presence of the Living God within us must be given full dominion over our four lower bodies: our physical actions, our etheric records and memories of the past, our thoughts and our feelings. Our creed or faith is not as important as it is that, through our creed of faith–whatever it may be–we contact the Presence of God blazing within our Hearts and become One with that resplendent Presence. Through this activity, God's Perfection will surge forth into our world.

It has been Cosmically ordained that the Permanent Golden Age must now manifest on Earth. A Golden Age is to be the permanent state of our Earth and all who are so blessed as to remain upon Her to continue their evolution back to the Heart of our Father-Mother God.

Those Lifestreams who choose not to move forward into the frequencies of Perfection with this Sweet Earth shall find hospitality on another star evolving at a slower pace, but this Planet and ALL WHO ARE WILLING shall move forward into Freedom. We can each assist through our own endeavors to become One with our God Presence, thus externalizing that Perfection in the physical plane of Earth.

As we become One with the Presence of God within, our four lower bodies become refined, and we develop a consciousness of Listening Grace. Then, in times of crisis, we will be the "open door" through which the Perfection of God will pour to Harmonize and Balance all Life. When we are in a state of Listening Grace, we are the hands and feet of God in the physical world of form. We are the lips through which He speaks. We are the eyes through which He blesses all Life. When our vehicles are unwieldy, when they are heavy and discordant, it is impossible for God to project the full force of His Radiant Assistance through us. If we are inharmonious at the moment when service is needed, God cannot direct a Ray of Light through us with sufficient intensity to reach the outer consciousness and earnest Hearts of Humanity.

This is very important for us to comprehend, for in the days to come, GOD REQUIRES MIGHTY TRANSFORMERS, OPEN PORTALS OF LIGHT ALL OVER THE EARTH, Lifestreams in a constant state of HARMONY, BALANCE and LISTENING GRACE, ready to receive the Light from God in an instant. This is the responsibility of the Lightbearers on Earth at this critical time of Planetary Transformation. *You*, Dear Hearts, who have come to Love this Planet Free, are the Lightbearers and The Cosmic Moment is NOW!

VEDANTIC PRAYER

Oh, Thou Infinite Holy Presence of God, the Divine Source of all Life...Hallowed be Thy Sacred name! We bow before Thee in Gratitude, Praise, and Thanksgiving for Thy Supreme Presence in the Universe–because Thou art "I AM".

We return to Thee, Almighty One, all the Power and Dominion we have ever vested in any imperfect manifestation, visible or invisible, for Thou art the All-Power of the Universe, and there is no other Power that can act. Let Thy Will be done in and through us NOW. Let Thy Kingdom of Harmony be manifest across the face of this Earth through the Heart Flames of all who are so blessed as to Live upon Her now.

Oh, Supreme Beloved One, as we lift our Hearts, our Vision, our Consciousness toward Thee, release the Substance of Thyself to us, each according to our requirements, that as we move forward in Thy Name, and upon Thy Service, we shall not be found wanting.

We ask Forgiveness for all the transgressions of Thy Law of Love and Harmony, both for ourselves and all Humanity, the Forces of the Elemental Kingdom and the Kingdom of Nature. Endow us now with Thy Power and Desire to so Forgive all who have ever caused us distress back unto the very beginning of time.

Because we are One with Thee, we fear no evil, for there is no Power apart from Thee. Thou Art the Strength and the Power by which we move ever in the Path of Righteousness–and

NOW—Oh Father-Mother God—show us the FULL GLORY we had with Thee in the beginning before even this world was ...SO BE IT!

Group Avatar

AFFIRMATION OF DEDICATION AND CONSECRATION

O Thou Mighty Supreme Source of all Life, "I AM"! As I enter deep within the Balancing Flame of LOVE, WISDOM, and POWER within my Heart, I consciously ACCEPT THEE as the Creator and Giver of all things, and that Thou Art in all Life, and I KNOW that "I AM" is the LIGHT OF THE WORLD.

I relinquish NOW, in Thy Name, all the Power I have ever given to the outer self; all the Power I have ever given to others; all the Power I have ever given to the shadows I have created.

I DEDICATE and CONSECRATE my conscious mind and feelings to knowing that, as I think, speak and walk, the PRESENCE OF GOD within me is widening the BORDERS of THY KINGDOM OF HARMONY!

"I AM" A LIGHT BEARER!
"I AM" THE LIGHT OF THE WORLD!

"I AM" the Master Presence grown to full stature, clothed with the Immortal Victorious Three-fold Flame of God "I AM" and through the Power of the Almighty Presence of God "I AM"!

I HAVE SPOKEN! I HAVE DECREED! and
I HAVE COMMANDED WITH AUTHORITY!...for

"I AM" THAT "I AM" within these Invocations!
"I AM" THAT "I AM" WITHIN these Affirmations!
"I AM" THAT "I AM" within this Cosmic Power,
supplying, sustaining, and fulfilling it each hour!
AS GOD'S HOLY NAME..."I AM"!

Group Avatar

THE TWELVE UNIVERSAL LAWS

For quite some time the scientific world has studied the physical Laws on this Planet. Now, it is time for us to reach higher, and through the Ray of Clarity, evaluate the Spiritual Laws governing our Universe. As we understand more about these Laws and learn to Live our Lives in co-operation with them, our forward progress on the path to self-mastery will be greatly enhanced.

These Laws, which work together as one unified whole, bring only Harmony and Balance. Any conflict or turmoil we experience in the world is merely the end result of ignoring or misusing the Universal Spiritual Laws.

Spiritual Laws are the mechanisms which serve to keep the Universe in order, and which provide the Balance necessary for all existence. They are constant and have remained so since the beginning of creation. They are pure, true expressions of the Divine Ideal which exists in every part of Life. They are inviolate and will never be changed, distorted or eliminated.

All creation is, at some level of consciousness, aware of the Universal Laws, and also has the Free Will to choose whether or not to co-operate with them or obey them. The Laws do not change for circumstances, situations or individuals. The circumstances, situations or individuals may choose to disregard the Laws or violate them, but that does not alter the intent of the Law. We must realize, however, that if we disregard a Spiritual Law, a consequence is brought into existence because of that violation.

These Laws are mechanisms of Universal Harmony and Balance. For us to stray or deviate from these Laws means that we call into existence a disharmony that is in direct proportion to the magnitude of the deviation.

On an individual basis, this usually means there is something amiss or out of order in our personal Lives. On a collective level, the effects are, at times, cumulative. Mass transgressions result in massive consequences. Aggression, poverty, disease, turmoil, discomfort and tension are all ramifications of these consequences.

Sometimes it appears as though people are going through

challenges that seem out of proportion to their deviation of the Law. *This is never the case*. The Laws are accurate and just to the letter, and no one is a victim. We are always going through exactly the learning experience we need to be going through to propel us toward our Eternal Freedom. These challenges occur by Universal Law not to plague us or punish us, but rather, to allow us to experience the results of our actions, and to give us the opportunity to Transmute our misqualified energy. Through this process, we learn to co-operate with the Universal Laws.

This information on Universal Laws is for our OWN growth and self-mastery. *NEVER SHOULD IT BE USED TO JUDGE ANOTHER PERSON'S STATE OF AFFAIRS*.

Throughout Humanity's sojourn on Earth, these Laws have been in existence. Since the "fall of man", they have been misunderstood and misapplied. The severity of the disobedience has determined the severity of the consequence. There is a direct relationship between the chaos on Earth and the transgression of the Universal Laws.

Divine Order and Harmony are God's Will for this Universe. The Universal Laws have been implemented to insure the continuance of Divine Order and Harmony. They are self-regulating, self-perpetuating mechanisms. Everything is subject to these Laws, and the Laws influence everything. All work together as a Unified Whole. If we will contemplate these Laws and implement them into our Lives daily and hourly, moment to moment, we will experience a Balance and Harmony beyond our greatest dreams.

Truth, Honesty and Integrity are qualities that will enable these Laws to be maintained and expressed according to God's Will.

If we will base our actions in Life on these principles, Eternal Peace will be our experience. As our individual worlds begin to reflect this Peace, the world around us will likewise be influenced, and the effect of Eternal Peace will be exponential.

The Ninth Ray of Harmony and Balance is now securely anchored in the physical dimension of Earth. Gradually, the frequencies of this Magenta Ray will be experienced by all Life evolving here, and soon each Lifestream will more clearly perceive the reality of Balance and Harmony in all existence.

Contemplate these Laws now, and ask your God Presence to flash the Ray of Clarity through your conscious mind, empowering you to perceive deeper Truths than you have ever comprehended. This will enable you to clearly see how these Universal Laws apply to your everyday Life, thus giving you greater knowledge and understanding to fulfill your Divine Plan.

THE TWELVE UNIVERSAL LAWS

1. The Law of ENERGY – LIGHT
   THE FIRST CAUSE OF GOD
   "LET THERE BE LIGHT".

All that exists in the Universe is LIGHT–Electronic Light Substance–ENERGY. Every particle of Life existing in any frequency of vibration or dimension is comprised of electrons–energy vibrating at different frequencies and different densities. From the Heart of God there are sent forth on every breath, countless numbers of Electrons, intelligent Beings, all vibrating with the totality of God's Perfection. They are our Gift of Life. As this intelligent Life Energy pours forth from the Heart of God, it carries to all manifest form the gifts of Health, Illumination, Understanding, Prosperity, Love and every other aspect of God's God's Perfection. These Beings of Light, the Electrons, are given into the Heart of the Mighty "I AM" Presence of every Human Being. They likewise pour through every Elemental and Angelic Presence.

These precious Beings are selfless servants of God, and as they pour forth from the very Heart of God, they Joyously and anxiously await their opportunity to serve Life. They eagerly await passage from the unformed essence of Primal Light into the world of form. As the God Presence of each Lifestream receives these Beings of Light, they are blessed and sent forth to the human personality in a rhythmic pulsation. The Hope is that these pure Beings can pass through the consciousness of the person and give their gifts to the Universe without being contaminated with Humanity's misuse of Free Will.

Unfortunately, since the "fall of man", as these Beings of Light leave the aura of the individual "I AM" Presence, they are catapulted by the emotions, thoughts, and vibratory actions of the human personality, and thus, their journey into the Universe is completely disrupted by the disintegrating forces of the uncontrolled consciousness through which they must pass. Their radiant Light is all but extinguished, and they pass from the person's Heart into the physical plane with practically no animation or Light left in their Beings.

Our responsibility now to this First Universal Law, is that we must stop desecrating our precious Gift of Life. We must lift up in consciousness and recognize what a sacred privilege it is to be given the honor of allowing these Beings of Light to pass through us as we use our creative faculties of thought and feeling. When we truly cognize the magnitude of this privilege, we will develop a Reverence for Life that will prevent us from ever thoughtlessly using our Gift of Life in a way that would reflect anything other than the Perfection of God. We will also selflessly commit to Transmuting the mass accumulation of Humanity's misqualified energy back to its original vibration of Perfection, restoring its radiant emanation of LIGHT. Then, the First Cause of God—PERFECTION FOR ALL THINGS—will be fulfilled.

2. The Law of AS ABOVE, SO BELOW
ENLIGHTENMENT

Everything in the Higher Realms of Perfection is reflected in the physical world of form onto matter, resulting in HEAVEN ON EARTH.

In the original Divine Plan, our purpose was to perceive the Perfection of the Heavenly Realms through the eyes of our God Presence, then project that Perfection onto physical matter through our creative faculties of thought and feeling. Through this process, we were to become Masters of physical energy, co-creators with God, and attain our Enlightenment.

With the "fall of man" and the creation of the veil of maya

or illusion around the Planet, we lost consciousness of our God Presence, and we lost the ability to perceive the Heavenly Realms. When this occurred, the Second Universal Law could no longer be accurately applied by Humanity; consequently, the Earth plane began to reflect disease, chaos and disintegration instead of Heaven on Earth—AS ABOVE—SO BELOW.

The physical plane is, at any given moment, a reflection of Humanity's consciousness. As we raise up in vibration and lift Humanity's consciousness, we will begin to, once again, perceive the Octaves of Perfection, and we will Heal the self-inflicted separation from our God Presence. Then, we will tap the Divine Ideas held in the Mind of God, and we will attain what is known as Enlightenment. Our Glorious God Presence will once again hold dominion within us, and our consciousness will reflect only Perfection. Through our creative faculties of thought and feeling, we will project the Perfection held within the Mind of God onto the physical matter of Earth, and this Blessed Star will once again reflect the verdant splendor of Her Divine Birthright—Heaven on Earth. The Second Universal Law will then be correctly applied by Humanity, and *AS ABOVE, SO BELOW* will be a Reality.

3. The Law of DIVINE LOVE
THE COHESIVE POWER OF THE UNIVERSE

DIVINE LOVE is the Cohesive Power of the Universe which has caused to come into being ALL manifest form, every Sun and Planet in the Galaxy; every Galaxy in the Universe; every Electron of precious Life energy. DIVINE LOVE is the matrix—the nucleus—the magnetic, cohesive Power around which the electronic substance is drawn to create all form. Without the Cohesive Power of Divine Love, all form would cease to be. All in the Universe would return to the unformed, and become again a part of primal Life. Without the Law of DIVINE LOVE, nothing is permanently accomplished. DIVINE LOVE is constancy under the most trying of circumstances and action at the moment when it is required most.

DIVINE LOVE alone is the reason for Humanity's Be-ing. God individualized Himself that there might be more foci through which the DIVINE LOVE principle might flower, and as each individualization of God evolves into the fullness of DIVINE LOVE, there will be Eternal Peace, Security, Contentment and Freedom.

DIVINE LOVE is the enfolding radiance of every part of Life and Intelligence. From the moment we were called forth as innocent Spirit Sparks from the Heart of our Universal Father-Mother God, DIVINE LOVE has sustained us.

The LOVE of our Father-Mother God is incomprehensible to our finite minds. It is an all-encompassing Presence which fills the Universe, and there is no manifest space where DIVINE LOVE does not abide. For us to experience the Law of DIVINE LOVE, we must invoke Its Radiance through our HEART FLAMES, and that LOVE, flowing through us toward the object of our affection, will well up in our Hearts, filling our Beings with Its Ecstasy. As we experience DIVINE LOVE, the Flame of Divinity in our Hearts will expand, and pulsating bands of Light will flow forth from us to bathe all Life. Our Hearts will entwine in PURE DIVINE LOVE with every particle of creation, and, through this association, miracles can be performed to return this Sweet Earth to Her pristine beauty.

We must never underestimate the Power of Divine Love. The more we grow in understanding of this Universal Law, the more we will desire to forge ever onward into the Heart of the One Supreme Source of all Love.

4. The Law of VIBRATION
   ALL THAT EXISTS IS IN PERPETUAL MOTION.
   THE ASCENSION OF MATTER INTO PURITY.

VIBRATION and radiation are co-existent with form. Every electron of Life, even a blade of grass, a flower, a rock or a tree, emits a rate of vibration which affects the Cosmos as a whole, and which, by the undulation of its energy, rearranges the atoms of the entire Universe. Thus, all Life is constantly contributing to the change of the cosmos. The slower the vibration of the electrons comprising the physical form, the denser the matter; the faster the vibrations comprising the physical form, the more refined and rarified the matter.

We are multi-dimensional Beings, functioning simultaneously in several dimensions. The reason we don't usually perceive the other dimensions is because they are vibrating at frequencies beyond the spectrum of our limited physical senses. Our purpose for being in the physical plane is to become masters of energy and VIBRATION. We are being trained, through our Life experience, to influence the vibratory rate of the electronic substance of the Universe in a way that is consciously co-operating with the Divine Design of our Father-Mother God. Our conscious control of the electronic substance, in accordance with God's Plan for Earth, results in our becoming co-creators with God, and it enhances our ability to embrace God Consciousness.

When we comprehend the Law of Vibration, even partially, we will be well on our way to self-mastery. The Power we have to create and change vibration is not only our responsibility, but it is an oportunity by which we can each experience our own Divinity through the Power of Ascending Light.

For millions of centuries we, by accepting individuality, have created vibrations which move from the center of our Beings to the periphery of the Cosmos. We are constantly, throughout the entire course of our individualization, affected by every electron within that cosmic orbit to some degree—just as when we drop a pebble into a pool of water, and we see the ripples expand out in ever-widening circles until they reach the periphery. The ripples then return again to the center, so everything in the pool is affected by the vibrations caused by the activity at the center. From the very moment we took individualization as "I AM", the electronic Light, in obedience to the decree of our Father-Mother God, became our servant. Through our Gift of Free Will, we were allowed to use our creative faculties of thought and feeling to charge the electronic substance with any VIBRATION we desired. As we began to charge the Light substance with vibrations of chaos, the frequencies became slower and denser.

Now, it's time for us to reverse that downward spiral. As we develop the skills and the discipline necessary to Live within the Universal Spiritual Laws, the vibratory rate of our four lower bodies will increase, as well as energy in the Cosmos, through our expanded ripples. Through this process, we will ASCEND in consciousness, and we will become tangibly aware of the Octaves of Perfection. We will then not only believe we are Divine Beings, but we will clearly SEE and KNOW the Reality of that Truth. We will K NOW the Oneness of all Life and Eternally affirm "The Father and I are One".

Through VIBRATION–perpetual motion–change is eminent. Change and growth are natural states of Being and imperative to Life. When we try to cling and hold on to old patterns and forms of existence, it is like trying to still VIBRATION. The end result is great distress and even physical and emotional pain. If we will observe what is taking place on the Earth today, we will see the tangible proof of the pain created when we try to stop VIBRATION or change. Our Planet is not only in a state of change, She is going through a quantum acceleration in VIBRATION. Those Lifestreams resisting the move forward in VIBRATION are experiencing what feels like a "grinding of the gears", literally the "screaming and gnashing of teeth". This is causing excruciating pain, and it is being reflected in every aspect of Life-finances, health, relationships, careers, physical, mental, emotional and spiritual well-being. In order to eliminate the pain, we must *let go* of the old programming, concepts and beliefs of the past that are keeping us stuck. We must accept the opportunity for CHANGE IN VIBRATION Joyously. If we let go of the old frequencies of vibration that are now obsolete, and move forward into the VIBRATIONS of Illumined Truth now pouring into the Planet, we will experience nothing less than the Pure Land of Boundless Splendor and Infinite Light. From this level of awareness, we can consciously charge the vibratory rate of the electronic Light Substance of the Universe with God Qualities of Perfection.

Envision now the unformed electronic Light with every intelligent electron receptive, obedient and alert, waiting to be charged with God's Perfection. We feel the perfect God Quality pulsating through our Heart Flames. The energy waves radiate out from our Hearts in ever-widening circles. We experience the obedient electrons bringing a Healing Benediction to all Life, and we absorb the increased frequency of VIBRATION, as this Planet and all Her Life ASCEND into the Octaves of PURITY.

5. The Law of CYCLES
   THE OUTBREATH AND
   THE INBREATH OF EXISTENCE
   DEDICATION AND CONSECRATION OF LIFE

There are two activities to the cycles of Life and creation. One activity is the OUTBREATH, expressed through radiation, expansion and projection. The other activity is the IN-BREATH, expressed through magnetization, contraction, and absorption. When we observe nature and the evolution of Humanity, we see constant, spiraling cycles of change through the process of involution–OUTBREATH–and evolution–INBREATH; cycles of birth and death; changing of the seasons; ebb and flow of the tides; rising and setting of the Sun; breathing in and breathing out; cause and effect; giving and receiving; silence and sound; stillness and activity; consuming and assimilating; wake and sleep, are reflections of the cycles of OUTBREATH and INBREATH of existence.

The balanced pulsation of these cycles is critical to the fulfillment of our Divine Plans. On the OUTBREATH or the cycle of radiation, expansion, and projection, we breathe out the full gathered momentum of Perfection pulsating within our God Presence "I AM" into the world of form. It expands, Blessing all Life as It flows to the periphery of the Universe. On the INBREATH or the cycle of magnetization, contraction and absorption, we breathe in as we extend in consciousness, inwardly reaching up through our Heart Flames to the Source of never ending Perfection, absorbing greater and greater frequencies of Divinity to Bless and CONSE-CRATE all Life.

On the cycle of the INBREATH, we are literally "filling the cup of our consciousness."

On the cycle of the OUTBREATH, we are giving all Life a "drink from our cup."

When we maintain the perfect BALANCE of these two CYCLES, we will Joyously fulfill our Divine Plans, DEDI-

CATING and CONSECRATING ourselves to the original pathway for our return journey home, the ever-spiraling, upward cycles into the Heart of our Father-Mother God.

6. The Law of CAUSE AND EFFECT
   THE LAW OF THE CIRCLE
   MINISTRATION AND DEVOTION

The Law of Cause and Effect is reflected in many of the terms used to express the scientific principles of physics, such as action and reaction; like attracts like; radiation and magnetization. Simply stated, the Law of Cause and Effect indicates that whatever energy we send out through our thoughts, words, actions and feelings (CAUSE), returns to us in our everyday Life experience (EFFECT). At any given moment, our individual Lives are reflecting the accumulated energy we have used during our sojourn on Earth. Our Lives also reflect how we have chosen to use our Gift of Free Will, and how we have chosen to qualify the electrons we have been given by God as our precious Gift of Life.

The situations, conditions and experiences now manifesting in our Lives are the direct result of the thoughts, words, actions and feelings we have chosen to express in the past. Our behavior patterns and belief systems are the CAUSE that continually create their EFFECT in our Lives. We need to evaluate our present Life situations and see if we need to change or improve the CAUSE we are setting into motion. We need to ask ourselves:

Am I healthy?
Am I financially free?
Am I involved in Loving relationships?
Am I happy and thrilled with Life?
Am I accomplishing my purpose?
Am I growing spiritually?
Am I reaching my highest potential?

If the answer to any one of these questions is anything less than a resounding YES!, then we need to change what we are projecting onto the electronic substance of Life through our thoughts, words, actions and feelings, and create NEW CAUSES that will result in NEW EFFECTS. We are the creators of circumstance, not victims. What we put our attention and energy into, what we think and feel, we bring into form. If we will only change our thoughts, feelings and behaviors (CAUSES), we will change our Lives (EFFECTS). Then we will fulfill our purpose, and through our Ministration and Devotion to all Life, we will set this Blessed Planet Free.

7. The Law of TRANSMUTATION
THE LIGHT OF GOD IS ALWAYS VICTORIOUS

Darkness cannot be sustained in the presence of Light! All discord is a misqualification of our precious Gift of Life, and is therefore, a HUMAN creation. Only Perfection is eternally sustained, and all discord will, one day, be Transmuted into Light by the very Powerful Universal Law of Transmutation.

We now have the opportunity to invoke the Violet Flame of Transmutation into every electron of discord on Earth, and offer ourselves as an open portal through which *ten times* as much Perfection as has ever been misqualified by us or any part of Life will pour into Earth. We must know and feel *"I AM" THE OPEN DOOR WHICH NO ONE CAN SHUT*.

As we consciously draw the Light of Transmutation into our four lower bodies and all of the physical substance of Earth, the Light will act as an atomic accelerator as It flows into each electron. Each electron will begin to spin more rapidly in its orbit, gradually increasing the vibratory rate of our four lower bodies and all of the physical substance of Earth. This action, if sustained by conscious effort, will bring all Life on Earth to a state wherein discord and imperfection will no longer exist. Through the use of God's limitless Light, we have the ability to rise up and be FREE.

8. The Law of POLARITIES
CLARITY

All energy vibrates with the dual aspects of the Masculine and Feminine Polarities of God.

The Masculine Polarity of God reverberates with the quality of DIVINE WILL. The Feminine Polarity of God reverberates with the quality of DIVINE LOVE. In order for electronic Light substance (primal Life) to manifest as physical form, both the Masculine Polarity (Divine Will) and the Feminine Polarity of God (Divine Love) must be present. As we continue to grow and evolve on Earth, we begin to realize that the balancing of these two polarities within our own Beings is the goal of every Living form. The Masculine Polarity of God is expressed through the left brain hemisphere; the rational, logical, verbal side of our thinking. The Feminine Polarity of God is expressed through the right brain hemisphere; the intuitive, creative, nurturing side of our thinking.

As these two polarities are brought into perfect balance within us, we begin to experience what is known as the birthing of the Son/Daughter Principle of God which is–THE CHRIST–Divine Wisdom, Enlightenment and Understanding–THE CLARITY OF GOD. It is only by Ascending into this level of consciousness that we Heal the self-inflicted separation from God we created through the misuse of our Gift of Life, and return to the realization of our own Divinity. That is why Beloved Jesus brought to us the knowledge and wisdom of the Christ through the example of His perfectly balanced nature of Divine Will and Divine Love. As these polarities of God came into perfect balance within Him, He became the Son of God–The Christ–revealing to all the world the Path of Attainment. In Truth, He spoke "no one returns to the Father except through me–THE CHRIST." It is only through the perfect balance of the Masculine and Feminine Polarities of God that we are raised into the Son/Daughter of God–THE CHRIST–and it is only through this path to Enlightenment that we return to our Father-Mother God.

9. The Law of Harmony
   THE HARMONY OF OUR TRUE BEINGS
   IS OUR ULTIMATE PROTECTION.

Harmony is the Law that lifts us up out of the frequencies of chaos and confusion. If we invoke the Law of Harmony into our Lives, we do not need to do "battle" with the negativity and discord manifesting in the world around us. We need merely accept the flow of God's Harmony, and accelerate our vibratory rate up beyond its reach.

If we surround ourselves with Harmony in every aspect of our Lives; our homes, workplaces, relationships, thought, feelings, etc. and ask God to project the Divine Essence of Harmony into our every activity, we will begin to truly understand what Inner Peace really is.

Harmony is a quality and a Natural Law that enables us to experience the Octaves of Perfection on Earth. It Heals all separation and lifts us into the Oneness of God.

10. The Law of BALANCE
ETERNAL PEACE

Balance in all of our Life experiences enables us to bring into Eternal Peace, the relationship between our physical, mental, emotional and spiritual aspects of Being. Balance brings us to the center of our God Presence. It results in the birth of the Christ within, and brings us into alignment with both the physical and spiritual realms.

Balance enables us to unfold our entire potential, our total God Self. Balance prevents us from creating extremes that lead us astray into confusion.

Balance in all things is the Key to Eternal Peace and Freedom.

11. The Law of PERFECTION
DIVINE PURPOSE, ENTHUSIASM AND JOY
THE FIRST CAUSE OF GOD IS PERFECTION

Divine Will is Perfection in all things. Our purpose and reason for Being is to learn to use our faculties of thought and feeling to create the Perfection of God's Will in the world of form with both Enthusiasm and Joy. Within all manifest form there is a Divine Blueprint known as the Immaculate Concept. The Immaculate Concept for all Life is held in the Mind of God. As we reach up into our God Presence "I AM", we become one with the Mind of God. Then, we are able to clearly see the Divine Blueprint contained within all Life.

Every person, place, condition or thing contains within it the Blueprint of Perfection. Within the core of poverty still pulsates the Perfection of God's Abundance. Within the core of disease still pulsates the Divine Blueprint of Vibrant Health. Within the core of hate still pulsates the Immaculate Concept of Divine Love.

The First Cause of God is only Perfection, and that core of Purity within every electron is invincible. The Law of Perfection assures us that the Perfection of God is the only thing that is Eternal. Anything less than God's Perfection will one day fade away.

12. The Law of ONENESS
    ALL THAT EXISTS IS PART OF
    THE ALL ENCOMPASSING PRESENCE OF GOD.
    TRANSFORMATION

GOD IS Omniscient, Omnipresent, Omnipotent. God is all there is. Every electron of precious Life energy that exists in any dimension is a cell in the Body of God. Every electron has color, sound, fragrance and vibration. All Life is growing, evolving, changing. As we grow, evolve and expand our consciousness, God likewise grows and expands His infinite Body of Perfection. This constant integration and expansion creates never-ending Octaves of Perfection. All Life is interrelated. Every electron of Life affects every other electron of Life. As we evolve and raise ourselves up in vibration and consciousness, all Life is lifted up with us. Every positive thought or feeling we have Blesses all Life on Earth.

It is time for us to grasp the magnitude of what the Oneness of all Life really means, and accept responsibility for our expenditure of energy, thus qualifying our Gift of Life only positively. Then, our Lives will be Transformed as we bless all Life.

As we absorb into the very fiber of our Beings the Truth and Reality of the Twelve Universal Laws, and strive to apply them to our Lives, miraculous things will begin taking place.

AGAIN, REMEMBER, *ANY CONFLICT OR TURMOIL WE EXPERIENCE IN THE WORLD IS MERELY THE END RESULT OF IGNORING OR MISUSING THE TWELVE UNIVERSAL SPIRITUAL LAWS.*

We must ask ourselves what are we contributing to the Universe–depression, confusion, shadow or Harmony, Wisdom, Healing, Peace and Supply of every good thing? Let's resolve each day to bring Peace and Harmony everywhere we move and to the Lives of everyone we come in contact with. The Power to do this is a gift given to us by our Father-Mother God through the Twelve Universal Laws. We can allow this Loving Light to flow in, through and around us as easily as we turn the electric light switch on to Illumine a room. Let's be practical in the application of this knowledge. Every electron which enters our Hearts through the silver cord from our own God Presence "I AM" becomes our responsibility. It flows through our four lower bodies into our world, and eventually returns to us on the Law of the Circle. Therefore, let's daily qualify every thought, word, action or feeling with the Love and Faith of God, renouncing all that is not of the Light. Let's accept and know that we can be the masters of the conditions affecting our Lives on this Earthly plane. Let's correctly apply the Twelve Universal Spiritual Laws and be TRANSFORMED.

Available Tape Associated With This Chapter Is:
    L. HARMONY
See page *xxiv* for more information and order blanks.

CHAPTER 10

THE TENTH ASPECT OF DEITY IS ETERNAL PEACE

COLOR – GOLD
TENTH RAY

THE TENTH UNIVERSAL LAW
OF BALANCE

THE ATTRIBUTES OF PEACE ARE:

THE GREAT SILENCE
INNER CALM
COMFORT
LIBERTY
SPIRITUAL FREEDOM
BALANCE

THE GREAT SILENCE

Silence great!
Silence sweet!
Silence deep within!
COME I now;
HERE I bow...
To Thy LOVE sublime!
QUIET, STILL;
Holy Will...
Here ALL is Divine!
Deep Within...
We are ONE...
SILENCE...
GREAT "I AM"!

The Bridge To Freedom

The Golden Rays of Eternal Peace are now pouring into the Planet on frequencies of Light beyond anything Humanity has ever experienced. Contained within the essence of this perfect Peace is the Great Silence. In the Great Silence we abide within the Heart and Mind of God. We can reach into the Great Silence by going within on the Holy Breath into the Victorious Immortal Three-fold Flame in our Hearts. Within the Great Silence, the Heart and Mind of God await the opportunity to project, through each of us, the gifts and perfection to bless all Life. The hour has now come in our Universal progress, and the Cosmic Fiat has been issued for each Heart Flame to be given full Liberty and Freedom of expression. Our Holy Christ Selves rejoice in the Divine Edict and will, at our invocation, give us every possible assistance in becoming one with the Heart and Mind of God. As this occurs, each one of us will become a Lord of the Flame in accordance with our Divine Destiny.

Within the Great Silence we achieve Perfect Balance in our emotional, mental, etheric and physical vehicles. This enables our God Presence to release the latent Powers within us, and it also enables the abilities we have already developed to be balanced into a state of true mastery.

As the primal Life essence flows to us from the Heart and

Mind of God through the Great Silence into the Three-fold Flames in our Hearts, the Blue Flame qualifies that energy with the Power to do practical works in God's name. The Yellow/Gold Flame Illumines the outer mind as to the constructive use of such Power. The Pink Flame directs the Illumined Power, through Love, for the Blessing of all Life. As we realize what is happening on Earth, we become aware of how very important it is for us to enter the Great Silence, and abide in the Forcefield of Eternal Peace.

These are days of great acceleration. The Earth's axis is being permanently straightened, and the Planet and all Her Life are moving forward in the Light. The vibratory action within our four lower bodies is being stepped up the maximum we can withstand every twenty-four hours. Because of this acceleration, we feel the tendency to hurry. Hurry always tends to bring stress of one kind or another. It is very necessary for us to clearly understand this at the present time, so we will consciously take the time to enter the Silence, and eliminate our feelings to hurry.

Once we enter the Great Silence through the Flame of Divinity within our Hearts, our God Presence "I AM" will flood our daily activities with Perfect Balance and help us to always take the MIDDLE WAY of Eternal Peace. This will enable us to enjoy the benefits of this natural acceleration of the Planet as the Earth moves forward into greater Perfection.

Remaining centered within the Great Silence enables us also to enjoy, in practical, daily Living, greater emotional stability, mental alertness, etheric clarity and more physical strength and energy. We will express balanced poise, dignity, general self-control and great inner Peace. From this extreme center of our Beings, the Virtues of God will stream out from our Hearts, blessing all Life. Our four lower bodies will cease acting independently of the direction of our God Presence, and no outer person, place, condition or thing will have the Power to draw us out of the center of our Being. All that abideth in the Great Silence—the Secret Place of the Most High Living God—shall abide within the Light, Radiation and Power of the Almighty. When we are centered within the Silence of our Heart, we are in control of the vibrant energies that flow from the Heart of God, and we become a Power that can never be thrown off balance.

What usually happens is that in our desire to serve, we rush forth from the center of our Beings, and attach our energies through thought and feeling to those people who require our help and assistance. This actually causes us to forfeit our mastery and interferes with our ability to help and serve them.

If, however, we abide in the Silence of the center of our Being, the Light and Power of our Father-Mother God will beam forth and be the Healing, Comfort, Guidance, Balanced Control, and Peace Commanding Presence of whatever is required to help someone at any given moment. There will be no fear, no uncertainty and no doubt when we dwell within the Great Silence. We can BE all things and DO all things when we are One with the Heart and Mind of God.

From this center, our Father-Mother God moves through us. Our eyes become beams through which God's Light may shine; our hands become conductors of God's Almighty Power; our lips become the instruments by which God's word's are fashioned and directed into the world of form; our feet become the feet of the Master Presence "I AM" moving through the Earth, and our energy becomes a conductor of whatever God desires to do through us at our point in the Universe.

As we are being raised up in vibration and consciousness, we are beginning to understand and know that the Presence of God abiding within the Great Silence of our Hearts is the Hope of our ultimate personal salvation and individual mastery over the substance and energy of any dimension in which our consciousness is required to dwell. The Presence of God "I AM" is within us NOW. It is not some ephemeral Being Who, at some future time, will Transform, Transmute and sublimate all the tendencies, conditions, effects and personal limitation we are manifesting in our Lives. If we will contemplate the Truth that the Presence of God within the Silence of our Heart is capable of Transformation and sublimation of all negative conditions NOW, we will bring the Hope of Glory and Eternal Peace into this very moment.

"The Kingdom of Heaven is at hand." NOW!!!

It is necessary for each of us to go within to the Silence of our Heart, and become STILL often throughout the day, so that the energy, directives, radiation and Power of our God Presence will flow into our four lower vehicles and nourish our outer consciousness.

In the East, the practice of concentrated meditation upon the Supreme Source of all Life prefaces all activity, but in the western world, where the requirements of each hour seem to demand so much of our attention and energy, this process of spiritual communion is often neglected. We rarely take time to "be still and know that 'I AM' God!"

We usually allow the "demands" of our four lower bodies to distract us from quieting ourselves sufficiently to hear the directives of our God Presence. These vehicles: physical, etheric, mental and emotional, must be purified and disciplined until they again recognize that they are supposed to be our SERVANTS, and assume their proper position, instead of controlling us with their appetites and promptings. As we diligently and persistently still the scattered energies of our mental bodies, calm the surging sea of our emotional bodies, Transmute the failures and disillusionments of the past festering in our etheric bodies, and control the rampant appetites of our physical bodies, our God Presence will take command and guide these vehicles back to a state of Harmony and Peace. This takes time, patience, constancy and strength, but it is well worth every electron of energy it takes, for, as our vehicles are brought into alignment and control, the "still, small voice" of our "I AM" Presence will be easily heard.

In Chapter Seven we discussed the importance of invocation, but after we invoke the Light and guidance of our God Presence and the Company of Heaven, there comes a point when we must rest IN THE SILENCE and accept the radiation that we invoked. Many times, we will continue to make our requests, decrees, prayers and petitions all through the period of application. When we do this, it does not allow our inner bodies to become quiet enough to accept the gifts we've invoked. It is very necessary for us to BALANCE the giving of our energy in invocation and the accepting of the Light of God and gifts we have invoked.

The activity of truly entering the SILENCE cannot be over-emphasized. As we strive to attain this state of consciousness, our four lower bodies must be disciplined to "be STILL." These vehicles must be trained to direct their energies toward their SOURCE–our God Presence "I AM"–and should never be allowed to "play" at that time with various distracting thoughts, feelings, memories or physical lassitude that often accompany our relaxation from physical work. It is easy to make invocations, decrees and visualizations that actually employ the energies of the lower bodies, but it is very difficult to complete the spiritual exercise by holding our lower bodies still in the Silence in order to RECEIVE the Blessings given to us from on High. Usually, we either fall Peacefully to sleep, or we allow numerous irrelevant thoughts and feelings to flood our consciousness, thus preventing us from reaping the benefits of this period of contemplation.

All Good, whether it is Abundant Supply of all good things, Health, Illumination, Faith, Success, Love, Strength, Purification or Freedom, COMES FROM GOD, the Universal Source of all Life, and these gifts are dispensed by God and the Beings of Light Who are the Messengers of God. It is critical that we realize we cannot receive the fullness of these gifts until we have disciplined our four lower bodies and have learned to ALLOW the Spiritual Grace which we have invoked to enter our Beings. We must speak to our bodies and command: "Peace! Be Still!" Persistence is the key. We need to daily practice communing with our God Presence in the SILENCE until we receive the abundant flow of God's Blessings.

We have, unfortunately, lost the rhythm of our four lower bodies, so that instead of functioning as a Harmonious unit directed by our "I AM" Presence, they spin erratically out of control. Their vibratory rate is slowed down by any discordant thought, feeling, memory or physical action that happens to grab our attention for the moment. We are unable to receive the Peace and Benediction of our God Presence and the Divine Beings when we are scattered and our vehicles are fragmented. Until we still the chaos and align our vehicles, we will not be able to return in consciousness from our spiritual exercises renewed in mind, feelings, body and soul as we should.

The SILENCE can become an actual substance that will give Protection to our physical bodies, as well as Illumination to our minds and Peace to our feelings. Many people have built a momentum in giving verbal invocations and decrees, but there is a need to BALANCE this activity by going into the SILENCE as well.

The demands upon our time, energy, attention and service in everyday Life form a great stumbling block to our individual, spiritual progress unless we learn how to consciously quiet the energies of our world, so new Strength, Faith and Power may be supplied by our "I AM" Presence and the Divine Beings Who are so willing to assist us. Many times, we have a tendency to rush forth to serve others without taking the necessary time to "fill our cups" at the Cosmic Fount. We cannot be of lasting service to our spiritual work or anything else at hand unless we understand the importance of taking undivided time from the outer world to enter the SILENCE, and draw the necessary rejuvenating strength and sanctity from the Source of All Life. Then, we can go forth in Poise, Dignity and Loving Solicitude to fulfill our Divine Purpose.

The GREAT SILENCE is HOME in the truest, deepest sense. It is Security, Safety, Understanding, Love without censure and Peace without price. It is Light equivalent to the most exquisite sunshine our imaging faculties could ever conceive, and yet, It is as restful as the twilight. It is SILENT as the Sun in the Heavens in the performance of Its Cosmic Service, yet, It is filled with the Music of the Spheres. The GREAT SILENCE is the Ultimate Goal toward which all Life is journeying, and It can be experienced by the evolving consciousness of any unascended Being who becomes STILL enough.

Once we have entered the GREAT SILENCE, we will meet within the exquisite STILLNESS every Being Who has mastered the outer self, and we will perceive the full design of God's Plan for every part of Life. Once we have experienced this Realm of Blissful Peace, we will never leave it again. We will work perpetually from within the Heart of the Silence–

abiding in Perfect Peace—allowing the Joy and Happiness of the SILENCE to blaze forth from us, giving Its blessings to every particle of Life we contact. Thus, we will fulfill our reason for being.

Know always, only those who have learned the way of the SILENCE, only those who have learned to master the energy which flows in such magnificent opulence from the Heart of God into their four lower bodies, ONLY THOSE become the conductors of the Gifts of God into the world of Humanity.

Preparation of the Four Lower Vehicles to Enter the GREAT SILENCE

With this exercise you will begin to experience first hand the assistance being given Humanity from on High. This activity is dedicated to re-establishing the Divine Pattern and Plan...the Immaculate Concept...within your physical, etheric, mental and emotional vehicles.

Through this exercise you will energize the Perfect Thoughtform within each vehicle until a pulsating force of Divine Reality is within that vehicle, thus regenerating health and order physically, etherically, mentally and emotionally.

To begin...sit comfortably in a chair with your arms and legs uncrossed and your spine as straight as possible. Breath in deeply, and as you exhale, completely relax and gently close your eyes. Feel yourself enveloped in an invincible Forcefield of Protection which prevents anything not of the Light from interfering with this Sacred Activity. This is a journey in consciousness that will physically manifest through the Power of your true God Reality "I AM."

Visualize yourself standing before a magnificent Crystalline Temple of Healing in the Realms of Illumined Truth. You ascend the steps, and pass through the massive doors. You pass through the alabaster hallway and enter the sacred, central chamber. As you stand within the central chamber, you notice that there are four surrounding chambers at the cardinal points. Pulsating in the center of the central chamber is a radiant crystal Lotus Blossom, and blazing within the center of the Lotus Blossom is a crystalline White Flame with a Madonna Blue aura. It is the Flame of the Immaculate Concept.

An Angelic Being beckons you, and you enter the crystalline Lotus Blossom and stand within the scintillating essence of the Immaculate Concept. You begin to experience the vibratory rate of your four lower bodies being accelerated. Your consciousness is raising, and you perceive, more clearly than ever before, the Divine Blueprint for each of your vehicles.

Pouring forth now from the very Heart of God is a tremendous Ray of Light that is pulsating with the God Qualities of Restoration, Transformation, Healing, Eternal Youth and Radiant Beauty. This shaft of Light enters the Flame of the Immaculate Concept, and then expands out to each of the outer chambers at the cardinal points which are dedicated specifically to one of the four lower vehicles of your Life's expression.

You now consciously project your emotional body and all of your feelings into the chamber at the cardinal point to the East. God's Holy Light begins blazing in, through and around this vehicle, Transmuting every trace of imbalance. Your God Presence now projects the Divine Blueprint for your emotional body through this vehicle, and it begins pulsating as a Light Pattern, Transforming this vehicle instantly into the Immaculate Concept of your Divine Plan.

You now consciously project your mental body and all of your thoughts into the chamber at the cardinal point to the West. God's Holy Light begins blazing in, through and around this vehicle, Transmuting every trace of imbalance. Your God Presence now projects the Divine Blueprint for your mental body through this vehicle, and it begins pulsating as a Light Pattern, Transforming this vehicle instantly into the Immaculate Concept of your Divine Plan.

You now consciously project your etheric body and all of your memories and records of the past into the chamber at the cardinal point to the North. God's Holy Light begins blazing in, through and around this vehicle, Transmuting every trace of imbalance. Your God Presence now projects the Divine Blueprint for your etheric body through this vehicle, and it begins pulsating as a Light Pattern, Transforming this vehicle instantly into the Immaculate Concept of your Divine Plan.

You now consciously project your physical body, every cell, atom, gland, muscle, organ and function, into the chamber at the cardinal point to the South. God's Holy Light begins blazing in, through and around this vehicle, Transmuting every trace of imbalance. Your God Presence now projects the Divine Blueprint for your physical body through this vehicle, and it begins pulsating as a Light Pattern, Transforming this vehicle instantly into the Immaculate Concept of your Divine Plan.

Now, one by one, you magnetize these purified, balanced vehicles back into the Flame of the Immaculate Concept where they are brought into perfect alignment: first the physical, then the etheric, then the mental, then the emotional. Your vehicles are now balanced, and once again returned to the service of your God Presence "I AM" as you prepare to enter the GREAT SILENCE.

SEALING AFFIRMATION

Through the Flaming Presence of God anchored in my Heart, I ask that this Transforming Activity of Light be maintained, Eternally self-sustained, daily and hourly increased moment by moment until each of my four lower vehicles is outpicturing the Perfection ordained for me, and "I AM" wholly Ascended and Free.

It is Done!
So Be It! "I AM"
BE STILL AND KNOW THAT "I AM" GOD

AFFIRMATIONS

During the following Affirmations we should feel, deeply within our own Beings, the Truth of the statements being affirmed.

"I AM" a constant expansion of the Perfection of the Beloved Presence of God "I AM" within me.

I now realize and accept my UNLIMITED ABILITY to do whatever I desire in order to establish and EXPAND PERFECTION in my own world, or anywhere upon the Planet where I direct my Life Energy toward that accomplishment. "I AM" the Mighty Balancing Activity of Life in, through and around every part of Life upon the Planet Earth–eternally sustained.

"I AM" THE SILENCE! I Live in the Silence! I move in the Silence! The daily activities of my very Being are held within the Power of the Great Silence! "I AM" THE SILENCE–eternally sustained.

In the Name, Love, Wisdom and Power of my own Beloved "I AM" Presence, I call to You, great Ascended Host of Light, to CHARGE, CHARGE, CHARGE the Cosmic Power of Light, Love, Illumination, Peace, Freedom and ALL PERFECTION from the Great Silence into the mental and feeling worlds of all Humanity. Hold this forever sustained until these Divine Powers MANIFEST in the Beings and worlds of everyone upon this Planet.

I so decree it in God's Most Holy Name…"I AM"

"I AM" enfolded in a Mighty Pillar of the Violet Transmuting Fire that goes before me–dissolving and Transmuting every imperfect thing that I contact into God's eternally sustained Perfection of the Great Silence.

The Light, Love and Protection of my own Beloved "I AM" Presence and the great Ascended Host of Light enfolds me now and forever. As I proceed about the Business of my Father-Mother God each day, I COMMAND that everyone and everything I contact be Illumined and set Free from all distorted human concepts, and that these be replaced with the Essence of God's Truth.

"I AM" within the Great Silence! I speak only when the Presence of God has something to say through me. Then is my every word charged with God's Love, Illumination and Perfection—eternally sustained. "I AM" a Lightbearer! "I AM" the Light of the World! I have spoken in God's Most Holy Name "I AM."

ETERNAL PEACE, THE GATEWAY TO SPIRITUAL FREEDOM AND LIBERTY

"I AM" THE PEACE OF TRANQUILITY
"I AM" ITS FULL RELEASE
"I AM" THE PEACE OF TRANQUILITY
"I AM" GOD'S COSMIC PEACE
"I AM" THE PEACE OF TRANQUILITY
"I AM" GOD'S COSMIC POWER
"I AM" THE PEACE OF TRANQUILITY
GOD DOUBLES PEACE THROUGH ME EACH HOUR

The Bridge To Freedom

Peace is a conductor of Healing Light, and must precede all permanent Healing of body, mind, soul and affairs. When we are in a state of turmoil, our auras repel the Healing Light we desire, but when we are enveloped in the radiance of Eternal Peace, our auras allow the Rays of Healing to penetrate deep into the atomic, cellular structure of our Beings and worlds. Peace is a positive Power, and as we progress toward the permanent Healing of this Blessed Planet, we can clearly see the need for the Light Rays of Eternal Peace to flood the Earth and all Her Life NOW. As we offer ourselves as the open portals through which the "Cosmic Peace that passeth the understanding of the human mind" will pour into Planet Earth, we will begin to experience, once and for all, the completion of Humanity's imbalance, and our transition into Planetary Harmony and Divine Order.

The Solar Rays of Cosmic Peace are now, as never before, entering the atmosphere of Earth and Humanity from the Great Central Sun. If we will lift up our consciousness and open our Hearts to this Glorious Light, we will become Powerful Peace Commanding Presences, blessing all in our spheres of influence. Peace is the Victory of the Divine Plan fulfilled!

"I AM" PEACE

"I AM" the open door for the Solar Rays of Cosmic Peace from the Great Central Sun.

"I AM" Eternal Peace, now established in the Heart centers of ALL Humanity.

"I AM" the Golden Light of Eternal Peace pervading all Life.

"I AM" claiming every cell, atom and electron of this Sweet Earth and all Her Life into the Heart of Peace.

"I AM" Eternal Peace, reflecting Humanity's Victory NOW in all our experience.

"I AM" in the world, but I dwell in the consciousness of the Peace of the Great Solar Quiet.

At this critical moment on Earth the Solar Ray of Eternal Peace is establishing a fundamental inner Peace which will ensure Humanity's Victorious Accomplishment in the Light. This Ray of Peace shall steady Humanity in the process of becoming One with our true God Reality, and it will create within us the profound inner Peace Beloved Jesus knew when He walked the Planet, thus enabling us to deal sublimely with even the most difficult circumstances. As this expanding inner Reality of Peace bursts upon the Screen of Life, It will fulfill all the prophecies of the Kingdom of

Heaven manifesting on Earth. We began in Peace and Completion, and now we must return to this perfect state of consciousness—the Cosmic Peace of Divine Completion.

The Solar Ray of Eternal Peace now entering Earth will allow Humanity to quickly and successfully master the difficult lessons facing us in the reawakening of our true Reality. This Forcefield of Peace is initiating a process whereby all that needs to be completed, all energy that needs to be Loved Free, will come to the fore to be recognized and Transmuted into Light for its ultimate completing and Freedom. Humanity is the superior Kingdom on Earth, and we are accountable for all of the imbalances presently existing here. Consequently, we are also responsible for the purifying and rebalancing of every electron of misqualified energy involved.

The humanly created imbalances are surfacing on Earth at an accelerated pace, and they are being placed before Humanity's Consciousness in a rather forceful way. This is causing a very turbulent awakening, as the mass consciousness begins to realize the urgent need to change our ways of thinking, feeling and acting. These difficult experiences will, however, produce three very important results: first, we will attain the permanent Wisdom and Understanding that comes from a lesson hard won. Second, we will clearly prove to ourselves the efficacy of the Violet Transmuting Flame, as we invoke Its radiant Light into the atomic and subatomic Life Force within all of our karmic debt, so it can be Loved Free before it manifests, acts or is further sustained in our Lives. Third, Unity will result from the sheer necessity of Humanity coming together in very fundamental ways to overcome the adversity manifesting upon the Screen of Life.

If we, as Lightworkers, hold our attention on God, we will greatly assist in establishing the goals of God Illumination, Truth and Unity in the feeling nature of Humanity.

The Solar Radiation of Peace now blessing the Earth is a tremendous accelerator of the *inner Spiritual stability* of all Beings It makes contact with. We need to hold this awareness in the forefront of our Consciousness in order to maintain this Reality for the masses, while the temporary illusion of imbalance manifests around them in their daily Lives. We will then be the Peace Commanding Presences we have committed to be.

Humanity has always sought solace, Peace and the security of God when adversity becomes great. If we hold our attention on these pure God Qualities, they will manifest within Humanity. Through our principal radiation of Eternal Peace, God Illumination, Truth and Unity, Humanity will more readily acknowledge the Divinity within, and in FREE WILL, turn toward the Light.

Eternal Peace is THE NEXT STEP in our Planetary Healing. Peace is the core of everything permanent, as well as the aura around every Perfected part of Creation.

"I AM" the Golden Ray of Solar Peace entering the Planet,
re-establishing the Reverence for all Life on Earth.

Even though imbalance may flash upon the Screen of Life–REMEMBER–the building *inner Reality* shall be PEACE. The All-Seeing Eye of God sees only Peace–the Golden Radiance of Peace within every cell, atom and electron of Life on Earth. This shall be our perception and growth likewise, as Spiritual Beings. As we *become* the All-Seeing Eye of God, visualizing our own Reality through the eyes of our God Parents, this will soon become the only Truth of our Lives, and we will KNOW the "Kingdom of Heaven" is Solar Peace–the very breath of the Great, Great Silence. When thousands and thousands of Lightworkers have manifested this Solar Peace within their radiation, then Humanity will be sealed within this radiance in our entirety. This will draw forth the Peace Vibration of the Holy Christ Self pulsating in every human Heart. The inner Peace will capture the attention of Humanity, and no matter what inharmony may tend to pass over the Screen of Life, each one will be centered in their inner experience of Peace, thus detaching from the imbalance manifesting around them. Humanity will then be able to SEE things for what they are, the lessons of God Illumination that Humanity must learn, without attaching any "misery" to them. With a fundamental foundation of Inner Peace, we will learn quickly, for it has been fear that has blinded us to the path of Wisdom and higher learning. During this Cosmic moment on Earth, the Wisdom of the REVERENCE FOR ALL LIFE shall become a core constituent in the feeling nature of Humanity, even as the outer Screen of Life reveals the effects of the lack of such Wisdom.

COSMIC PEACE ENFOLDING ALL

In the Name of the Infinite Presence of God "I AM" . . . I call to my God Presence . . .

Enfold me now in your Mighty Presence of Peace until I radiate that Essence to all with whom I come in contact.

"I AM" Peace. "I AM" Peace. "I AM" Peace.

I now behold the entire Planet enfolded in the Golden Essence of Peace, and I behold the Pink Essence of Love joyously crowning every electron of that Peace.

I decree that, from this day and this moment forward, every expression I make shall be qualified with Divine Peace. The Cosmic Flame of Peace through me is now blessing all Humanity, all the Forces of the Elements, the Kingdom of Nature, the Angelic Kingdom and every Living thing in every realm according to their various needs. The Earth is a Sea of Peace. Peace reigns in every Heart evolving upon this Planet—Freedom's Holy Star.

I accept this call fulfilled . . . As God's Most Holy Name . . . "I AM"

Available Tape Associated With This Chapter Is:
    M. ETERNAL PEACE
See page *xxiv* for more information and order blanks.

CHAPTER 11

_∽⁖⁘⁖⁘⁖⁘⁖∾_

THE ELEVENTH ASPECT OF DEITY IS DIVINE PURPOSE

COLOR – PEACH
ELEVENTH RAY

THE ELEVENTH UNIVERSAL LAW OF PERFECTION

THE FIRST CAUSE OF GOD IS PERFECTION IN ALL THINGS

THE ATTRIBUTES OF DIVINE PURPOSE ARE:

FULFILLMENT
SELFLESS SERVICE
LOVING LIFE FREE
HAPPINESS
JOY
ENTHUSIASM
VICTORY
THE COSMIC MOMENT OF
VICTORIOUS ACCOMPLISHMENT

HAPPINESS AND JOY
OUR DIVINE BIRTHRIGHT—OUR CHOICE

Happiness is a quality of God that is imperative to our personal unfoldment. The buoyancy of Happiness forms a magnet, drawing into our Lives all of the Gifts of God we need to attain our Cosmic Momentum of Victorious Accomplishment. This enables us to reach our highest potential and fulfill our Divine Purpose.

The seed of God Happiness naturally abides within every human Heart, and it is the decree of God that this seed shall be nourished, developed and expanded *now* to bear its manifest fruit in the Beings and worlds of all evolving on Earth.

Happiness is a most positive quality. It is a vibratory action which we must cultivate and practice through our Free Will choice everyday. We cultivate Happiness and Joy through the conscious control of our thought processes, our feeling worlds, our memories and our physical activities. Every person who radiates the power of Happiness and Joy into the world adds to the overall frequency of uplifting energy on the Planet. So many times we are caught up in the challenges of our everyday Lives, and we become "heavy" and somber. Often, even our Spiritual work is too serious and intense. We need to recognize that our opportunity of being on Earth at this extremely significant time is a sacred privilege beyond our greatest dreams. Serving God and all Life on Earth can, and should, be an incredibly Joyous experience. All we have to do is open our feeling worlds to the God Quality of Happiness and accept It into our Lives. When we open ourselves up to the frequency of Happiness, the radiance of this energy can, and will, requalify the vibratory action of our vehicles permanently—IF WE WILL ONLY CHOOSE TO ACCEPT IT. Then the accumulation of past failures, disillusionments and depressions that keep us in unnecessary limitation, will be dissipated.

In general, Humanity seems to be a very unhappy lot. If we look into the eyes of people we encounter every day and observe the reports of people around the world brought to us through the media, it is easy to ascertain Humanity's present level of misery. It is ironic that Happiness appears to be such an illusive quality, because we have sought Happiness through every conceivable avenue of endeavor. Humanity has pursued every emotional indulgence and pastime, every mental and physical excess...all to no avail. We continually fail to learn the lesson that *there is no permanent Happiness for any Lifestream until we finally Heal our self-inflicted separation from our own God Presence "I AM," and once again surrender control of our four lower vehicles to that radiant Presence of Light.* When this Healing takes place, we will then KNOW "the Father and I are One. All that the Father has is mine." In this Octave of Consciousness, Happiness is our natural state of Being.

When our God Presence is once again in command of our vehicles, our thoughts, feelings, memories and actions will reflect and accept our Purpose and reason for Being. Our mental bodies will receive the Divine ideas from the Mind of God, and those ideas will flow forth to Illumine our path. Then, our emotional bodies will develop those ideas in Living, grateful Enthusiasm and Joy. Our etheric bodies will record the Divine patterns and ideas within their substance, and our physical bodies will make the ideas practical by bringing them into manifest form for the Blessing of all Life. Thus, our Divine Purpose is brought to fruition.

Through this Unification with our God Presence, we will become radiating Suns of God's Light, and all who are drawn into our spheres of influence will be instantly and permanently assisted, as God's Light Illumines their own consciousness. This benediction of God's Light, flowing through us, will assist in releasing Humanity from distress. It will, likewise, Illumine Humanity as to the cause of the distress and reveal the solutions to the distress as well, so that conscious endeavors will be made by Humanity not to create the distress again.

When our vehicles are continually filled with God's Happiness and Joy, our physical forms will be buoyant and luminous, expressing perfect health, eternal youth and radiant beauty. Our physical bodies merely reflect our consciousness. Therefore, if we are sincere in wanting to be exponents of eternal yough, perfect health, beauty and the magnificence of God's Perfection, remember always, we must remain in the blissful frequencies of God's Joy and Happiness.

We can dramatically change our Lives by altering our thought patterns and letting go of the distorted programming of our past. When we replace old, limiting thought patterns with constructive thought patterns that work, the effect is truly Transformational. The Happiness and Success we are longing for will begin to manifest in our Lives naturally and automatically.

Because of our confused perception, most of us don't even realize we have the power and the God-given right to create Happiness and Joy every moment of our Lives. Very often, those of us who do realize we have the ability to live Lives of Happiness choose not to put forth the effort necessary to create them.

Most of us are unhappy because we don't realize we can be Happy, or we have too many habit patterns that are contrary to Happiness. These habit patterns keep us stuck where we are if we don't motivate ourselves to change. Happiness, like everything else that is worthwhile, does take work and discipline. That work begins with Transmuting our past and changing our destructive habit patterns and thought processes.

Once we accept that our behavior patterns, belief systems and thought processes are important factors in determining our Happiness, we will be well on our way to creating more fulfilling Lives. We must develop the discernment to recognize which of our thought patterns are accurate and which are inaccurate. We must learn to perceive what patterns we need to change to improve our Lives–which patterns serve our highest good and which do not.

Many times we mistakenly believe Happiness is a direct result of good things happening to us. In reality, Happiness has nothing to do with circumstances we are in or the environment around us. Happiness *is not* a result of good things happening to us. Instead, Happiness is the result of our attitudes and free will CHOICE.

We are taught that Happiness comes when we have more income, more Loving relationships, better health or more fulfilling jobs. This belief creates a victim role for us. If Life's circumstances are favorable, we feel like winners, which "allows" us to be Happy. When circumstances are not to our liking, we feel like losers, which "forces" us to be unhappy. When we play this game, we are pawns, being buffeted around by the environment, over which we believe we have very little control. The environment fluctuates tremendously. The erratic ups and downs put us under extreme emotional stress that is destructive to our well being.

Remember, our environment is a reflection of our consciousness

HAPPINESS IS NOT A RESULT OF
OUR ENVIRONMENT...

OUR ENVIRONMENT IS A RESULT OF
OUR HAPPINESS...

We have the power and the right to be Happy in each moment of time no matter what challenges we are going through. We can be Happy and successful, regardless of problems and setbacks.

OUR HAPPINESS IS A MATTER OF CHOICE,
NOT CHANCE!

HAPPINESS IS A MATTER OF CONSCIOUSNESS,
NOT CIRCUMSTANCES!

Life is simple. To be Happy and Successful, all we have to do is Harmonize ourselves with this simplicity. To experience Happiness DAILY, we need merely shift our consciousness and accept this Truth.

We usually believe we will be Happy if we acquire more income, better relationships, better health, more fulfilling jobs. But, the Truth of the matter is, we must first CHOOSE Happiness as a context from which we will accomplish all of our Life objectives.

When we operate from a consciousness of Happiness and Joy, our incomes will increase, our relationships will improve. We will be healthier, and we will know greater fulfillment and success in our jobs. An abundant Life is the natural *effect* of the *cause* of Happiness.

Happiness is a state of mind, an attitude and consciousness, not something we pursue. We bring Happiness into the experiences of our Lives. We do not expect the experiences of our Lives to bring us Happiness.

Once Happiness is our constant state of consciousness, it will perpetually lead us on to Victorious Accomplishment in every facet of our Lives.

"I AM" HAPPINESS

Through the Power of God, blazing in my Heart, I offer myself as a conductor of God's Limitless Happiness and Joy into the world of form.

I invoke every part of Life which has ever contributed to the Cosmic Fount of Happiness and Joy since the beginning of time to come now and pour the Flame of Happiness through me to bless all Life evolving on this Sweet Earth.

Blaze the Flame of Happiness and Joy through all physical, etheric, mental and emotional substance on Earth, until all is raised into the embrace of God's Heart.

Illumine each part of Life with the Wisdom and Understanding that according to their ACCEPTANCE of this precious gift, will it manifest daily in their Life experiences.

I dedicate myself now to be the perpetual open portal through which the full-gathered momentum of God's Happiness and Joy will flow to bless all Life Eternally.

It is Done! So be It! "I AM"

FULFILLING OUR DIVINE PURPOSE
A STEP BY STEP PROCESS

A reactivation and initiation into multi-dimensional awareness has occurred on Earth, and all Life evolving here has been lifted up in vibration. The pre-encoded memories implanted deep within our cellular patterns aeons ago, as we progressed through our Earthly experience, have now been activated. These patterns contain within them the blueprint of our Divine Plan, our Purpose and Reason for Being. We are beginning to experience an awakening, and we are beginning to remember our Divine Heritage.

As the acceleration in vibration took place on Earth, the

frequencies of the physical third dimensional plane ascended higher and entered the frequencies of the ethereal Fourth Dimensional Plane. This enabled us to take THE NEXT STEP and pass through the doorway into multi-dimensional awareness. Humanity has now been empowered with an even higher octave of rarified Light from the Fifth Dimension. This Light reflects the totality of God, the Twelve-fold Aspect of Deity from the Great Central Sun.

Moment to moment, this radiant Light is intensifying the activation of the pre-encoded memories of our Divine Purpose. These memories are registering at a physical, cellular level within our four lower bodies. As this occurs, the blueprint of our Divine Purpose reverberates through our creative centers of thought and feeling. This allows the currents of Wisdom and Illumination, which are revealing our Divine Purpose, to pass through our conscious minds. As they do, our God Presence sends a Ray of Light into our consciousness to help us tangibly grasp each Divine idea. Through this Sacred Activity, the knowledge of our Divine Plan is now available to us as never before. To grasp it, we need only reach up in consciousness and tap the Octaves of Illumined Truth.

VISUALIZATION FOR PERCEIVING YOUR DIVINE PLAN

Become quiet and relaxed.

Go within your Heart Center and experience a feeling of perfect Peace.

See yourself sitting on the Golden Throne in the "Secret Place of the Most High Living God."

Ask your God Presence to bring into focus before you the image of your Purpose and reason for Being.

Observe this image clearly and see how it reflects your natural gifts and talents.

Experience, deep within your Heart Flame, the innermost longing to fulfill this Purpose.

Now, reach higher into the Octaves of Illumined Truth, and ask your Higher Self to reveal to you how you can begin to implement this Purpose into your daily Life.

See the avenues of opportunity unfold before you.

Experience the feeling of elation as you begin to fulfill your Divine Plan.

Observe that, as each opportunity presents itself, you Joyously seize it and feel a greater sense of accomplishment and self-worth than ever before.

You realize that in the simple act of fulfilling your Purpose your self-esteem is restored, and you feel whole and complete.

The emptiness that you have continually been trying to fill from the outside is now pulsating with the meaning and warmth of your Divine Plan.

You understand now, with greater awareness, that as you take advantage of each opportunity to fulfill your Purpose, the Universe presents another one on the horizon.

Thus, your Divine Plan unfolds for you step by step.

After completing the above visualization, gently return your consciousness to the room, and take a pencil and paper and write down what you perceived to be your Divine Purpose.

MY DIVINE PURPOSE

As clearly and comprehensively as possible, evaluate your Purpose. Assume there are no barriers or limitations to prevent you from accomplishing this wonderful Purpose. Now, write it down in detail.

Expand your Purpose to include all of your Life's roles. This Purpose serves as a foundation from which you will be more complete and balanced in each of your roles:

Parent
Spouse-Partner
Businesswoman/Man

Co-worker
Homemaker
Son/Daughter
Community Participant
Friend
Planetary Steward
Spiritual Being

ELIMINATING THE BARRIERS TO OUR PURPOSE

In order for us to begin fulfilling our Purpose, we must first discover and eliminate the barriers we have created, which prevent us from realizing and expressing that Purpose. Embarking on a successful course in Life that is filled with Purpose and Happiness involves changing habit patterns and perspectives that do not serve us. As we improve, our Lives improve. For our Lives to get better, WE must first get better.

Since all Life is interrelated, the success and Happiness we create in our Lives today will effect generations for milleniums to come. Think about that. Is your Life presently reflecting the legacy with which you want to bless future generations? In most cases the answer will be no, but we have the absolute Power to change that legacy now.

IT IS NOT THE CHALLENGES IN OUR LIVES, BUT RATHER HOW WE HANDLE THE CHALLENGES THAT DETERMINES WHETHER THEY ARE DEVASTATING TRAGEDIES OR POSITIVE OPPORTUNITIES FOR GROWTH.

Every emotional response we have is a direct result of a conscious choice or an indirect result of a learned habit. We are responsible for how we feel and respond. It's time for us to learn to create feelings that work for us in a positive way, regardless of the situations or circumstances occurring in our Lives. Any emotional response or feeling that does not support our commitment to our Purpose is not working for us. Regardless of what habit patterns motivated us in the past, we must now re-examine those patterns and see if they serve us. So many times, our habits are ingrained to the point that

we have an automatic reflex response to the challenges aris-
ing with no conscious thought or awareness at all. This is
definitely NOT the path to self-mastery we are seeking. Self-
mastery means just that, that we are the Masters of our
thoughts, words, feelings, actions and behavior patterns,
not the victims of our Lives' experiences, buffeted about by
the changing tides of emotion and circumstance.

When we are the Masters of our Lives and on Purpose, we
realize that we not only have the ability to be Happy and Fulfilled in each moment of time, but we have the RESPONSI-
BILITY to do so as well. In order to be Happy and Fulfilled,
we must give up habits that hinder us from reaching our
goals. We have all heard the invocation of the Lord's Prayer,
"THY KINGDOM COME, THY WILL BE DONE ON
EARTH AS IT IS IN HEAVEN." Heaven on Earth is available
to us now, not in some distant future time, but right here
and now. Creating Heaven in our Lives RIGHT NOW,
RIGHT HERE, is our assignment for being on Earth at this
time. It is a major facet of our Divine Purpose.

The moment we take responsibility for being Happy and
Fulfilled internally, we begin to influence our external world.
Our environment is merely a reflection of our consciousness.
At this moment, we all have the Happiness and Fulfillment
we deserve, according to the reflection of our consciousness.
If we want more, we must deserve more by changing our
consciousness. Most of us don't deserve optimum Happiness and Fulfillment by virtue of the way we Live and respond to the challenges of each day. Frequently, our habitual
mode of operation will be the reflex response of anger, frustration, greed, selfishness, rudeness, lack of consideration,
impatience, intolerance, disgust or disappointment. Iron-
ically, we are seldom willing to work at improving these very
uncomfortable emotional reactions until we are completely
fed up with our Lives.

The "good news" is, once we start taking responsibility for
our Lives, our circumstances will automatically improve.
Our present Lives are reflections of our actions and attitudes
of the past. Therefore, we must Transmute and COMPLETE
our past in order to experience optimum enjoyment and success in our present. We COMPLETE our past by telling the

TRUTH about our past and TRANSMUTING all misqualified energy associated with each transgression of the
Law of Love and Harmony.

Every time we judged another, lied, stole, blamed another
or failed to communicate what needed to be said, due to fear,
embarrassment or uncertainty, we created an incompletion
in our past. These incompletions must now be faced and
dealt with, so we can move forward into Lives of Happiness
and Joy as we fulfill our Divine Purpose. We cannot erase the
past, and we cannot move forward into the Joy of Heaven on
Earth, dragging the negative baggage from the past with us.
our *only* option is to complete and Transmute our past, thus
Freeing ourselves to create a Glorious present and future.

The first step in completing our past is telling the TRUTH.
The TRUTH must be completely communicated to the person or people involved, and any possible restitution must be
made. Through this process, we begin to clear the space, the
murky, swamp water that is creating a barrier to our Happiness and Fulfillment, preventing us from accomplishing our
Divine Purpose. The price we have paid for allowing our
four lower bodies to rage out of control has been too high.
Our minds have deceived us. Our feelings have manipulated us. Our memories have held us stagnant in the past,
and the appetites of our physical bodies have held us in a
grip of oppression and limitation.

The awakening taking place within us now is creating a
sense of urgency, and the drive for our God Presence to take
full dominion of these vehicles once again is intense.

IT IS THE ONLY WAY TO LIBERATION

Our four lower bodies are, in part, the distracting forces in
us that manifest the rationalizations and deviations from our
Purpose.

Our God Presence "I AM" is the aspect of ourselves that is
created in God's Image. It is the part of our consciousness
that is continually prodding and prompting us on to reach
our highest potential, keeping us on course, as It supports
us in fulfilling our Divine Purpose.

Now is the time for each of us to allow our God Presence
to take full dominion of our four lower bodies as we clear the

space and eliminate the barriers that are preventing us from accomplishing our Divine Purpose.

COMPLETING AND TRANSMUTING THE PAST

STEP ONE:

Write a list of all the transgressions and incompletions of the past you can remember.

STEP TWO:

Tell the Truth to the appropriate person or people about each transgression or incompletion.

STEP THREE:

Do all you can to correct the situation by completing the transgression or incompletion to the offended person's satisfaction.

STEP FOUR:

Recommit to a lifestyle of total Honesty and Integrity by acknowledging to your God Presence "I AM" that you are committing, now and forever, only to Integrity and Honesty with every person, place, condition or thing in your Life.

As a result of telling the TRUTH, we regain our Integrity, which is a key element in our character. As we complete our incompletions, we begin to feel better about ourselves, and our Lives begin to automatically get better.

It takes strength, courage and confidence to fulfill our Divine Purpose. We need to recognize our self-worth and accept our own Divinity. In order to have self-confidence, we must have self-esteem.

TRUTHFULNESS IS A
PREREQUISITE FOR SELF-ESTEEM

Self-confidence gives us the courage and strength necessary to fulfill our Purpose.

KNOW THE TRUTH,
AND THE TRUTH WILL SET YOU FREE!

The TRUTH nourishes new seeds of self-esteem, Love of others, and a willingness to let others Love us. From the

TRUTH springs a worthiness that adds to every dimension of our Prosperity, Success, Health, Loving Relationships and Rewarding Careers. From the TRUTH flows the confidence and INNER PEACE we so desperately tried to achieve by violating Life's Law of Integrity. From the TRUTH comes a realization—a knowingness that is greater than faith or belief—of our Oneness with God. God has given us three TRUTHS to sustain us as we complete our pasts:

"I have come that you may have Life and have it more abundantly."

"'I AM' the Way, the TRUTH and the Life. No one comes to the Father except through me."

"'I AM' the Lord, your God. You must have no other gods before Me."

The first statement is one of PURPOSE. The second statement is one of CHARACTER. The third statement commands us to avoid getting off of our Divine Purpose by allowing any of our objectives to be more important to us than our own INTEGRITY.

NO ACHIEVEMENT IS WORTH THE PRICE WE MUST PAY FOR IT IF WE PAY WITH OUR INTEGRITY.

Contemplate and absorb these statements. They are guideposts to point us toward our new, abundant Life. We must daily apply them to our Lives.

THOSE WHO *KNOW* THE LAW ARE *NOT* EQUAL TO THOSE WHO *LIVE* BY THE LAW.

LIST OF TRANSGRESSIONS AND INCOMPLETIONS
Releasing Exercise

The purpose of this exercise is to help us unlock and release, then complete and TRANSMUTE, the destructive vibrations of past thoughts, words, actions and feelings.

The negative energy that we have released during our Earthly sojourn pulsates in, through and around us. By unlocking, releasing, completing and Transmuting these heavy discordant vibrations, we literally open the door for our God Presence to take full dominion, thus creating a contact and communication with our God Self that will guide us unerringly toward our highest potential.

INVOCATION

"I AM" now enveloped in an invincible Forcefield of Protection. From this focus "I AM" able to review my Life as an objective observer. I ask my God Presence to push to the surface of my conscious mind every single experience, both known and unknown, that is, in any way, preventing me from attaining my highest good.

Blazing in, through and around my four lower bodies (physical, etheric, mental and emotional) is the full power of the Violet Transmuting Flame. This Light, from the very Heart of God, instantly Transmutes these negative thoughts, words, actions, feelings and memories back into their original perfection.

"I AM" at Perfect Peace.

As this information surfaces, I easily write it down, so I can complete it, and I effortlessly let it go, without emotion, without pain and without fear.

I simply experience this negative energy passing through me to be Transmuted back into Light, as I complete it and Love it FREE!

Appearing before my mind's eye are the transgressions and incompletions of my past. I now list every lie I have ever told, every item I have stolen, every judgment or blame I have ever made and all my current, undelivered communications.

I ignore the resistance of my lower mind.

I listen to my God Presence. This part of my consciousness does want me to make the list and be FREE of the past. This is the part of me who longs for a more abundant Life.

Through this activity, I will regain my *INTEGRITY* and attain true character.

REPUTATION is what other people BELIEVE I am.

CHARACTER is what God KNOWS "I AM".

As long as I persist in incompletions, my Life remains incomplete, no matter how much energy I put into it. I choose, now, to complete and Transmute all of the transgressions and incompletions of my past as I list them one by one.

1.
2.
3.
4.
5.
6.
7.

(Use as much paper as you need to complete your list.)

Now that we have completed the first step, we must accept the responsibility of completing the other three steps:

STEP ONE:

Write a list of all the transgressions and incompletions of the past you can remember.

STEP TWO:

Tell the Truth to the appropriate person or people.

STEP THREE:

Do all you can to correct the situation by completing the transgression or incompletion to the offended person's satisfaction.

STEP FOUR:

Recommit to a lifestyle of total Honesty and Integrity by acknowledging to your God Presence, "I AM" that you are committing, now and forever, only to Integrity and Honesty with every person, place, condition or thing in your Life.

To further complete our past experiences, I would like to share with you the following thoughts. Contemplate them and apply them to any relationship or situation you are having trouble letting go of or completing.

THE DISCIPLINE TO FREEDOM

Transference is clinging to an outmoded view of reality –the way we perceive and respond to the world which is developed in our childhood. This is usually appropriate to the childhood environment, but INAPPROPRIATE when transferred to our adult environment.

Truth or reality is avoided when it is painful. We can revise old programming only when we have the discipline to overcome that pain.

To have such discipline, we must be totally dedicated to Truth.

Truth must be more vital to our self-interest than our comfort.

Conversely, we must consider personal discomfort relatively unimportant in the search for Truth.

Mental Health is an ongoing process of dedication to reality at all costs.

A Life dedicated to Truth means continuous and never-ending, stringent self-examination.

Self-examination is often painful, but when one is dedicated to Truth, this pain seems relatively unimportant.

Consequently, self-examination is less and less painful the farther one proceeds on the path of Truth.

A Life of dedication to Truth also means a willingness to be personally challenged.

The only way that we can be certain our concept of reality is valid is to expose it to the criticism and challenge of other concepts of reality.

Often, because of the pain involved in revising our view of reality, we seek to avoid any challenges to its validity.

Total dedication to the Truth means total Honesty.

It means a continuous process of self-monitoring to assure that our communications invariably reflect, as accurately as possible, the Truth or reality as we know it.

Such Honesty is sometimes painful. The reason people are untruthful is to avoid the pain of challenge and its consequences.

The force that lies in back of, and provides the motive and energy for, the discipline of Honesty and Truth is LOVE.

LOVE includes self-Love. We are incapable of Loving anyone unless we Love ourselves.

LOVE gives us the WILL and the courage to challenge ourselves for the purpose of enabling our spiritual growth and our adherence to TRUTH.

As we grow in the discipline of Truth, Love and Life, our understanding of the world and our Purpose in it naturally grows.

The result of this evolving process is self-mastery, bringing with it FREEDOM on all planes of existence.

COMPLETING THE LEARNING EXPERIENCE OF PAST RELATIONSHIPS

1. Evaluate the relationship objectively. Each relationship is a reflection of our own Being. What were the lessons being presented?
2. Do you feel you learned the lessons being presented?
3. How have you grown from the experience?
4. What concepts or attitudes did you develop about yourself and other people as a result of your experience?
5. What have you learned about yourself?
6. What have you learned about your ability to relate to other people?

7. Evaluate how you have changed as a result of your relationship.

8. What insight does this awareness give you about yourself?

9. Do you feel the relationship was the result of mis-qualified energy, negative thinking patterns or low self-esteem?

10. Have you effectively Transmuted the negative energy so you will not have to repeat the experience?

11. Has your relationship given you greater understanding and compassion regarding other people's pain?

12. Because of your experience, can you learn more easily by observing other people's behavior patterns?

13. Is the learning experience completed?

14. Have you released and let go of the pain of the relationship?

15. Are you able now to close the door behind you and move forward more Illumined into a Life of Joy?

MOVING INTO RIGHT RELATIONSHIPS
WITH OUR PARENTS

1. Sometimes the greatest weakness in a parent or other relationship is the quality we are needing most to overcome in ourselves, a weakness in our own Being.

2. What we see as a parent's greatest weakness may be covering up a great strength.

3. Pick out the most beautiful quality in your parents you feel the most removed from.

4. Often, our relationships with other people are a direct reflection of the patterns we fall into with our parents.

5. In order to Free ourselves, we must develop true independence, which is an inner state and has nothing to do with what is said or done outwardly.

6. Freedom is attained through a gradual emergence of grateful and respectful feelings for who our parents are—not how well they have played their roles.

7. If we will begin to truly look at our parents, we will begin to see them maybe for the first time, not only as parents, but as human beings with Joys as well as pains, Happiness as well as sadness, Victory as well as failure.

8. This re-evaluation can Heal the weak links in a long chain of Love and strengthen the relationship with a new warmth.

9. When we see beauty in our father or mother, our relationship is Healed.

10. When we experience our parents as Children of God, like ourselves, we become wiser channels for the Perfection of God to express through us. Our Hearts can then open to all of the Children of God— to all Humanity and all Life.

11. There comes a time in our relationships with our parents, when we must stop seeking their approval and begin approving of them.

12. When we continually seek approval from outside sources, we will always be disappointed and frustrated.

13. Our concentration needs to be changed from wanting to receive Love to looking for ways of giving Love.

14. This simple act can have a tremendous impact in all of our relationships.

15. We receive appreciation by appreciating others.

16. If we begin to focus on all of the beautiful aspects of the people in our relationships and find ways to express our appreciation for them, it will have a very FREEING effect.

17. When we Heal our relationships with our parents, we are Healing a deep part of ourselves, and this will enhance all of our relationships, enabling us to Joyously fulfill our Purpose.

ILLUSIONS

How we interpret things that are communicated to us in relationships affects our ability to communicate. The following is a list of some of the *ILLUSIONS* we buy into:

1. Life hurts–Life is the pits.
2. Love hurts.
3. My opinions don't count.
4. My feelings don't count.
5. I'm insignificant.
6. I have no value.
7. I have no control over what happens to me.
8. People are basically selfish and uncaring.
9. My problems are caused by other people or social circumstances beyond my control. Therefore, it is up to other people or society to solve my problems.
10. Nobody cares what I have to say.
11. Nobody listens to me.
12. I'm not smart enough to solve this problem.
13. I can't express my thoughts clearly.
14. People will laugh at me and think I'm stupid.
15. It's not worth discussing. Nothing's going to help.
16. You can't fight "city hall".
17. What if I'm wrong?
18. I don't trust anybody.
19. My feelings are too important to me. I don't dare share them with anyone else.
20. There's "right" and there's "wrong"–no in between.
21. I'll take the path of least resistance, even if I don't agree, just to avoid an argument.
22. So what–who cares?
23. Other people's problems are trivia compared to mine. I'm not even going to listen to them.
24. Why bother? It's like talking to a brick wall.
25. What difference can I possibly make?
26. If I just keep quiet, maybe it will go away.

PLEASE HEAR WHAT I'M NOT SAYING

Don't be fooled by me.

Don't be fooled by the faces I wear, for I wear a mask.

I wear a thousand masks, masks that I'm afraid to take off, and none of them are me.

Pretending is an art that's second nature with me, but don't be fooled.

For God's sake, don't be fooled.

I give you the impression that I'm secure, that all is sunny and unruffled with me, within as well as without, that confidence is my name and coolness my game, that the water's calm, and I'm in command and that I need no one.

Don't believe me. Please.

My surface may seem smooth.

But my surface is my mask, my ever varying, ever concealing mask.

Beneath dwells the real me in confusion, in fear, in aloneness, but I hide this–I don't want anybody to know it.

I panic at the thought of my weakness and fear being exposed.

That's why I frantically create a mask to hide behind a nonchalant, sophisticated facade, to help me pretend, to shield me from the glance that knows.

But such a glance is precisely my salvation, my only salvation, and I know it.

That is, if it's followed by acceptance, if it's followed by Love, it's the only thing that can liberate me from myself, from my own self-barriers that I so painstakingly erect.

It's the only thing that will assure me of what I can't assure myself, that I'm really worth something.

But I don't tell you this.

I don't dare. I'm afraid to.

I'm afraid that deep down I'm nothing, that I'm just no good, and that you will see this and reject me.

So I play my game, my desperate, pretending game with a facade of assurance without and a trembling child within.

And so begins the parade of masks, the glittering but empty parade of masks, and my Life becomes a front.

I idly chatter to you in the suave tones of surface talk.

I tell you everything that's really nothing, and nothing of what's everything, of what's crying within me.

So, when I'm going through my routine, do not be fooled by what I'm saying.

Please listen carefully and try to hear what I'm not saying, what I'd like to be able to say, what for survival I need to say, but what I can't say.

I dislike hiding. Honestly!

I dislike the superficial game I'm playing, the superficial, phony game.

I'd really like to be genuine and spontaneous and me, but you've got to help me.

You've got to hold out your hand, even when that's the last thing I seem to want or need.

Only you can wipe away, from my eyes, the blank stare of the breathing dead.

Only you can call me into aliveness.

Each time you're kind and gentle and encouraging, each time you try to understand because you really care, my Heart begins to grow wings, very small wings, very feeble wings, but wings.

With your sensitivity and sympathy and your power of understanding, you can breathe Life into me.

I want you to know that.

I want you to know how important you are to me, how you can be a creator of the person in me, if you choose to.

Please choose to.

You alone can break down the wall behind which I tremble.

You alone can remove my mask.

You alone can release me from the shadow world of panic and uncertainty, from my prison world, my lonely, prison world.

So, do not pass me by.

Please do not pass me by.

It will not be easy for you.

A long conviction of worthlessness builds strong walls.

The nearer you approach to me, the more blindly I may strike back.

It's irrational, but despite what the books say about man, I am irrational.

I fight against the very thing that I cry out for, but I am told that Love is stronger than walls, and in this lies my hope, my only hope.

Please try to beat down those walls with firm hands, with gentle hands, for a child is very sensitive.

Who am I?

I am someone you know very well.

by Peter Lehmann
Author of "Masks"

REALITY

THERE ARE THINGS OUR HIGHER SELVES WILL REVEAL TO US, WHEN WE TAKE THE TIME TO ASK AND LISTEN, THAT WILL DISPEL THE ILLUSIONS:

1. I am not a victim of circumstance. "I AM" a creator of circumstance.
2. I have a Purpose and Reason for Being.
3. The people I come in contact with in my Life are there for a reason. Whether the relationship is intimate or casual, each interaction is an opportunity for learning and growth.
4. No one knows what another person's learning experience is. Consequently, I do not always know what is best for another person.
5. I can only perceive a situation from my own frame of reference, which may not accurately apply to the other person.
6. In other words—what is true for me may *not* always be true for someone else.
7. It's OK for me to share my perspective and opinion in a situation. It's also OK for the other person to perceive things differently from me.
8. This doesn't necessarily mean that one of us is right

and the other wrong. It merely means that we each have a different perspective, according to our wisdom and experience.

9. It does not diminish my value or self-worth if another person disagrees with me.

10. The greatest gift I can give another person is the Freedom to experience the lessons Life is presenting, according to his/her own Divine Plan.

11. I now realize that only my God Presence can guide me unerringly to my highest potential, and I now know this is true of every man, woman and child on Earth.

"I AM" VERY SPECIAL

"I Am" special...In all the world there is nobody exactly like me...

Since the beginning of time, there has never been another person exactly like me...nor will there ever be in the future...

No one has my smile, my eyes or nose, my hair, my hands or my voice. Nobody has my handwriting..."I Am" special...No one can paint my brush strokes. Nobody has my special taste in food or music or drama or art. No one in the world sees things just exactly as I do...

In all of time, there has never been anyone who laughs exactly as I do or cries or thinks exactly as I do...And what makes me laugh or cry or think in precisely my way might elicit a totally different reaction from someone else..."I Am" special. "I Am" different from every other person who has ever Lived or will ever Live in the history or future of the Universe...

"I Am" the only one in the whole of creation who has my particular set of abilities...Now, there is always someone who is better than "I Am" at one thing or another because every human being is superior to every other person in at least one regard...But, "I Am" special... And "I Am" superior to each other person in at least one regard...

No one in the Universe can reach the quality of the combination of my talents, my abilities, my feelings, my heart, my head, my hands... Like a room full of musical instruments–some may excel alone–but none can match the symphonic sound made when all are played together..."I Am" a unique symphony...

Through all eternity, no one will ever look, walk, talk, think or act exactly like I do..."I Am" special..."I Am" rare... And in all of rarity, there is enormous value. ... Because of my great value, I need not imitate any other person... I will accept, verily, celebrate my differences because..."I Am" special.

And it is no accident that "I Am" special... I must realize that God has made me special for a specific Purpose... He has chosen a job for me to do that no one else can do as well as I can... out of the billions of applicants, only one is qualified... Only one has that unique, right combination of what it takes... And "I Am" that one...

"I Am" special..."I Am" very special...*AND SO IS EVERY OTHER HUMAN BEING.*

Author Unknown

AFFIRMATIONS AND INVOCATIONS TO COMPLETE THE TRANSMUTATION OF ALL PAST MISQUALIFIED ENERGY

GIVING MY GOD PRESENCE DOMINION

Mighty "I AM" Presence... take command of my outer self this day.

Take command of my every thought, feeling, spoken word, action and reaction.

Produce Your perfection, hold Your dominion.

Put and keep me always in my right and perfect place.

Show me the perfect thing to do, and through me,

do it perfectly.
So be it, Beloved "I AM".

A PREPARED VEHICLE

In the Name of the Cosmic Law of Love and
Forgiveness, which I now Invoke:

"I AM" Transmuting my human consciousness by
Violet Fire. (Three times)

Oh, Sacred Fire, blazing as a radiant
spiraling Light within my Heart:

Charge my physical vehicle into a higher physical
consciousness. (Three times)

Charge my etheric vehicle into a higher etheric
consciousness. (Three times)

Charge my mental vehicle into a higher mental
consciousness. (Three times)

Charge my emotional vehicle into a higher emotional
consciousness. (Three times)

And grateful for this Sacred Fire...

"I AM" now sublimated, refined, accelerated and
Transformed by the currents of Sacred Fire
and a prepared vehicle for the expression of my God
Self, and the fulfillment of my Divine Purpose
on this Planet.

So Be It, Beloved, "I AM".

GREATER PRESENCE IN ACTION

(To be used regularly and/or for specific problems
in your Life or service, especially if you have been
thrown off center by a problem.)

In the Name of the magnificent Flame of Life "I AM"...

I do now affirm that in all areas of my Life and service:

"I AM" relinquishing self and human will (Three times)

As the embodied Flame "I AM"...

I KNOW there is a greater Power than myself
in action here. (Three times)

I KNOW there is a greater Wisdom than myself
in action here. (Three times)

I KNOW there is a greater Love than myself
in action here. (Three times)

I know this is the Victory of the Light in Action through
me! I accept this as the Truth in all areas of my Life and
service. "I AM" that Greater Presence here in action...

"I AM" that "I AM". SO BE IT!

RESTORATION OF MY LIFE

My Divine Essence...I Love and adore you. Shine
through my every effort at becoming ONE WITH
THEE. Oh, Flaming Presence of Light, let the gift of
Divine Love which is Yours alone to give, flow
through me to set Life Free. I ask that I might be Love's
open door.

And as I accelerate my journey toward Eternal Oneness
with You, I consciously draw back to myself all my own
energies that "I Am" so desirous of Loving Free. Help
me, Oh, Flame in my Heart, to Love myself Free...all
returning energy...as "I Am" about my Father's Business of LOVING ALL LIFE FREE.

In Thy Name, I now accept that in all my day-to-day
experiences "I AM" reclaiming all my energies back
into the Heart of Love. (Three times)

"I AM" the Violet Fire in action, Loving me Free.
(Three times)

"I AM" grateful to the Sacred Violet Fire, the most
powerful aspect of Love that instantly Transmutes
all outstanding energy back into Perfection.

"I AM" again made Whole with Thee!

As God's Most Holy Name..."I AM".

Group Avatar

BRINGING OUR DIVINE PURPOSE INTO FORM

Without adequate planning, our dreams and goals have
little chance for success. Even the most challenging opportunity or the most difficult situation can be handled in small

increments. A written plan allows us to systematically approach Life one step at a time.

What I have shared in the first part of this chapter are very necessary steps in preparing to fulfill our Divine Purpose. We must complete each of them before proceeding to the process of setting goals.

PREPARATION

1. COMMITMENT TO HAPPINESS AND JOY
2. WRITE A STATEMENT OF MY DIVINE PURPOSE
3. COMPLETION OF MY PAST TRANSGRESSIONS AND INCOMPLETIONS
4. COMMITMENT TO TOTAL HONESTY AND INTEGRITY

THE PURPOSE IN GOAL SETTING IS TO IMPEL US TOWARD FULFILLING OUR HIGHEST POTENTIAL–OUR DIVINE PURPOSE

For our Lives to be more complete, we must be more complete. To create external conditions of excellence, we must first create an internal order of excellence. What we BECOME in the pursuit of our highest and noblest goals is far more important than the achievement of those goals.

Goals set the direction and the speed of the changes in our Lives.

Goal setting keeps us current with the rapid changes taking place all around us.

Goals allow us to clearly perceive how far we've come, how far we have to go, and THE NEXT STEP we need to take.

By building character and by keeping us on course, goal setting is a powerful tool to keep us aligned with our Divine Purpose and commitment to excellence.

Setting balanced goals requires that we establish goals in several areas of our Lives. Many areas will overlap, but we should establish goals in the following categories:

Personal goals: health, appearance, attitude, habits, diet, exercise.

Relationship goals: parents, children, spouse/partner, other close relationships, friends, co-workers, associates.

Financial and career goals: income, savings, investments, job, volunteer work, community service, planetary service.

Social goals: group activities, traveling, interaction with friends, the performing arts, social functions.

Spiritual goals: application of spiritual disciplines and exercises, prayer, church or spiritual activities, tapes, lectures, research, study.

Mental goals: independent study and research, tapes, books, lectures, formal and informal education and seminars.

Make a list of anything you could *be, do* or *have* to make each of these areas more complete. Look carefully for areas of incompletion and possible improvement. We will then use this worksheet to create a valuable Life Plan that will Transform our Lives.

ACHIEVEMENT PLAN

My list of possible improvements in this area:

Personal Goals

1.
2.
3.
4.
5.
6.
7.

Relationship Goals

1.
2.
3.
4.
5.
6.
7.

Financial and Career Goals

1.
2.
3.
4.
5.
6.
7.

Social Goals

1.
2.
3.
4.
5.
6.
7.

Spiritual Goals

1.
2.
3.
4.
5.
6.
7.

Mental Goals

1.
2.
3.
4.
5.
6.
7.

Now that we have completed the preparation and established our goals, we're ready for the next step, which is to
bring our goals and Divine Purpose into form. The following
guidelines will accomplish just that. Follow them carefully,

and experience for yourself the Joy of creating a Life of Fulfillment, Happiness and Purpose.

STEPS TO VICTORIOUS ACCOMPLISHMENT

STEP ONE

Reread the statement you wrote of your Divine Purpose. Compare it to your list of goals, and make any necessary additions or adjustments. Then, DEDICATE YOUR LIFE ENERGY TO THE FULFILLMENT OF THAT PURPOSE.

STEP TWO

Commit to a Life of total Happiness and Joy. Moment to moment, make the conscious choice to be Happy. Affirm continually, *"I willingly accept God's limitless flow of Happiness and Joy into my Life now!"*

STEP THREE

Invoke your God Presence "I AM" to lift you into the highest Octaves of Honesty and Integrity. With all past transgressions and incompletions Transmuted and completed, consecrate yourself to a Life filled only with HONESTY and INTEGRITY.

STEP FOUR

Spend time each day communing with your God Presence and opening your creative centers to the Realms of TRUTH. Read inspirational books, listen to motivational tapes, meditate, pray. "BE STILL AND KNOW THAT 'I AM' GOD."

STEP FIVE

After your quiet time with your God Presence, write down all the thoughts and ideas you received. Don't edit or censor anything at this point. Just allow the creativity to flow. Later, evaluate the material, and see how it will assist you in bringing your Divine Purpose into physical manifestation.

STEP SIX
Put your goals in a priority list: short term goals, long term goals (one, three, five, ten years) and Lifetime goals. Then, on a blank piece of paper, write the word "BE". On another piece of paper write the word "DO", and on a third piece of paper write the word "HAVE". Evaluate your Divine Purpose and your prioritized goals. Then, write them on the appropriate piece of paper. Are they things you want to BE, DO, or HAVE? Be sure you cover all of the areas listed on your "Achievement Plan".

Your "Achievement Plan", coupled with this creative list, comprises your personal *Master List* of all the improvements you want to make in your Life.

Now, go over the lists, and determine which of the items are really important. Which are the most worthy of your time and effort? Which assist you in fulfilling your Divine Purpose and reaching your highest potential?

STEP SEVEN
Now, create a MASTER LIST. List the specific goals you have chosen to work on on the MASTER LIST.

MASTER LIST

PERSONAL GOALS:
RELATIONSHIP GOALS:
FINANCIAL AND CAREER GOALS:
SOCIAL GOALS:
SPIRITUAL GOALS:
MENTAL GOALS:

Each day after your quiet time with your God Presence, spend some time comparing your creative thoughts to your MASTER LIST. If appropriate, update your MASTER LIST. This allows your goals and your Divine Purpose to grow and evolve. It also enables you to see just where you are and helps you know what action to take next to move toward the accomplishment of your plan. This daily attention charges your goals with the Power of God's Light.

STEP EIGHT:
Visualize your goal already completed in every detail. Work continually in the moment of NOW. Incorporate all of your senses in your vision: touch, taste, smell, sound and sight. Feel the elation of your Victory. Make it real in your thoughts and feelings in every respect.

STEP NINE:
The ninth step in goal setting is to see yourself enjoying the goal as if you had already achieved it. This is a step beyond visualization. This creates a powerful, magnetic force that draws it into your Life. In this step, you focus on the reasons for desiring your goal. What you want is important. *Why* you want it is even more important. Act as though you have already achieved your goal NOW!

STEP TEN:
Plan out exactly what action you need to take to accomplish your goal. Write down your plan in detail. This gives you a positive thoughtform to refer to daily to keep you motivated and ON PURPOSE.

STEP ELEVEN:
Don't discuss your goals with anyone unless you are working on joint goals. Discuss your goals only with those individuals whom you know will support them and nurture your efforts. Many people will be indifferent or not interested in your achievements. Others may be afraid you will be disappointed. Some may even hope you fail. Sometimes, people will feel uneasy about themselves when they witness your growth. They may even feel threatened by your success. All of these negative attitudes will dissipate your efforts and delay your goal. So, only share your goals with those who share your dreams.

STEP TWELVE:
Create a "Completed Goal File". Write ACCOM-

PLISHED across the face of all your completed goals and keep them in a file. On those days when you are feeling down or stuck and unmotivated, you can review the file and prove to yourself that you have the absolute ability to succeed in your Purpose.

These twelve steps will give you the self-confidence and support you need to bring your goals and your Divine Purpose into Perfect Victorious Accomplishment.

All the Universe rejoices in the fulfillment of your Divine Purpose, as you achieve and accept your true Heritage as a Child of God.

"THE FATHER AND I ARE ONE.
ALL THAT THE FATHER HAS IS MINE."

Available Tape Associated With This Chapter Is:
   N. DIVINE PURPOSE
See page *xxiv* for more information and order blanks.

CHAPTER 12

THE TWELFTH ASPECT OF DEITY IS TRANSFORMATION

COLOR – OPAL
TWELFTH RAY

THE TWELFTH UNIVERSAL LAW OF ONENESS

ALL THAT EXISTS IS PART OF THE ALL-ENCOMPASSING PRESENCE OF GOD

THE ATTRIBUTES OF TRANSFORMATION ARE:

**TRANSFIGURATION
REBIRTH
REJUVENATION
THE SACRED SUBSTANCE OF THE
SPIRIT OF HUMANITY
FOCUS ON THE FIRE ELEMENT**

TRANSFORMATION

Our *personality*, our LITTLE SELF, often referred to as the EGO, is created from a synthesis of all the activities we express through our four lower bodies—thoughts, words, actions, feelings and beliefs. This part of our identity manifested gradually through our Earthly sojourn as we experienced Life through our limited physical senses. Humanity gave the outer personality so much power and attention that we actually grew to believe this limited, struggling self is who we really are. We separated ourselves from our true God Self, and consequently, we bound ourselves to function within the extreme limitations of our distorted human personality.

We are now on the threshold of individual and planetary TRANSFORMATION. This unparalleled activity of FREEDOM will occur, not through some supernatural phenomenon, but through a slight adjustment in our consciousness. We have become so attached to the limitations of our outer personalities, it seems as though we are light years from the FREEDOM of TRANSFORMATION, but I assure you, it is only a breath away. Transformation will occur the instant we integrate the outer personality with our true God Self.

Our God Self is One with our Father-Mother God, and It is the part of us that strives for balance and prods and prompts us on to complete our Earthly lessons. When our personality is integrated with our God Self, we move into a state of Mastery and exceptional attainment. When we are functioning through our God Self, we receive guidance and direction from the Realms of Illumined Truth that will enable us to fulfill our Divine Purpose and Plan. In that state of consciousness, we clearly KNOW "all that the Father has is mine", and we realize Perfection is possible in every aspect of our Lives now. The Harmonious integration of our God Self with our outer personality allows us to attain Enlightenment, Wisdom and Understanding.

The frequency of TRANSFORMATION pouring into the Planet NOW is available specifically to bring about the integration of our God Self with our human personality. The Power of this Light is working to eliminate the blocks and resistance in our personalities that are preventing the integration from taking place. As we utilize this gift from God, we will experience our outer personalities becoming one with our God Selves, and we will begin to function as Divine Humans on Earth.

The purpose of our embodiment on Earth, during this unprecedented time, is to Renew and Rejuvenate our bodies and the bodies of this Blessed Planet, until all are reunited with the Presence of God "I AM". Thus, the vibratory rate of physical matter will increase, until the entire Planet is TRANSFORMED, as She Ascends into the Octaves of the Fourth Dimension on Her return journey to the Heart of our Father-Mother God.

Our bodies become purified, literally refined and rarified, as we draw the qualities of God through our Heart Flames in selfless service to Humanity and all Life. Selfless, giving service is, literally, the fastest pathway "Home". As we learn to continually focus on the Divinity within our Hearts, the Immortal Three-fold Flame expands, creating an ever-increasing magnet to draw God's precious qualities into our realms of service. This enables us to unify our minds and Hearts, for TRANSFORMATION cannot occur on a mental level alone. It must resonate through a selfless, serving Heart.

TRANSFORMATION occurs when the Divinity pulsating in our Hearts becomes so integrated with our outer human personality and our four lower bodies that the dense substance of the physical plane can no longer hold dominion. Through this integration, physical matter is purified by the Power of God within.

Deep within the sanctuary of our Hearts where Truth abides, we understand that we become masters of our Lives, not only by attaining Victory over our human personality, but by becoming masters of the Power of Divine Love through selfless, giving service and the Reverence of all Life as well. Divine Love is the greatest Power in the Universe. It is a magnet for Transformation, and It is the cohesive essence which Unifies, yet gives complete Freedom. Divine Love is Power. Divine Love is Wisdom. This Holy Trinity–Love, Wisdom and Power–is inseparable. When Transformation is applied to this Holy Trinity, Victory is always assured.

This is the Cosmic Moment on Earth when matter will

be TRANSFORMED. The DNA in our cells is being repro-grammed by our God Presence "I AM" to accept the higher frequencies of energy pouring into the Planet from the Heart of God. Through this activity, our four lower bodies will be purified, and we will experience their Ascension into the Light Body of our God Presence. From this level of Perfection, our ability to effectively serve Life will be greatly enhanced, and the process of Planetary Transformation will be accelerated.

THE REWARD FOR SERVICE IS MORE SERVICE…

But, one thing we must hold in mind is that, when we begin to experience the rewards and fulfillment pouring into our Lives as a result of our selfless service, we will Joy-ously welcome the new opportunities presented to *Love Life FREE!*

I would like to share with you now several exercises and affirmations designed to lift our four lower bodies into the Light Body of our God Presence. These exercises will also assist in integrating our outer human personality into our God Presence. Once we are again One with God, our ability to be Powerful Lightworkers will intensify immeasurably. Thus, our selfless service expands, quantum leap by quan-tum leap.

INTEGRATING OUR FOUR LOWER VEHICLES INTO OUR FOUR HIGHER VEHICLES

The pyramid has always been symbolic of the journey of the developing consciousness. Through this exer-cise, we will unify all of our diverse aspects into com-plete Oneness, readying us for our Spiritual journey into self-mastery.

Our Pyramid of Light has four sides to its base, repre-sented by the four lower vehicles of our worldly experi-ence (physical, etheric, mental and emotional). To gain the stability of a four square base, from which the sides of our pyramid will ascend, each lower vehicle must be equal to and balanced with the next, none demanding more energy than its due. Upon the balanced, four square base, we must then magnetize the four equal sides of our pyramid, represented by our four Divine Vehicles.

First, we magnetize our Higher Mental Body (often referred to as the Holy Christ Self). We see this vehicle ascending as the first side of our pyramid from the four square base. This vehicle operates as a mediator between the "I AM" Presence and the lower self. The Higher Mental Body steps down the vibration from the Higher Self and transmits to the lower vehicles the maximum amount of energy they can withstand, according to our frame of mind at any given moment.

Next, we magnetize our Causal Body. We see this vehicle ascending from the four square base as the second side of our pyramid. This vehicle is known as our storehouse of good. Every electron of energy we have ever released that is qualified with Light is stored in this vehicle for us to draw on to expand the Light of the World, as we proceed in selfless service.

Next, we magnetize our "I AM" Presence. We see this vehicle ascending from the four square base as the third side of our pyramid. This is the individualized Presence of God that is known as "The Father within." This is our God Presence, our true God Reality.

Finally, we magnetize our White Fire Being. This vehicle ascends as the fourth side of our pyramid from the four square base. This is the Spark of Divinity that is first called forth from the Heart of God. It is the vehicle that is One with the all-encompassing Presence of God and exists prior to our awareness of individual identity as "I AM".

When the balanced four lower vehicles merge into perfect alignment with the four Divine Vehicles, the spiritual Pyramid is topped with the Capstone Point of

Light, which is our union with Infinity, the formless Eternity of God. At this point, Transformation occurs, and we become One with the Presence of God "I AM".

Visualize yourself now in the center of your large Pyramid of Light. Beneath you is your perfectly proportioned base of worldly experience. You feel stable on this base, remaining safely balanced in the world. Surrounding you are the four vehicles of God expression. As you experience these unified vehicles, you come to know your full expression of Divinity. Above you is the point of Transformation, Ascending and blending your Light with all Light...everywhere...the Great "I AM". You know of your Immortality. You are Divine Consciousness created with the actual Flaming Substance of your own Permanent Atom, your own Three-fold Flame, with all the spiritual Gifts imaginable at your feet, preparing you for the journey into mastery. In your hands are the Rod and Scepter of Power, given by God to one who has assumed his full identity as a Being of Light who has conquered his outer world. Thus, you are prepared for the full manifestation of the Light of the COMPLETE YOU while yet having vehicles of expression for service to Humanity and to the Planet.

This is the Consciousness of the Ascension into "I AM" through the process of Transformation, knowing and using the various vehicles of expression, but Living in the permanent identity of the Unity of All in a glorious Whole. Practice knowing, accepting and BEING this Electronic pattern in your visualizations, your affirmations and in the Silence of your Heart.

As the reality of this Truth permeates your consciousness, you will grow to understand, know and ACCEPT...

"I AM" a Being of Flame, and "I AM" Its Light.

"I AM" part of an Activity reacquainting all human beings with their Flame and their Light.

"I AM" the Flame which is the Vibration of the Godhead. "I AM" the Flame which is the cohesive Love which holds the Sun and Stars in place. "I AM" the Flame whose power projects Light Rays from the Sun. "I AM" the Flame which fills all the Universe with the Glory of Itself.

"I AM" the Flame, the animating Principle of Life. Wherever "I AM", there is God Activity. "I AM" the Alpha and Omega of Creation. "I AM" the beginning, and "I AM" the end of manifestation, all externalization, for "I AM" the Flame which is the Source of all and into which all returns.

The Flame which "I AM" is a Power. The Flame which "I AM" is a Substance. The Flame which "I AM" is the all of everything: energy, vibration and consciousness in Action, ever fulfilling the Divine Plan of Creation. The Flame which "I AM" shall restore this Planet Earth and set Her Free Eternally.

The Flame which "I AM" is a Fourth Dimensional Activity. The Flame which "I AM" is the Higher Law of God come to assert Its full Dominion over all the lesser laws of the third dimensional world of Humanity. It is Master over every vibration less than Itself. It is all-Loving, all-Knowing and all-Powerful, and "I AM" that Flame in action amongst Humanity.

Within the Flame which "I AM" is every good and perfect thing, every thought and feeling the God Parents have ever had for the Blessing of Their Creation. This Perfection is externalized as Light. Within the Flame is the seed of all things, and within the Light is the full manifestation of all things. "I AM" the Flame, and "I AM" Its Light.

The Flame which "I AM" is available like air or water. It is everywhere present, available to those who perceive It and accept It. This is my reason for Being—The Flame and the Light embodied in a form acceptable to Humanity. "I AM" the Flame, again reaching the withering souls of Humanity, filling them with Light . . . the Substance of myself, my Holy Self. "I AM" embodied for this reason and no other.

For "I AM" part of an Activity designed to reacquaint all mankind with their Flame and their Light.

"I AM" a Being of Flame, and "I AM" Its Light.

"I AM" the Flame of Life.
"I AM" that "I AM".

Group Avatar

THE HAND OF GOD

In the Name of the Father-Mother God "I AM", as Their True Son/Daughter, the Arisen Christ...

"I AM" the Opal Flame of Transformation in Action! (Three times)

"I AM" the Sacred Fire Breath of God charging through me, *Loving Life Free!* (Three times)

As a Lightworker, I have come to set right the vibratory action of all energy and substance in my world and in all the world. As a Lightworker, "I AM" the Sacred HAND OF GOD, moving through this world, instantly re-establishing Divinity wherever this Sacred Fire is applied. I invite, invoke, focus, concentrate, manifest and sustain the Opalescent Transformation Flame. "I AM" a director of the Flame of Transformation, and "I AM" humble before Its Magnificent Presence, grateful to unleash Its Power of Love on the Earth...(pause)...

"I AM" the Hand of God, CHARGING the Electronic Substance, in, through and around all Life with the Opalescent Flame of Transformation. (Three times)

In Oneness of Consciousness with the Holy Christ Self of all involved, "I AM" the Cause of this Blessing of God. "I AM" the Bridge over which It flows, and "I AM" Its final effects of Divinity, re-establishing the Divine Plan now made manifest in the world of form.

So Be It! As God in Action, "I AM"!!!

ONE WITH THE DIVINE MIND

Visualize the Heart and Mind of God as a blazing Sun, radiant with the Opalescent Flame of Transformation. A Light Ray is directed out from the Center of the Sun into the Heart of every member of the human race. Feel that Universal Light as the Life and intelligence of every man, woman and child. Remain still until that Consciousness of Oneness permeates your feelings. Then, visualize that Light rise from the Heart into the Head, making the entire head area a miniature sun. See every human being with an expanding aureole of Light around the head area, a rapidly moving succession of electrons connecting the human mind with the Divine Mind of God. Looking again into the Mind of God, see the Impulses of Divine Directives arise within That Mind and travel along the Rays into the intellectual consciousness of Humanity, restoring each person according to their specific requirements...(pause)

"I AM" consciously and constantly connected with
the Universal Mind of God
and "I AM" about my Father's business.

"I AM" creating, through My God Intelligence, perfect
conditions of Peace, Harmony and Supply
in my world and environment.

"I AM" receiving the pure Light of God, which is also
now expanding within the mind and brain
consciousness of all Humanity...
Healing, Purifying and Illuminating
all our faculties, senses and organs.

"I AM" conscious only of God's Will, manifesting
through the intelligent and conscious co-operation
of all individuals in positions of trust and authority.
They are all now working together in Harmony
to produce World Peace and World Progress...

By the Power of the Divine Mind of God. ..SO BE IT!
"I AM"!!!

Group Avatar

THE OPAL RAY:
TRANSFORMATION OF THE MIND AND
THE PHYSICAL BRAIN

Through the Sacred Fire of Divinity anchored within my Heart, I call to The Presence of God, and I invoke, from God's Great Cosmic Heart, an Opal Ray of Light into my mental vehicle, my etheric mind and physical brain structure, so that I may see and hear the beauty of my God Presence. I humbly request God's assistance in maintaining this purifying activity of the Opal Ray of Transformation. Keep this Sacred Flame pulsating constantly through each cell, molecule, atom and electron of my brain structure, until my mind and brain are restored and rejuvenated to their original crystal Purity of substance. Help me to be, once again, fully alert to the impressions of Divinity, so that I may achieve great dexterity in transmitting the thoughts of Divinity into expression.

EXPAND the Harmony of my true Being to fill my four lower vehicles, Healing them with the Tones of Cosmic Harmony and drawing them back into Divine Alignment with my God Presence "I AM". Assist me in constantly maintaining my outer mind at Peace, instantly dissolving, with the Opalescent Transformation Flame, all thoughts of self-generating expression that manifest. Like the sea reflecting the Sun, help me to keep my brain constantly open to the Divine Plan of the Universe, and then, seeing and knowing that Plan, assist me in going forth to express it.

Dear Father-Mother God, bathe the Earth and Her atmosphere in Oceans of Your Cosmic Melody, Color and Harmony, so that all Life may feel AT ONE with Your exquisite, prismatic, cascading sea of sound and color.

What I ask for myself, I call forth for all Life evolving on this Planet, and I bow in gratitude to You for this tremendous assistance to me and the Humanity of Earth.

With all the Love from my Heart...I thank You! I thank You! I thank You!

With deep Gratitude, I accept this call fulfilled RIGHT NOW...as the MOST HOLY NAME OF GOD "I AM"!

BREATHING IN THE LIGHT
OF TRANSFORMATION

We owe much to our Physical Sun. The Sun pours forth Light and Lifegiving Substance to all creation. We, of course, are aware of the Sun, but we must also know that we can, by our attention, draw into our Beings, through Love and Gratitude, the beneficial Radiation, which is the Sun's pleasure to bestow upon all who Live, move and have their Beings on this Earth.

In the following breathing exercise, I ask that you face the Sun if possible—if not, visualize the Sun in your mind's eye. As you breathe in, raise your arms out and up from your sides until you form a Cross, palms facing upwards. This position symbolizes complete surrender to our Heavenly Father-Mother God.

Standing straight with your feet together, visualize the Opalescent Light Rays of the Sun pouring toward you, as you take a deep, slow breath to the count of four while raising your arms to form the Cross. Breathe these Rays of Transformation into your Heart. Hold the breath to the count of four as the Light Rays are absorbed into every fiber of your Being. Exhale to the count of four as you lower your arms. Feel the breath as Opalescent Light expanding out through every pore of your body. Now, rest to the count of four with your arms at your side. Repeat the breath seven times. Then decree with *deep feeling*...

"I AM" TRANSFORMED..."I AM" TRANSFORMED ..."I AM" TRANSFORMED..."I AM" DRAWING INTO MY BEING THE BLESSING AND LOVE OF GOD. "I AM" ABSORBING THIS LIGHT INTO EVERY CELL OF MY BODY. "I AM" RADIANT WITH THE LIGHT. "I AM" FILLED WITH THE LIGHT. "I AM" GRATEFUL, GRATEFUL, GRATEFUL TO THE LIGHT, AND I LOVE THE LIGHT.

As you conclude this Breathing Exercise, kindly remember that rhythm is important in all lasting manifestation. As you breathe rhythmically, there will be a noticeable acceleration of your Spiritual Progress.

By continually using the Breath and practicing this exercise daily, you will, through perseverance, draw the Light from the Heart of God into every cell and atom of your Being, bringing about a state of excellent health, youthful vigor and clear thinking, as well as Wisdom, Prosperity and Transformation.

"I AM" THE BREATH OF TRANSFORMATION FLOWING THROUGH MY BEING INTO THE GREAT COSMIC BREATH OF GOD WHICH UNIFIES ALL PERFECTION...EVERYWHERE!!! (Three times)

SCIENTIFIC BREATHING

Visualization: Contemplate the Sacred Presence of your God Self. Feel the Holy Breath of God breathed into the Universe and sustained as the atmosphere of Earth by the rhythmic Inspiration and Exhalation of the Holy Spirit. Then, connect your individual Life breath with this Holy, Pure, Inspirational Cosmic Breath and draw Its vitalizing Spiritual energies into your lungs.

Feel this Fiery Breath expanding within your chest area and filling your individual soul with the Light of Transformation, New Life, Aspiration, Courage and the Will of God to fulfill your own Divine Plan. Then, as you exhale, qualify the breath you are releasing into the Universe with Transformation, Purity, Blessing, Love, Mercy and Godliness.

When you have completed your individual contemplation, repeat the activity for the entire human race.

As all individuals embodied on the Earth share the breath and must participate in the general conditions of the atmosphere, inner as well as outer, there is a marvelous opportunity for treating the entire race by your individual, conscious qualification of the universal blanket of air with God Receptivity, Transformation and all the God Qualities that will arise within your own mind as you proceed with this fundamental visualization.

Think and feel the following statements at least three times a day while breathing as deeply as you can:

1. *"I AM" inbreathing the Fiery Substance of the Holy Spirit, activated by His Flame, and It is now cleansing and energizing my emotional, mental, etheric and physical bodies with the Power of Transformation. (Three times)*

2. *"I AM" inbreathing the electronic substance of unending Peace, inexhaustible Strength and Health and Infinite Supply, now manifest in my Being and world. (Three times)*

3. *"I AM" breathing out Transformation, Peace, Strength, Health and Supply to all Humanity and the Kingdom of Nature. (Three times)*

THE RHYTHMIC BREATH
OF TRANSFORMATION

(Inbreathing Slowly)
"I AM" Inbreathing the Opalescent Flame of Transformation.
(Holding Breath In)
"I AM" Absorbing the Opalescent Flame of Transformation.
(Exhaling Slowly)
"I AM" Expanding the Opalescent Flame of Transformation.
(Holding Breath Out)
"I AM" Projecting the Opalescent Flame of Transformation.

(Repeat Seven Times)

"I AM" THE DIVINE IMAGE OF GOD!

"I AM" a Flaming Presence of God now made manifest in the physical world of form.

With every thought I think, every word I speak, every action I take, "I AM" expanding the borders of the Kingdom of our Father-Mother God throughout Infinity.

Every electron of elemental energy—the Earth, the Air, the Water and the Fire, will receive a healing benediction through the radiance of my physical presence.

"I AM" projecting the deep purple Law of Forgiveness and the Violet Transmuting Flame through all Life evolving on this Sweet Earth with every breath I take.

The vibratory rate of every electron in the four lower vehicles of each Lifestream that enters my sphere of influence will be raised to the Perfection of their Holy Christ Selves, instantly.

The God Virtues of all Twelve Rays: God's Will, Illumined Faith, Power and Protection; Wisdom and God Illumination; Divine Love; Purity and Hope; Truth, Concentration, Healing and Consecration; Peace and Ministration; Invocation, Freedom, Mercy, Transmutation and Forgiveness; Clarity; Harmony and Balance; Eternal Peace, Divine Purpose, Enthusiasm and Joy; and Transformation, are activated within my Being and continually pulsate through the Creative Fire in my Heart into the physical world of form.

Because the Father and I are One, God Supply and Perfection are externally sustained in my Being and world.

"I AM" All Light!

"I AM" That "I AM"!

PREPARING FOR
THE EARTH'S ASCENSION INTO
THE FOURTH DIMENSION

Breathing in the Holy Breath of God "I AM", slowly and rhythmically, I enter a consciousness beyond the physical plane. My eyes remain closed, and yet, I see great visions of Light and Color. I hear the Music of the Spheres, and I know perfect calm in my mind and great ecstacy in my feelings, for I have entered through the Christ into "I AM" Consciousness...into my own "I AM" Presence of Being. Here I know "I AM" Present.

In this Presence and Being, I realize that a great Rod of Light anchors through me. It is my Solar Spine, the Finger of God Almighty pointing to Planet Earth from out of the great Realms of Light saying, "HERE...I AM". Along this Rod of Solar Fire, I see and feel the Twelve Chakric Forcefields of "I AM" Consciousness and Being. I increasingly accept Their radiant Presence as my True Being. This is what "I AM"...the Twelve-fold Aspect of Deity. Into this "I AM" Presence I now gently assimilate my Seven-fold nature of Planetary Being. "I AM" both of these natures: Solar and Planetary, for "I AM" the Christ...the Divine Mediator between man and God. I serve through a planetary body, but I dwell in the Consciousness of the Great "I AM".

In this accelerated Consciousness of "I AM", I know my Presence on Earth as a Rod of Light projected out of the Fourth Dimension, anchoring the Planet and Humanity into that Homeland. Through my inner sight, I see millions of such Rods of Light anchoring through the Lightworkers in Humanity, and I know that God Almighty has reached out to claim this Earth. I now see horizontal Rods of Light flowing from Heart to Heart, uniting all embodied anchorage points of Light on the Earth, establishing a mighty planetary Forcefield, a Grid System of Light, throughout Humanity.

In my own Being, I feel the Ray of Polaris (The Masculine Polarity of God), the North Star, anchoring through the top of my head and the Ray of Magnus (The Feminine Polarity of God), the South Star, anchoring through my feet. These Solar Light Rays meet at my Heart Center in perfect balance and unity of the Masculine and Feminine Polarities of God, igniting as an expansion of Freedom's Flame at my Heart. On the top half of my aura are the dazzling Lights of Aurora Borealis (the Northern Lights) and on the bottom half of my aura, the shining Lights of Aurora Australis (the Southern Lights). "I AM" enveloped in this interstellar Forcefield within my own aura. I now realize that this is simultaneously occurring in all Lightworkers in the Grid System of Light within Humanity, until the Earth itself is completely enveloped in the Northern and Southern Lights of Polaris and Magnus, within Their interstellar Forcefield of *Planetary Security*.

Into this great Forcefield, I now invoke the Light from the Entire Company of Heaven assisting this Planet. My own Immortal Victorious Three-fold Flame magnetizes the Pink Flame of Love into the atmosphere from directly above the Earth, the Illumined Gold Ray of Wisdom from directly in front of the Earth and the Cosmic Blue Ray of Power from directly below the Earth. I magnetize these Rays of Light, Love, Wisdom and Power into my own Heart Flame, and I radiate the Light forth into Humanity. I again realize this is simultaneously occurring through the Lightworkers worldwide, linking Humanity with Divine Assistance from the Heavenly Octaves of Perfection.

I now feel myself as One with all these Magnificent Forces of Light, readying the Earth for transfer into the Fourth Dimension. Through the Lightworkers, the Grid System of Light within Humanity, I now know, with certainty, that Humanity is being assimilated into this Forcefield of *Planetary Security* for transfer into the Fourth Dimension. I dwell in the Twelve-fold Consciousness of "I AM", even as I serve in this Seven-fold Body of planetary existence. "I AM" at Peace in this duality of the Christ Nature, One with God, One with Humanity.

DECREE TO POLARIS AND MAGNUS

Beloved Presence of God "I AM", which I know "I AM"...

I send my Heart's Love to the Great North Star Polaris and to The Great South Star, Magnus, those glorious Beings Whose Light forms the Axis of the Earth and holds this Planet in Cosmic Orbit.

I consciously ACCEPT and KNOW that "I AM" aligned with, and form a cable from, that Axis of Light into the very substance of this Planet.

I accept the responsibility to daily direct my attention to this Merciful Activity of Light, and I know that this

Scepter of LIGHT, LOVE, WISDOM, and POWER will keep the Earth on Her destined course in the Cosmic Advancement of the Planets, according to Divine Edict.

I make this affirmation of Faith...as the Holy Name of God..."I AM"

CHANNELING THE LIGHT OF LOVE, WISDOM AND POWER

In the Name of the Almighty Presence of God "I AM" and the Creative Fire pulsating in every human Heart...

"I AM" the expansion of the Light of Love, Wisdom and Power, as It is released through the Heart of our Father-Mother God, the Hearts of the Beloved Directors of the Four Elements, and the Mighty "I AM" Presence of all Beings belonging to or serving the Earth at this time. "I AM" the open door though which the Legions of Light from the Realms of Perfection CHANNEL the currents and Essence of Their Vibratory action into the Earth and Her evolutions.

I send Gratitude and Love to those Glorious Beings Who have come to render our Earth a Service at each strategic point where the Light of Love, Wisdom and Power enters the Earth, strengthening and holding this Blessed Planet in Pillars of Light and Protection.

I send my deepest Love and Gratitude to ALL of the Blessed Angels, Who are encircling the Planet Earth at this very moment, twenty-four hours a day, filling all Life hereon with Cosmic Love, so that when the Earth is ready to enter the orbit where She truly belongs, *ALL* Life may proceed with Her.

I accept this call FULFILLED...IN GOD'S HOLY NAME ..."I AM".

GOD'S WILL SHALL BE MANIFEST!!!

VISUALIZATION FOR
PLANETARY TRANSFORMATION

Coming forth now from the very Heart of God is a Sapphire Blue Ray of Light that is pulsating with the full Power of God's Will and Protection. This Ray of Light enters the top of my head and descends into my Heart Center. As It merges with the Spark of Divinity in my Heart, It begins to expand through my four lower vehicles as a tremendous starburst, cutting Free anything that is not of the Light and preventing anything that is not of the Light from penetrating into this private space around me. "I Am" now enveloped in an invincible Forcefield of God's Will and Protection.

"I Am" going within to the Golden Throne Room of my Heart, the Secret Place of the Most High Living God. There, I kneel before the altar of Love and offer my ALL in service as I surrender my lower human personality to the Perfection of my God Self, my true Reality.

I then sit upon the Golden Throne, and all of my vehicles are brought into Perfect alignment. My Twelve Chakras are balanced and spinning in Their Perfect direction. Each one is a convex vortex of energy, completely nonrecordant to the illusion of imperfection now appearing in the outer world.

I feel the Presence of The Christ anchored in my Heart, and "I AM" enveloped in a magnificent Lotus Blossom of The Immaculate Concept–The Divine Blueprint for All Life. From within this Forcefield of Love, I begin to perceive clearly, my Divine Plan of Service.

"I AM" now donning my seamless garment of White Light, and instantly, I begin to soar up a spiraling shaft of Light, piercing into the very Heart of God. I take a drink from the Golden Chalice and absorb the Elixir of Immortality and Transformation through every fiber of my Being, and "I AM" instantly the Perfection of my true God Reality, now made manifest and sustained by Holy Grace.

From this Focus within the Heart of God, I will serve all Life on this Sweet Earth, until all are wholly Ascended and Free.

"I AM" now a Lightbearer, and I offer myself as a CUP, a HOLY GRAIL, One Breath, One Heartbeat, One Body, One Energy and Vibration, One Consciousness of Pure Thought and Feeling, One Love and One Desire …through which to pour and anchor the Light, Illumination, Wisdom, Truth, Virtues and Instructions, Gifts and the Blessings of God to the Children of Earth.

"I AM" THE RESURRECTION AND THE LIFE
OF THE ONE CUP…
THE HOLY GRAIL OF THE NEW AGE.
"I AM" THE RESURRECTION AND THE LIFE
OF THE ONE BREATH…
THE HOLY SPIRIT OF THE NEW AGE.
"I AM" THE RESURRECTION AND THE LIFE
OF ONE BODY…
ONE ENERGY AND VIBRATION OF THE NEW AGE.
"I AM" THE RESURRECTION AND THE LIFE
OF THE ONE CONSCIOUSNESS
OF SPIRITUAL FREEDOM FOR THE NEW AGE.

I now breathe in deeply the Sacred Essence of the Holy Breath from the Holy Spirit, and my vehicles begin to expand and expand, until they engulf the entire Planet Earth.

The Planet Earth is now located in the upper portion of my body, and the Three-fold Flame in my Heart is anchored in the center of the Earth. All Life, belonging to or serving the Earth at this time, is within my Being, and every prayer or call for assistance I make for myself, I make for all Life evolving here.

Through the pulsation of my Heart Flame, I now visualize the Planet Earth being Transformed into a luminous sphere, giving off the soft Pink radiance of pure Divine Love. Encircling this Planet are the hands of all nations, joined together in an invincible Forcefield of Unity. In the atmosphere above the Earth is the Cosmic Dove of Eternal Peace, pouring the Golden Rays of Peace through all Life. From the Divine Momentum within the center of the Earth, the Emerald Green Healing Power of Living, Loving Truth pierces outward into the receptive consciousness of all Humanity.

At the cardinal point to the North is a Being of Light standing on a Rainbow Arc of the Twelve Rays, pouring forth the God Reality of the Twelve-fold Aspect of Deity into all Life. At the cardinal point to the South is a Being of Light projecting forth, from His Heart, a Three-fold Lotus Blossom, cradling this Sweet Earth in the Divine Balance of Love, Wisdom and Power. At the cardinal point to the East is a Divine Being blazing forth the radiance of a Violet Light with a sunshine Yellow aura, filling all Life with the Power of Transmutation through Illumination, Wisdom and Understanding. At the cardinal point to the West is a Divine Being Who is blazing forth a Violet Light with an Aquamarine aura, filling all Life with the vibration of Mercy, Compassion and Forgiveness through the Power of God's Will, Truth and Clarity.

This entire Forcefield is sealed in the vibratory frequency of Spiritual Freedom and Supreme Harmony...

AND NOW...

THE PERFECTED KEYNOTE OF THE
PLANET EARTH RESOUNDS THROUGHOUT
A REJOICING UNIVERSE.

We watch, in breathless awe, as the Transformation of Planet Earth is Fulfilled.

Beloved Mother Earth sheds Her cloak of darkness and dawns Her new resplendent garment of Victorious Light. The fullness of God's Perfection expands within every electron of Life on Earth.

Every Heart Flame dances with Joy. Our Victory is assured.

The Elemental Kingdom: the Earth, Air, Water and Fire, accepts Humanity's plea for Forgiveness. Amends are made, and Unity is restored.

The Angles are singing, "Glory to God in the Highest. Peace on Earth, Good Will toward ALL!"

The Heavens open, and the Earth Ascends through the multi-dimensional doorway. She moves to THE NEXT STEP of Her evolutionary journey back to the Heart of our Father-

Mother God.

The Solar Beings from the Fifth Dimension welcome the Earth and all Her Life, as the Earth takes Her rightful position in the Fourth Dimension.

Those Beings from the Heavenly Realms, Who came to assist the Earth through the doorway, are now released to return "Home" to Their own System of Worlds.

Other Beings from the Octaves of Perfection volunteer to remain with the Earth until ALL evolving here are Ascended and FREE!

The clarion call sounds as a mighty trumpet throughout the Universe to all Great Beings of this mighty Cosmos, summoning Them to come and see the miracle taking place on Earth. These Great Ones behold Humanity experiencing God Awareness in their Lives and on their planetary home. The Great Ones see, too, the increased GLORY of the ASCENSION FLAME, blazing brilliantly in, through, and around every Lifestream. The Human Race serves all of Life Joyously and adopts as their Supreme Law, these Truths:

I LOVE THE GREAT UNIVERSE WITH ALL MY BEING...
MY HEART, SOUL, MIND AND STRENGTH!

I LOVE GOD'S LAW LIKEWISE, AS THE GREAT
LAW LOVES ME!

I LOVE THIS BEAUTIFUL, MIRACULOUS PLANET
AND TREAT THIS GREAT BEING WITH INFINITE CARE,
AND I LOVE MY SISTERS AND BROTHERS IN ALL
ELEMENTS OF LIFE WITH THE GREAT UNIVERSAL
LOVE THAT IS SO FREELY POURED FORTH TO ME!

The rejoicing is tremendous! The Heavens ring with the songs of Angels and of Humanity. It is the SEVENTH DAY of EARTH, the PLANET of GODHOOD!

And God responds, "How magnificent You are, O Spirit Sparks!"

"Welcome Home!"

Available Tape Associated With This Chapter Is:
    O. TRANSFORMATION
See page *xxiv* for more information and order blanks.

INDEX

AVAILABLE TAPES

THE NEXT STEP
by
Patricia Diane Cota-Robles

This is a very important series of tapes filled with knowledge, wisdom, practical tools, exercises and visualizations that will help you reunite with the part of your Being and Consciousness that always aspires to the highest level of EXCELLENCE.

The purpose of these tapes is to provide you with the insight, wisdom and techniques that will enable you to develop the skill to TAP THE POWER WITHIN YOUR OWN BEING. Then, once you have reconnected with your Higher-Self, your God Presence, It will guide you perpetually as you create for yourself a Life of *JOY, FULFILLMENT, PURPOSE, ABUNDANCE* and *SUCCESS*.

To gain the most benefit from the tapes, listen to each one in the series. Then, quiet yourself and ask the Presence of God, pulsating in your Heart, to reveal which tape you should concentrate on first. Your God Presence always knows exactly what THE NEXT STEP is for your own individual path and will guide you, unerringly, to the correct tape.

Once a tape has been selected, listen to it again carefully. Focus on the information presented. *Apply* the tools and exercises to your Life and practice them daily until you have developed the necessary skills that will set you FREE from your present state of lack and limitation. When you feel a sense of completion with that particular tape, ask your God Presence to reveal to you the next tape you should concentrate on. Continue this process until you have experienced ALL of the tapes.

As you proceed through these lessons, you will find yourself becoming more and more Illumined and FREE. Your Life will change, and It will begin to reflect the Harmony and Success you have been striving to achieve for as long as you can remember. As you develop the skills taught in the series of tapes, you will experience more Loving Relationships, Vibrant Health, Prosperity, Happiness, a Fulfilling Career, Spiritual Growth, Joyous Selfless Service, Inner Peace, Optimism and Total Self-Mastery.

A. **GOD'S WILL**

   THE WILL OF GOD IS PERFECTION–HUMANITY'S FALL FROM THE WILL OF GOD–EXPOSING THE WORLD OF ILLUSION IN THE LIGHT OF REALITY–HUMANITY'S RETURN JOURNEY BACK TO THE WILL OF GOD–EFFECTIVELY UTILIZING GOD'S WILL IN OUR DAILY LIVES.

B. **THE WORLD HEALING MEDITATION**

   THIS MEDITATION TAPE CLEANSES OUR FOUR LOWER BODIES AND PREPARES US TO BE THE CLEAREST POSSIBLE CHANNELS OF HEALING LIGHT.

C. **ENLIGHTENMENT**

   "YE ARE GODS"–IN THE BEGINNING…"I AM"–THE ORIGINAL DIVINE PLAN–EARTH'S RETURN JOURNEY HOME.

D. **DIVINE LOVE**

   THE POWER OF DIVINE LOVE–LOVE…AND LET IT BEGIN WITH ME–THE CHILDREN OF LOVE: TOLERANCE, PATIENCE, KINDNESS, HUMANITARIANISM, REVERENCE, BALANCE–COMMUNICATION; THE KEY TO HARMONIOUS RELATIONSHIPS.

E. **PURITY**

   PURITY IS THE HEART OF CREATION–THE MIRACLE OF RESURRECTION–RESURRECTING THE DIVINE PATTERN WITHIN–THE IMMACULATE CONCEPT–THE GOAL OF LIFE IS THE ASCENSION.

F. **TRUTH**

   THE EMPOWERMENT OF ALL GOD QUALITIES ON EARTH THROUGH THE SUPREME INITIATION.

G. **MINISTERING GRACE**

   MINISTRATION IS AN ACTIVITY OF GRACE. THE

FOURTH DIMENSION IS ESTABLISHED ON EARTH–
THE OPENING OF THE SEVENTH AND FINAL AN-
GELIC VORTEX–ACCEPTING THE POWER WITHIN:
BECOMING THE DIVINE IMAGE EMBODIED IN
FLESH.

H. STAR∗LINK 88
THIS IS A POWERFUL ACTIVITY OF LIGHT IN WHICH
HUMANITY UNITES WITH THE ANGELIC KINGDOM
TO ASSIST THIS SWEET EARTH AS SHE ASCENDS
INTO THE REALMS OF HARMONY AND BALANCE.

I. TRANSMUTING THE PAST THROUGH THE POWER OF FORGIVENESS
UTILIZING THE POWER OF TRANSMUTATION, THE
VIOLET FLAME OF FORGIVENESS AND FREEDOM.

J. FREEDOM
SEVEN STEPS TO PRECIPITATION: THE SCIENCE OF
SUCCEEDING IN YOUR PURPOSE–VIOLET FLAME
CLASS.

K. CLARITY
THE REBIRTH OF OUR PLANETARY IDENTITY IN-
TO OUR GOD IDENTITY–THROUGH THE RAY OF
CLARITY, THE TRAPS OF THE WORLD OF ILLUSION
ARE REVEALED.

L. HARMONY
HARMONY AND BALANCE: THE PATH TO OUR
ETERNAL FREEDOM–THE TWELVE UNIVERSAL
LAWS.

M. ETERNAL PEACE
THE GREAT SILENCE–ETERNAL PEACE, THE OPEN
DOOR TO SPIRITUAL FREEDOM AND LIBERTY.

N. DIVINE PURPOSE
HAPPINESS AND JOY: OUR DIVINE BIRTHRIGHT,
OUR CHOICE FULFILLING OUR DIVINE PURPOSE,
A STEP-BY-STEP PROCESS.

O. TRANSFORMATION
TRANSFORMATION–PREPARING FOR THE EARTH'S
ASCENSION INTO THE FOURTH DIMENSION.

ORDER FORM FOR TAPES AND BOOKS

Please send me _____ copies of the *book* THE NEXT STEP.

I am enclosing a check or money order made out to The New Age Study of Humanity's Purpose, Inc. for $14.98 per book plus $2.00 postage and handling for the first copy and $1.00 for each additional copy.

TAPE ORDER

Please send me the following tapes:
NUMBER
OF COPIES

A. _____ GOD'S WILL
B. _____ THE WORLD HEALING MEDITATION
C. _____ ENLIGHTENMENT
D. _____ DIVINE LOVE
E. _____ PURITY
F. _____ TRUTH
G. _____ MINISTERING GRACE
H. _____ STAR*LINK 88
I. _____ TRANSMUTING THE PAST THROUGH THE
           POWER OF FORGIVENESS
J. _____ FREEDOM
K. _____ CLARITY
L. _____ HARMONY
M. _____ ETERNAL PEACE
N. _____ DIVINE PURPOSE
O. _____ TRANSFORMATION
P. _____ ENTIRE SET OF TAPES

I am enclosing $9.00 per tape or the special discount price of $120.00 for the ENTIRE SET OF 15 TAPES.

Postage and handling for the first tape is $1.50 and 50¢ for each additional tape. If ordering the entire set of tapes, postage and handling is $5.50

Please make check or money order payable to:
THE NEW AGE STUDY OF HUMANITY'S PURPOSE, INC.
P.O. BOX 41883, TUCSON, ARIZONA 85717

NAME _____

ADDRESS _____

CITY _____ STATE _____ ZIP _____

COUNTRY _____

ORDER FORM FOR TAPES AND BOOKS

Please send me _____ copies of the *book* THE NEXT STEP.

I am enclosing a check or money order made out to The New Age Study of Humanity's Purpose, Inc. for $14.98 per book plus $2.00 postage and handling for the first copy and $1.00 for each additional copy.

TAPE ORDER

Please send me the following tapes:
    NUMBER
    OF COPIES
A. _____ GOD'S WILL
B. _____ THE WORLD HEALING MEDITATION
C. _____ ENLIGHTENMENT
D. _____ DIVINE LOVE
E. _____ PURITY
F. _____ TRUTH
G. _____ MINISTERING GRACE
H. _____ STAR∗LINK 88
I. _____ TRANSMUTING THE PAST THROUGH THE
              POWER OF FORGIVENESS
J. _____ FREEDOM
K. _____ CLARITY
L. _____ HARMONY
M. _____ ETERNAL PEACE
N. _____ DIVINE PURPOSE
O. _____ TRANSFORMATION
P. _____ ENTIRE SET OF TAPES

I am enclosing $9.00 per tape or the special discount price of $120.00 for the ENTIRE SET OF 15 TAPES.

Postage and handling for the first tape is $1.50 and 50¢ for each additional tape. If ordering the entire set of tapes, postage and handling is $5.50

Please make check or money order payable to:
THE NEW AGE STUDY OF HUMANITY'S PURPOSE, INC.
P.O. BOX 41883, TUCSON, ARIZONA 85717

NAME _____

ADDRESS _____

CITY _____ STATE _____ ZIP _____

COUNTRY _____

ORDER FORM FOR TAPES AND BOOKS

Please send me _____ copies of the *book* THE NEXT STEP.

I am enclosing a check or money order made out to The New Age Study of Humanity's Purpose, Inc. for $14.98 per book plus $2.00 postage and handling for the first copy and $1.00 for each additional copy.

TAPE ORDER

Please send me the following tapes:

NUMBER
OF COPIES

A. _____ GOD'S WILL
B. _____ THE WORLD HEALING MEDITATION
C. _____ ENLIGHTENMENT
D. _____ DIVINE LOVE
E. _____ PURITY
F. _____ TRUTH
G. _____ MINISTERING GRACE
H. _____ STAR*LINK 88
I. _____ TRANSMUTING THE PAST THROUGH THE POWER OF FORGIVENESS
J. _____ FREEDOM
K. _____ CLARITY
L. _____ HARMONY
M. _____ ETERNAL PEACE
N. _____ DIVINE PURPOSE
O. _____ TRANSFORMATION
P. _____ ENTIRE SET OF TAPES

I am enclosing $9.00 per tape or the special discount price of $120.00 for the ENTIRE SET OF 15 TAPES.

Postage and handling for the first tape is $1.50 and 50¢ for each additional tape. If ordering the entire set of tapes, postage and handling is $5.50

Please make check or money order payable to:
THE NEW AGE STUDY OF HUMANITY'S PURPOSE, INC.
P.O. BOX 41883, TUCSON, ARIZONA 85717

NAME _____

ADDRESS _____

CITY _____ STATE _____ ZIP _____

COUNTRY _____

ORDER FORM FOR TAPES AND BOOKS

Please send me _____ copies of the *book* THE NEXT STEP.

I am enclosing a check or money order made out to The New Age Study of Humanity's Purpose, Inc. for $14.98 per book plus $2.00 postage and handling for the first copy and $1.00 for each additional copy.

TAPE ORDER

Please send me the following tapes:

NUMBER
OF COPIES

A. _____ GOD'S WILL
B. _____ THE WORLD HEALING MEDITATION
C. _____ ENLIGHTENMENT
D. _____ DIVINE LOVE
E. _____ PURITY
F. _____ TRUTH
G. _____ MINISTERING GRACE
H. _____ STAR*LINK 88
I. _____ TRANSMUTING THE PAST THROUGH THE
             POWER OF FORGIVENESS
J. _____ FREEDOM
K. _____ CLARITY
L. _____ HARMONY
M. _____ ETERNAL PEACE
N. _____ DIVINE PURPOSE
O. _____ TRANSFORMATION
P. _____ ENTIRE SET OF TAPES

I am enclosing $9.00 per tape or the special discount price of $120.00 for the ENTIRE SET OF 15 TAPES.

Postage and handling for the first tape is $1.50 and 50¢ for each additional tape. If ordering the entire set of tapes, postage and handling is $5.50

Please make check or money order payable to:
THE NEW AGE STUDY OF HUMANITY'S PURPOSE, INC.
P.O. BOX 41883, TUCSON, ARIZONA 85717

NAME _____

ADDRESS _____

CITY _____ STATE _____ ZIP _____

COUNTRY _____

ORDER FORM FOR TAPES AND BOOKS

Please send me _____ copies of the *book* THE NEXT STEP.

I am enclosing a check or money order made out to The New Age Study of Humanity's Purpose, Inc. for $14.98 per book plus $2.00 postage and handling for the first copy and $1.00 for each additional copy.

TAPE ORDER

Please send me the following tapes:

NUMBER
OF COPIES

A. _____ GOD'S WILL
B. _____ THE WORLD HEALING MEDITATION
C. _____ ENLIGHTENMENT
D. _____ DIVINE LOVE
E. _____ PURITY
F. _____ TRUTH
G. _____ MINISTERING GRACE
H. _____ STAR*LINK 88
I. _____ TRANSMUTING THE PAST THROUGH THE
           POWER OF FORGIVENESS
J. _____ FREEDOM
K. _____ CLARITY
L. _____ HARMONY
M. _____ ETERNAL PEACE
N. _____ DIVINE PURPOSE
O. _____ TRANSFORMATION
P. _____ ENTIRE SET OF TAPES

I am enclosing $9.00 per tape or the special discount price of $120.00 for the ENTIRE SET OF 15 TAPES.

Postage and handling for the first tape is $1.50 and 50¢ for each additional tape. If ordering the entire set of tapes, postage and handling is $5.50

Please make check or money order payable to:
THE NEW AGE STUDY OF HUMANITY'S PURPOSE, INC.
P.O. BOX 41883, TUCSON, ARIZONA 85717

NAME _____

ADDRESS _____

CITY _____ STATE _____ ZIP _____

COUNTRY _____

ORDER FORM FOR TAPES AND BOOKS

Please send me _____ copies of the *book* THE NEXT STEP.

I am enclosing a check or money order made out to The New Age Study of Humanity's Purpose, Inc. for $14.98 per book plus $2.00 postage and handling for the first copy and $1.00 for each additional copy.

TAPE ORDER

Please send me the following tapes:

NUMBER
OF COPIES

A. _____ GOD'S WILL
B. _____ THE WORLD HEALING MEDITATION
C. _____ ENLIGHTENMENT
D. _____ DIVINE LOVE
E. _____ PURITY
F. _____ TRUTH
G. _____ MINISTERING GRACE
H. _____ STAR*LINK 88
I. _____ TRANSMUTING THE PAST THROUGH THE
        POWER OF FORGIVENESS
J. _____ FREEDOM
K. _____ CLARITY
L. _____ HARMONY
M. _____ ETERNAL PEACE
N. _____ DIVINE PURPOSE
O. _____ TRANSFORMATION
P. _____ ENTIRE SET OF TAPES

I am enclosing $9.00 per tape or the special discount price of $120.00 for the ENTIRE SET OF 15 TAPES.

Postage and handling for the first tape is $1.50 and 50¢ for each additional tape. If ordering the entire set of tapes, postage and handling is $5.50

Please make check or money order payable to:
THE NEW AGE STUDY OF HUMANITY'S PURPOSE, INC.
P.O. BOX 41883, TUCSON, ARIZONA 85717

NAME _____

ADDRESS _____

CITY _____ STATE _____ ZIP _____

COUNTRY _____